SPARKNOTES®

WORKOUT in GERMAN

SPARK PUBLISHING

© 2007 by Spark Publishing

Contributing writers: Jeremy Berg, Deborah Bischof
Illustrations by Christina Berg Renzi.

SPARKNOTES is a registered trademark of SparkNotes LLC.

Spark Publishing
A Division of Barnes & Noble
120 Fifth Avenue
New York, NY 10011
www.sparknotes.com

ISBN-13: 978-1-4114-9677-4
ISBN-10: 1-4114-9677-9

Library of Congress Cataloging-in-Publication Data

Workout in German: practice for the tricky rules of German grammar.
        p. cm.—(Workout in)
   ISBN-13: 978-1-4114-9677-4 (pbk.)
   ISBN-10: 1-4114-9677-9 (pbk.)
   1. German language—Textbooks for foreign speakers—English. 2. German language—Problems, exercises, etc. 3. German language—Self instruction.

PF3129.E5W67 2007
438.2'421—dc22

2007028610

Please submit changes or report errors to www.sparknotes.com/errors.

Printed and bound in Canada

10 9 8 7 6 5 4 3 2 1

A Note from SparkNotes

There's a saying that goes, *if you can speak three languages, you're trilingual; if you can speak two languages, you're bilingual; and if you speak only one language, you're American*. If you're a student who dreams of bilingual fluency—or who just dreams of passing that German final exam—you've come to the right place.

We've designed the *Workout In* series to be the hammer that helps you nail down your studies. The 100 workouts you're holding in your hands cover all of the trickiest grammar rules. Whether you're taking your first course in a language, moving from a beginner to an intermediate level, or coming back for a little refresher course, these bite-size lessons and power-packed exercises will give you the help you need.

This book is organized by subject, some of which include Nouns, Verbs, Adjectives, and Adverbs. Sample sentences show you how to apply these rules, and English translations and bolded text help you zero in on the words being discussed. The following features make it easy to navigate around trouble spots that are likely to cost you points on a test:

→ **Achtung! boxes** provide tips and strategies to solidify your learning and alert you to potential pitfalls.

→ **Ausnahme boxes** call out exceptions to the rules.

→ **Alltagssprache boxes** explain some of the quirkier rules or point out where a rule may differ from colloquial usage.

This format makes it easy for you to get the information you need most. But reading a bunch of rules on grammar will get you only so far. The key to learning any language is practice—and you'll get lots of practice with this book. To go with all the rules and fancy features, each workout includes several sets of exercises in a variety of formats, from fill-ins, translations, and matching questions to crossword puzzles, writing prompts, and personal profiles.

We've also included a glossary of irregular and special usage words, as well as a handy reference for general grammar terms (just in case you don't know your preterite from your past participle). So dig in. Whether you thumb through and find help in the areas you need it most or read it cover to cover, this book will give you what you need to get to the next level.

Contents

An Introduction to German

German is spoken by roughly 120 million people in eight countries worldwide. At one time, German was considered *the* foreign language (second only to Latin) for budding American scientists to learn. The peak of popularity with Americans in general came around the time of *die Wende* (the fall of the Berlin Wall on November 9, 1989) and the German reunification that followed. In the past several decades, though, German has had to share that spotlight with other foreign languages. Even so, it remains popular among students in the United States. German is recognized for its importance in travel and business despite the large number of Germans who know English. German is not only spoken in Germany, Austria, and parts of Switzerland, but is also the most popular foreign language among students in most of the former East Bloc counties. For anyone wishing to do business in Central or Eastern Europe, German is the popular and sensible common language.

The standard German (Brockhaus) known today did not emerge fully formed. It was the result of a mixture of dialects that became codified over time, primarily through the works of lawmakers, poets, and scholars. The first major work to standardize German was Martin Luther's 16th-century translation of the Holy Bible, written with the conscious intention to merge the various regional dialects in the hopes of bringing that work to as many people as possible. From there, luminary works from literary masters such as Johann Wolfgang von Goethe and Friedrich von Schiller further solidified the standard German language among the populace.

English is a Germanic language, and when it comes to some words, such as *Haus* (house), *Maus* (mouse), *Brot* (bread), *Garten* (garden), *Wein* (wine), *Bier* (beer), *Mann* (man), and *Wasser* (water), the similarities between German and English can be easily seen and heard. But in spite of the similarities and a common origin, the structure of German is quite different from English. German nouns have both gender (masculine, feminine, or neuter) and case (nominative, accusative, dative, or genitive). One result is that German has 16 possible equivalents of *the, a,* or *an*. Word order in German is in some ways more flexible than in English: Many more parts of speech are likely to begin a sentence than in English. In other ways, though, German word order is quite strict and varies greatly from English. The differences between the two languages can be overwhelming, but with time and practice they can become second nature. One of the beauties of the German language is its logic compared to many other languages. Once a rule or pattern is learned, using it can be quite simple since there are generally few exceptions.

Despite its beauty and logic, German is not a language frozen in time. Since World War II, English has had a profound effect on the German language, particularly in recent decades as words borrowed from American advertising and technology are popularized by German youth. Some of the borrowed words have a slightly different pronunciation, and many have been *germanified* with, for example, German verb endings. Other English words, such as *Handy* (the German word for *cell phone*) have taken on a whole new meaning in German. Today, the German language includes common English words such as *cool, Body, Aroma, Blazer, Poncho, Story, Computer, Homepage, Internet, Software, Laptop, managen, babysitten, chatten,* and *downloaden*. Several of these, such as *Computer* and *Laptop,* have even edged out the German equivalents (*der Rechner* and *der Schlepptop,* respectively).

In addition to these culturally influenced changes, German has recently gone through an official spelling reform. Starting in 1998, educational materials have been published using new rules for spelling and grammar, though many non-educational materials and texts that are reprinted today use the old rules. As a result, it is possible to see variations in spelling and punctuation in many German texts. (All exercises and examples in *Workout in German* have been written using the new rules whenever possible. We've also dedicated one of the workouts to exploring some of the differences introduced by the spelling reform.)

1 Cases *Nominative and Accusative*

German nouns (which are always capitalized, regardless of where they are in a sentence) are said to be in one of four "cases," depending on their function within a sentence. The four cases are nominative, accusative, dative, and genitive.

Case is usually indicated through changes in the articles or adjectives that precede the noun or through changes in the pronoun used to replace the noun. The table below shows the nominative and accusative cases in the masculine singular form.

	Nom.	Acc.
Definite article	*der* Mann (the man)	*den* Mann (the man)
***Der*-word**	*dieser* Mann (this man)	*diesen* Mann (this man)
Indefinite article	*ein* Mann (a man)	*einen* Mann (a man)
Possessive adjective	*mein* Mann (my man)	*meinen* Mann (my man)
Personal pronoun	*er* (him)	*ihn* (him)

The nominative case is used primarily to indicate the subject of a clause or sentence. The subject is the person or the thing doing the action and expresses *who* or *what* did something.

> *Der Hund* bellt.
> **The dog** is barking.

The nominative case is also used to note a noun that follows a "linking verb," such as *sein* (to be) or *werden* (to become). In essence, verbs such as these equate the object that follows them with the subject.

> *Das ist **der Tisch**.*
> That is **the table**.

The accusative case is used primarily to note the direct object of a verb. The direct object is the person or thing that is receiving the action and expresses *whom* or *what* is being acted upon.

> *Backst du **einen Kuchen**?*
> Are you baking **a cake**?

The accusative case is also used to indicate the object of certain prepositions.

> *Ich laufe **durch den Park**.*
> I'm walking **through the park**.

Alltagssprache

The subject does not always come first in a German sentence. Context or emphasis can indicate the person or thing that is the subject. Also, the verb will always agree with the subject and the subject will always be in the nominative case.

Ich (nominative, subject) *kenne **Frau Meier*** (accusative, direct object).
I know **Ms. Meier.**

Frau Meier (accusative, direct object) *kenne **ich*** (nominative, subject).
I know **Ms. Meier.**

Ich is the subject: It is in the nominative case, and the verb is conjugated to agree with it. The direct object (*Frau Meier*) can be placed at the beginning of the sentence for emphasis.

Exercise 1

Circle the subject and underline the direct object of the verb in the sentences below.

1. Sie kocht die Suppe.
2. Er hat den Ball.
3. Mein Lehrer schreibt eine E-Mail.
4. Das weiße Haus an der Ecke hat ein neues Dach. (roof)
5. Seinen Vater ruft er jeden Tag an.

Exercise 2

Determine from context if the bold phrase is the subject (nominative case) or the direct object of the verb (accusative case).

1. **Meine Frau** kocht nur vegetarisch. nominative
2. Heinrich kauft **ein Buch**. accusative
3. Die Kinder schreiben **Aufsätze über die Sommerferien**. (essays) accusative

4. **Martha** mietet eine neue Wohnung. _nominative_
   (rents)
5. Der Mann kennt **sie** gut. _nominative_

Exercise 3

Describe each picture below by building simple sentences using the elements provided. Be sure to choose a verb that agrees with the subject.

Subjects (Nom. Case)	Verbs	Direct Objects (Acc. Case)
der Junge	werfen _throw_	das Haus
die Frau	malt _paints_	Kekse
das Mädchen	putzt _cleans_	den Ball
die Kinder	backt _bakes_	ein Bild

3. _Das Mädchen backt Kekse._

1. _Der Junge malt ein Bild._

4. _Die Kinder werfen den Ball._

2. _Die Frau putzt das Haus._

The dative case is used primarily to note the indirect object of a verb. The indirect object is the person or thing *to whom* or *for whom* an action is being carried out.

*Sie gibt **dem Mann** den Regenschirm.*
She gives **the man** the umbrella.

The dative case is also used to indicate the object of certain prepositions.

*Gehst du **mit deinen Freunden**?*
Are you going **with your friends**?

Achtung!

While the nominative and accusative cases show little difference from each other except in the masculine singular forms, the dative case is distinguishable in all forms.

	Nom.	Dat.
Definite article	*der Mann* (the man)	*de**m** Mann* (the man)
***Der**-word*	*diese Frau* (this woman)	*dies**er** Frau* (this woman)
Indefinite article	*ein Foto* (a photo)	*ein**em** Foto* (a photo)
Possessive adjective	*meine Stühle* (my chairs)	*mein**en** Stühlen* (my chairs)
Personal pronoun	*Sie* (you)	***Ihnen*** (you)

Exercise 1

To or for whom are the following actions being done? Underline the indirect object in the sentences below.

1. Ich kaufe meinem Freund ein Geschenk. *[io]*

2. Die Kinder kochen ihren Eltern Spaghetti. *[io]*

3. Die Schauspielerin zeigt dem Publikum ihren neugeborenen Sohn. *[io]* *(shows)(audience, crowd)* *(newborn)*

4. Er hat mir seine neue Adresse gegeben. *[io]*

5. Hast du deiner Tochter eine Geschichte vorgelesen? *[io]*

6. Meine Großmutter backt uns Kekse. *[io]*

7. Der Junge erzählte ihm mehrere Witze. *(tells) [io] (several)* *(jokes)*

8. Was hast du mir gekauft? *[io]*

Exercise 2

In the following sentences, circle the subject (nominative), underline the direct object (accusative), and use a wavy line to underline the indirect object (dative). Use the context of the sentences to help determine which case is being used.

1. Der Vater kocht der Mutter ein schönes Abendessen. *[s] [io] [do]*

2. Ich kaufe meinem Bruder ein neues Fahrrad. *[s] [io] [do]*

3. Der alten Dame neben uns schenken wir immer etwas zu Weihnachten. *[io] [s] [s] [do]*

4. Wir geben dem alten Mann eine Karte für das Konzert. *[s] [io] [do]*

Exercise 3

The noun phrases and pronouns given in bold below are in the dative case. Determine whether they are the indirect object of the verb (IO) or the object of a preposition (OP) that requires the dative case and circle the correct answer.

1. Oskar zeigt **ihm** seine Briefmarkensammlung.   IO ~~OP~~
shows   *stamp collection*

2. Wir fahren mit **unserer Familie** nach Köln.   IO (OP)

3. Wilhelm hat **mir** Rosen gekauft.   (IO) OP

4. Bei **der Ärztin** hat er eine Spritze bekommen.   IO (OP)
injection

5. Wer spricht mit **dem Mann** da drüben?   IO (OP)
over here

Exercise 4

Sabina is buying presents for her family members. Answer the questions below by saying what she is buying each person. Use the noun phrase to describe each person's relationship to her.

Family Member	Present
dem Bruder	ein Computerspiel
der Schwester	eine CD
der Tante	einen Roman
dem Onkel	eine Pfeife *whistle, pipe*
dem Vetter *cousin*	ein Buch

Beispiel: Wem kauft Sabina ein Computerspiel?
Sie kauft dem Bruder ein Computerspiel.

1. Wem kauft Sabina eine CD?

Sabine kauft der schwester eine CD.

2. Wem kauft Sabina einen Roman?

Sabina kauft der Tante einen Roman.

3. Wem kauft Sabina eine Pfeife?

Sabina kauft dem Onkel eine pfeife.

4. Wem kauft Sabina ein Buch?

Sabina kauft dem vetter ein Buch.

2

Cases *Genitive*

The genitive case is primarily used to show a possessive relationship between two people or things. The genitive case expresses *whose* or *of what*.

> *Das ist der Bruder **meines Onkels.***
> This is **my uncle's** brother.

> *Das Ende **des Films/Filmes** war wirklich gut.*
> The end **of the movie** was really good.

The genitive case noun is the person or the thing that *possesses* or *has* another person or thing. In English, this relationship is indicated with an apostrophe *s*, with the use of the preposition *of*, or with the phrase *belonging to.*

> *Das ist der Wagen **meines Bruders.***
> This **is my brother's** car.

> *Ich fahre den Wagen **meines Bruders.***
> I am driving **my brother's** car.

> *Wir fahren mit dem Wagen **meines Bruders.***
> We are going with **my brother's** car.

The genitive case is also used to indicate the object of certain prepositions.

> *Was machst du **während der Ferien**?*
> What are you doing **during vacation**?

The definite and indefinite articles undergo a change in the genitive case.

	Definite Articles	Indefinite Articles
M	*des*	*eines*
F	*der*	*einer*
Neuter	*des*	*einer*
Pl.	*der*	——

*Der Anfang **des Romans** ist wirklich spannend.*
The beginning **of the novel** is really suspenseful.

*Er ist der Bruder **einer Freundin.***
He is the brother **of a** (female) **friend** (of mine).

Masculine and neuter nouns in the genitive case add an *-s*. In the case of monosyllabic nouns, an *-es* is often added.

> *Böll ist der Name **eines berühmten Autors.***
> Böll is the name **of a famous author.**

> *Kennst du den Namen **des Mannes**?*
> Do you know **the man's** name?

Exercise 1

Relationships matter. Define the family members below by matching the genitive construction in column A with its definition in column B.

A		B
D	1. der Bruder meiner Mutter	a. meine Schwester
e	2. der Vater meines Vaters	b. mein Bruder
a	3. die Tochter meines Vater	c. meine Tante
c	4. die Schwester meines Vaters	d. mein Onkel
B	5. der Sohn meiner Mutte	e. mein Großvater

Exercise 2

Use context to determine the case of the nouns below. Circle the subject (nominative), underline the direct object (accusative), use a wavy line to underline the indirect object (dative), and use two lines to underline the person or thing possessed (genitive). Note: Not all cases will be used in each sentence.

1. Kennst du den Bruder dieses Mädchens?   *S DO TP*

2. Er spielt gern Tennis.   *S DO*

3. Die nette Dame liest den Kindern die Märchen der Brüder Grimm vor.   *S DIO DO TP*

4. Unser Großvater zeigt uns alte Fotos.   *S IO DO*

5. Hast du mir etwas gekauft?   *S IO DO*

6. Der Schwanz der Katze ist schwarz.   *S TP (tail)*

7. Wann gibst du mir endlich einen Tipp? (tip, hint)   *S IO DO*

8. Meine Schwester hat die Filme des Regisseurs immer gern.   *S DO TP (director)*

Exercise 3

Provide the equivalent of the nouns below using the definite article in the genitive case.

1. von der Frau

   dem Frau

2. von dem Mädchen

   des Mädchen

3. von dem Kunden (customers)

   des Kunden

4. von dem Arbeiter

   des Arbeiter

5. von der Familie

   dem Familie

Exercise 4

Translate the following sentences into German using the appropriate case.

1. Her mother's car is in the garage.

   Das Auto ihrer Mutter ist in der Garage.

2. The horse's leg is injured.

   Das Bein des Pferdes ist verletzt.

3. The cover of that book is new.   *den Einband*

   Der Einband das Buches ist neu.

4. Where is the owner of the red Mercedes?   *der Besitzer*

   Wo ist der Besitzer des roten Mercedes?

5. Did you see the neighbors' new carpet?

   Hast du den neuen Teppich der Nachbaren gesehen?

3

The German definite article is equivalent to *the* in English. **The definite article inflects according to the number, case, and gender of the noun.**

	Singular (M)	Singular (F)	Singular (Neuter)	Plural
Nom.	*der*	*die*	*das*	*die*
Acc.	*den*	*die*	*das*	*die*
Dat.	*dem*	*der*	*dem*	*den*
Gen.	*des*	*der*	*des*	*der*

Achtung!

With the exception of the masculine singular, the definite article is the same in the nominative and accusative in all forms.

Achtung!

In the dative plural, an *-n* is added to the end of the noun if it does not already end in one.

die Kinder → *den Kindern*
the children → to/for the children

The definite article is used to indicate a specific object as opposed to a generic object.

Eine Birne schmeckt gut.
A pear tastes good.

Die Birne schmeckt gut.
The pear tastes good.

The definite article is used in the name of certain countries, including *der Libanon* (Lebanon), *die Niederlande* (the Netherlands), *die Schweiz* (Switzerland), *die Slowakei* (Slovakia), *die Tschechische Republik* (the Czech Republic), *die Türkei* (Turkey), *die Ukraine* (the Ukraine), *die USA* (USA), *die Vereinigten Staaten* (the United States).

Die Schweiz bleibt neutral.
Switzerland remains neutral.

The definite article is often used in combination with the dative reflexive pronoun to indicate parts of the body.

Sie wäscht **sich die Haare.**
She is washing **her hair.**

Alltagssprache

The definite article is often used with first names when one is very familiar with someone.

Hast du **den** *Otto gesehen?*
Did you see Otto?

Exercise 1

Create a question-and-answer pair for each question below. First, ask if the person you are with sees the building (using the accusative case for the direct object), then answer that it is on the main street (using the nominative case for the subject).

Beispiel:

Siehst du das Hotel?
Das Hotel steht in der Hauptstraße.

1. _____
_____
_____

2. _____

   _____

3. _____

   _____

Exercise 2

Fill in the blank in the sentences below with the correct form of the definite article depending on the number, case, and gender of the noun. Determine if the noun is used as the subject, direct object, or indirect object.

1. Hast du _____den_____ Wagen gesehen?

2. _____Die_____ Frau wartet im Büro.

3. Sie kocht _____die_____ Suppe heute Abend.

4. Er wollte _____dem_____ Opa einen Roman schenken.

5. _____Der_____ Kugelschreiber liegt auf meinem Schreibtisch.
   (ballpoint pen)

Exercise 3

Who is writing what to whom? Write five sentences based on the chart below. Use definite articles for the objects (direct and indirect), including the first names. Since both objects are noun phrases, the indirect object should come before the direct object in each of your sentences.

Beispiel: Martin schreibt der Claudia das Gedicht.

Wer?	Was?	Wem?
ich	Karte	Oma
du	E-Mail	Andreas
Martin	Gedicht poem	Claudia
Sigrid	Brief	Michael
Elke und Jürgen	Geschichte	Kinder

1. Ich kaufe der Oma die Karte.
2. Du schickst dem Andreas die Email
3. _____
4. Sigrid schreibt dem M. den Brief.
5. Elke und Jürgen lesen den Kindern die Geschichte.

Exercise 4

Translate the following sentences into German using the correct case and definite article.

1. Where are the keys?

   Wo sind die schlüssel?

2. Is this the right house?

   Ist das das richtige Haus?

3. They live in Lebanon.

   Sie wohnen im Libanon.

In German, certain words, called *der*-words, change endings similar to the definite articles. The *der*-words include *dies-* (this), *jed-* (each/every), *jen-* (that), *manch-* (some), *solch-* (such), and *welch-* (which).

Der-words change form depending on the case of the nouns they qualify.

> **Diese** *Birne schmeckt gut.* (nominative)
> **This** pear tastes good.

> *Ich kenne* **solche** *Typen.* (accusative)
> I know **such** people (people like that).

> *Sie erzählt* **jener** *Frau eine Geschichte.* (dative)
> She is telling **that** woman a story.

> *Das Ende* **jedes** *Märchen ist das Gleiche.* (genitive)
> The end of **every** fairy tale is the same.

The *der*-words inflect according to the table below, which also shows their similarities to the definite articles:

	M	F	Neuter	Pl.
Nom.	der/dies**er** Löffel the/this spoon	die/dies**e** Gabel the/this fork	das/dies**es** Messer the/this knife	die/dies**e** Tassen the/these cups
Acc.	den/ dies**en** Löffel the/this spoon	die/dies**e** Gabel the/this fork	das/dies**es** Messer the/this knife	die/dies**e** Tassen the/these cups
Dat.	dem/ dies**em** Löffel the/this spoon	der/ dies**er** Gabel the/this fork	d**em**/ dies**em** Messer the/this knife	den/ dies**en** Tassen the/these cups
Gen.	des/dies**es** Löffels the/this spoon	der/ dies**er** Gabel the/this fork	des/dies**es** Messers the/this knife	der/ dies**er** Tassen the/these cups fork

Achtung!

In the dative plural, an *-n* is added to the end of the noun if it does not already end in one.

diese Kinder → *diesen Kinder**n***
these children → to/for these children

Exercise 1

Use the adjectives and the nominative form of *dies-* to describe each of the objects pictured below.

~~round~~ rund ~~small~~ hoch klein alt modern
~~high~~ hoch ~~old~~ alt

Beispiel:

Dieser Apfel ist rund.

1. dieses Gebäude ist hoch

2. dieses Haus ist klein

3. dieser Fernseher ist alt.

1. der Tisch/die Tische

welchen tisch möchten sie?
Möchten sie diesen tisch?
Nein, danke. solche tische
möchte ich nicht.

4. dieser stuhl ist modern

2. die Lampe/die Lampen

welche lampe möchten sie?
Möchten sie diese lampe?
Nein, danke. solche lampen
mag ich nicht.

Exercise 2

Determine if the noun is used as the subject, direct object, or indirect object and fill in the blanks below with the correct form of the *der*-word in parentheses.

1. jede (jed-) Frage ist wichtig.

2. solche (solch-) Bücher finde ich interessant.

3. welches (welch-) Mädchen kennst du?

4. Woher hast du diesen (dies-) Rucksack?

5. jedes (jed-) Kind soll das wissen.

6. welchen (welch-) Wagen fahren Sie gern?

7. welchem (welch-) Mann haben Sie das Handy gegeben?

8. manch (manch-) Häuser sind klein.

9. Das hat sie diesen (dies-) Leuten schon erzählt.

10. jenes (jen-) Kind hat er nichts gegeben.

3. die Vase/die Vasen

4. das Regal/die Regale bookcase

welches Regal möchten sie?
Möchten sie dieses Regal?
Nein, danke. solche Regale
mag ich nicht.

5. das Sofa/die Sofas

Exercise 3

A saleswoman (*Verkäuferin*) and customer (*Kunde*) are selecting home furnishings and decorations. Create short exchanges, based on the example, discussing the objects indicated. Inflect all the *der*-words to match the gender and number of each noun as indicated by the definite article.

Beispiel: der Stuhl/die Stühle
Verkäuferin: Welchen Stuhl möchten Sie?
Möchten Sie diesen Stuhl?`
Kunde: Nein, danke, solche Stühle mag ich nicht.

The indefinite article in German is *ein*, similar to *a/an* in English.

The indefinite article *ein* inflects according to the following table.

	M	**F**	**Neuter**
Nom. (subject)	*ein*	*eine*	*ein*
Acc. (direct object)	*einen*	*eine*	*ein*
Dat. (indirect object)	*einem*	*einer*	*einem*
Gen. (shows possession)	*eines*	*einer*	*eines*

Achtung!

There is no plural form of the indefinite article.

The indefinite article can be used to indicate something in general.

Die Birne schmeckt gut.
The pear tastes good.

Eine Birne schmeckt gut.
A pear tastes good.

Sie erzählt einem Mann den Witz.
She is telling **a** man the joke.

Ein can also mean the number one.

Ich möchte bitte ein Kilo Salami.
I would like **one** kilogram of salami, please.

Ich möchte einen von denen.
I would like **one** of those.

Ausnahme

When expressing the indefinite pronoun *one, man* is used in the nominative case, *einen* is used in the accusative case, and *einem* is used in the dative case.

Wenn der Lehrer einem etwas erzählt, dann muss man zuhören.
When the teacher tells **one (you)** something, then **one (you)** has (have) to listen.

Ein can also be used in expressions of time, in which it takes the accusative form.

Einen Augenblick, bitte.
One moment, please.

Das ist einen Monat nach dem Unfall passiert.
That happened **one** month after the accident.

Alltagssprache

Specific situations that in English would use the indefinite article do not take the indefinite article in German:

- To describe a role, position, religion, or nationality with the verb *sein* (to be) or *werden* (to become) unless an adjective is used modify the noun.

Seth ist Amerikaner.
Seth is **an** American.

Claudia wollte immer Ärztin werden.
Claudia has always wanted to become **a** doctor.

Sie ist eine gute Ärztin.
She is **a** good doctor.

- In phrases where the indefinite article means *every* or *per* in English. (The definite article is used in these situations.)

Ich besuche meine Mutter zweimal die Woche.
I visit my mother twice **a (every)** week.

Exercise 1

Use the correct form of *ein* to complete each sentence below. Determine if the noun is used as the subject, direct object, or indirect object.

1. Elisabeth sucht _____eine_____ Stelle.

2. Heinz-Peter schenkt mir jeden Morgen _____einen_____ Kaffee ein.

3. Katrin und Georg haben _____einen_____ Hund und zwei Katzen.

4. Ute erzählt _____einem_____ Kunden dieselbe Geschichte.

5. Oma hat Dominik _____ein_____ altes Foto gezeigt.

Exercise 2

Write a sentence indicating what each person below wants to be. Decide if an indefinite article should be used based on the information given. Write the English equivalent as well.

Beispiel:
Claudia, Ärztin
Claudia will Ärztin werden.

1. Rolf, Schauspieler

   Rolf will Schauspieler werden.

2. Miriam, effiziente Managerin

   Miriam will eine effiziente Managerin werden.

3. Stefan, effektiver Krankenpfleger *male nurse*

   Stefan will einen effektiver Krankenpfleger werden

4. Kirstin, Katholikerin

   Kirstin will Katholikerin werden.

5. Heinz, Deutscher

   Heinz will Deutscher werden.

Exercise 3

Use the indefinite article to indicate that each building pictured below is on the main street (subject, nominative). Then say that you need one nearby (accusative, direct object).

Beispiel:

Ein Hotel steht in der Hauptstraße.
Wir brauchen ein Hotel in der Nähe.

1. Eine Bank steht in der Hauptstrasse. Ich brauche eine Bank in der Nähe.

2. Ein Markt steht in der Strasse. Ich brauche einen Markt in der Nähe.

3. Ein Restuarant steht ... Ich brauche ein Restuarant...

6

13

7 Articles & Related Words *Ein-words*

Possessive adjectives indicate ownership or possession.

my	*mein*	our	*unser*
your	*dein*	your	*euer*
his, her, its	*sein, ihr, sein*	their/your (formal)	*ihr/Ihr*

All possessive adjectives take the same endings as *ein* and are referred to as *ein*-words. Though *ein* has no plural form, the possessive adjectives do since someone can possess more than one of something.

	M	F	Neuter	Pl.
Nom.	*mein*	*meine*	*mein*	*meine*
Acc.	*meinen*	*meine*	*mein*	*meine*
Dat.	*meinem*	*meiner*	*meinem*	*meinen*
Gen.	*meine*	*meiner*	*meines*	*meiner*

The ending taken by a possessive adjective is determined by the gender of the noun possessed, not by the gender of the person who possesses the noun.

Mein Vater heißt Martin.
My father's **name** is Martin.

Ich kenne seine Schwester.
I know **his sister.**

Er fährt mit ihrem Wagen.
He is driving **her car.**

Wo wohnt der Vater Ihrer Mutter?
Where does **your mother's** father live?

Achtung!
In the dative plural, an *-n* is added to the end of the noun if it does not already end in one.

meine Kinder → meinen Kindern
my children → to/for my children

Alltagssprache
In both spoken and written German, the *-e* before the *-r* in *unser* and *euer* is often dropped when adding an ending.

Sie will unsren Hund mitnehmen.
She wants to take **our** dog along.

Alltagssprache
When indicating parts of the body or articles of clothing, the possessive adjective is not used with reflexive verbs where the subject is the possessor. Instead, possession is shown by using the dative reflexive pronoun, and the definite article is placed before the noun.

Sie wäscht sich die Haare. (ihre Haare)
She is washing **her** hair. (**her** hair)

Ich ziehe mir die Jacke an. (meine Jacke)
I am putting on **my** jacket. (**my** jacket)

Achtung!
The pronoun *kein* (no) takes the same endings as the *ein*-words.

Exercise 1

The following questions ask if an item belongs to a specific person. Use *Nein, . . .* to negate the statement, then state the actual owner according to the clue in parentheses. Note: The nominative case is used with the linking verb *sein*.

Beispiele:
Ist das Ihre Jacke? (his)
Nein, das ist nicht meine Jacke. Das ist seine Jacke.

Ist das eure Wohnung? (their)
Nein, das ist nicht unsere Wohnung. Das ist ihre Wohnung.

1. Ist das sein Computer? (her)

_____

_____

2. Ist das unsere Haltestelle? (their)

_____

_____

3. Ist das meine Zeitung? (my)

_____

_____

4. Ist das ihr Handy? (his)

_____

_____

5. Ist das dein Wagen? (her)

_____

_____

Exercise 2

Fill in the blanks with the correct form of the _ein_-word given. Determine if the noun is used as the subject, direct object, or indirect object.

1. _____ (ihr) Vater arbeitet an der Universität.

2. Was schenkst du _____ (dein) Freund zum Geburtstag?

3. Sie kann _____ (ihr) Rucksack nicht finden.

4. Ich schreibe _____ (mein) Onkel einen Brief.

5. Wir verkaufen _____ (unser) Haus.

Exercise 3

Who is giving what to whom? Write five sentences based on the chart below. Use correct possessive adjective to correspond to the subject of each sentence.

Wer?	Was?	Wem?
ich	E-Mailadresse	Onkel
du	Handynummer	Kollegin
Maria	Rock	Schwester
Christian	Buch	Freund
Peter und Nina	Wagen	Sohn

1. _____

_____

_____

2. _____

_____

_____

3. _____

_____

_____

4. _____

_____

_____

5. _____

_____

_____

All German nouns are said to have one of three genders: masculine, feminine, or neuter.

The gender of a noun is indicated by the definite articles (*der, die, das*), which are usually learned together with the nouns.

der Hund (masculine)	the dog
die Katze (feminine)	the cat
das Kind (neuter)	the child

When referring to people, the gender of a noun usually mirrors the gender of the person.

der Mann (masculine)	the man
die Frau (feminine)	the woman

Ausnahme

Although *Mädchen* means *girl*, it literally means "little maid" and is neuter (*das Mädchen*). The diminutive ending -*chen* is always neuter.

Fräulein, which means *miss*, is also neuter (*das Fräulein*). The diminutive ending -*lein* is always neuter.

For many occupations (particularly those derived from verbs), the form changes depending on gender of the person performing the job. Masculine forms usually end in -*er*. The feminine is formed by adding -*in* to the end of the masculine form.

der Lehrer (the male teacher)
*die Lehrer**in*** (the female teacher)

der Maler (the male painter)
*die Maler**in*** (the female painter)

The feminine form of many diplomatic titles is formed by adding -in to the masculine form.

der König (the king)
*die König**in*** (the queen)

der Herzog (the duke)
*die Herzog**in*** (the duchess)

As in English, some animals have both a masculine and a feminine form in German. In these cases, the gender of the noun typically mirrors the gender of the specific animal.

der Kater (tomcat)	*die Katze* (female cat)
der Bulle (bull)	*die Kuh* (cow)

Exercise 1

The following nouns all refer to people and animals. Determine the gender of the following nouns and insert the correct definite article. Use the meaning of the noun as well as its ending to help.

1. _____ Tochter

2. _____ Chef

3. _____ Maklerin

4. _____ Bruder

5. _____ Balletttänzerin

6. _____ Arbeiter

7. _____ Mädchen

8. _____ Wissenschaftler

9. _____ Fräulein

10. _____ Hund

11. _____ Kuh

12. _____ Katze

13. _____ Vater

14. _____ Lehrling

15. _____ Touristin

16. _____ Politikerin

17. _____ Neffe

18. _____ Journalist

Exercise 2

Translate the following sentences into German. Pay close attention to noun gender.

1. Our daughter is a scientist.

   _____

   _____

2. Their son is a politician.

   _____

   _____

3. This is my dog.

   _____

   _____

4. His landlady's name is Mrs. Braun.

   _____

   _____

5. This girl is a ballet dancer.

   _____

   _____

Exercise 3

Change the following nouns from masculine to feminine.

Beispiel: der Student: <u>die Studentin</u>

1. der Flugbegleiter: _____

2. der Krankenpfleger: _____

3. der Verkäufer: _____

4. der Vermieter: _____

5. der König: _____

8

Some groups of inanimate objects are always a specific gender.

Masculine	Feminine	Neuter
days of the week	names of airplanes	names of cafés (*das Café*)
months	names of motorcycles	chemical elements
	seasons	names of ships
		names of colors
names for cars (*der Wagen*)		names of hotels (*das Hotel*)
names of trains (*der Zug*)		names of theaters (*das Theater*)
		nouns created from the infinitive form of a verb (*das Schwimmen;* swimming)

The following endings can be used to determine the gender of most nouns for inanimate objects.

Masculine	Feminine		Neuter
-er	*-ade*	*-ie*	*-chen*
-ig	*-age*	*-ik*	*-lein*
-ismus	*-anz*	*-ion*	*-ma*
-ling	*-e*	*-in*	*-ment*
-or	*-enz*	*-keit*	*-o*
	-ette	*-schaft*	*-um*
	-ei	*-tät*	
	-heit	*-ung*	

Alltagssprache

In some German dialects, the genders of nouns vary. In some regions, *Butter* is considered masculine; however, in standard, written German, only *die Butter* is considered correct.

Other nouns have officially recognized dual genders: *das/der Taxi* varies regionally between neuter and masculine, and both are considered acceptable. It may help to remember that a taxi is a car and that the two words for car are *Auto* (neuter) and *Wagen* (masculine).

The gender of a compound noun is determined by the gender of its last component.

> *die Maschine* (machine, F)
> > *die Flug**maschine*** (airplane)
> > *die Kaffee**maschine*** (coffee machine)
> > *die Brot**maschine*** (bread slicer)

Exercise 1

Determine the gender of each noun below based on its meaning and the word groups it belongs to and insert the correct definite article.

1. _____ Aluminium

2. _____ Februar

3. _____ Mayflower

4. _____ Montag

5. _____ U.S. Constitution

6. _____ Gold

7. _____ Rot

8. _____ Schwimmen

9. _____ Mercedes

10. _____ Frühling

11. _____ Silber

12. _____ Herbst

13. _____ Boeing

14. _____ Hilton

15. _____ Radfahren

Exercise 2

Determine the gender of each noun based on its ending and insert the correct definite article.

1. _____ Büchlein

2. _____ Gesundheit

3. _____ Reportage

4. _____ Rennauto

5. _____ Märchen

6. _____ Partei

7. _____ Diskussion

8. _____ Universität

9. _____ Sozialismus

10. _____ Museum

11. _____ Tageszeitung

12. _____ Demokratie

13. _____ Miete

14. _____ Butter

15. _____ Stigma

Exercise 3

Place the following nouns into the appropriate column: masculine, feminine, or neuter. Then rearrange the first letter of the words in each column to form three new words. Hint: Each new word will be the same gender as the list of words it came from.

Winter
Ritz
Lithium
Büro
Blockade
Einkommen

Universität
Studium
Gegner
November
Anfänger
Reaktion

Tätigkeit
Tendenz
Egoismus
Erholung
Indigo

Masculine	Feminine	Neuter

New words:

_____   _____   _____

Exercise 4

Translate the following sentences into German, paying close attention to the gender of each noun.

1. This is my street.

_____

_____

2. The *Titanic* was gigantic.

_____

_____

3. Realism is much more interesting.

_____

_____

4. The Café Kranzler is an old café in Berlin.

_____

_____

5. This scientist is interested in magnesium.

_____

_____

A noun may undergo several changes to form the plural in German, many of which must be memorized. The definite article for all plural forms, regardless of gender, is *die*. Words such as the definite article can help when identifying those plural forms in which there is no change in the noun itself.

Most nouns ending in *-er* are derived from verbs and undergo no change in plural form.

der Arbeiter (the worker) → **die** *Arbeiter* (the workers)

Some nouns form the plural by adding an umlaut to the vowel, if possible, and *-er* to the end of the singular form.

das Buch (the book) → *die B**ü**ch**er*** (the books)
das Kind (the child) → *die Kind**er*** (the children)

Some nouns form the plural by adding an umlaut to the vowel, if possible, and *-e* to the end of the singular form.

der Stuhl (the chair) → *die St**üh**l**e*** (the chairs)
der Fisch (the fish, singular) →
   *die Fisch**e*** (the fish, plural)

Some nouns form the plural by adding *-n* or *-en* to the end of the singular form. Feminine nouns that end in *-in* add *-nen* in plural form.

die Straße (the street) → *die Straße**n*** (the streets)
der Student (the student, male) →
   *die Student**en*** (the students, all males or
   mixed group)
die Studentin (the student, female) →
   *die Studentin**nen*** (the students, all females)

Achtung!

Although *Studenten* is the plural of the masculine form, it is used to specify either a group made up entirely of males or a group made up of both male and female students. The word *Studentinnen*, however, refers only to a group of female students. The same is true of all nouns with a feminine form ending in *-in* that refer to people, except for those that are masculine in nature and can only refer to males, such as *Vater* (father) and *Bruder* (brother).

Alltagssprache

In order to be more inclusive of females in mixed groups without using the masculine plural form, a more recent plural form of *Student* has developed; *StudentInnen,* spelled with a capital *I* mid-word. Similar plural forms that emphasize the inclusion of women in a mixed group can be made for any noun with an *-innen* ending by capitalizing the *i*.

Some nouns, often those borrowed directly from other languages, add *-s* to the end to form the plural.

das Sofa (the sofa) → *die Sofas* (the sofas)

Exercise 1

Give the plural form of each singular noun below. If needed, use a dictionary to determine the appropriate ending.

1. der Bleistift _____

2. die Zeitung _____

3. der Computer _____

4. das Handy _____

5. das Land _____

6. die Hose _____

7. die Prinzessin _____

8. der Tisch _____

9. der Film _____

10. die Tasse _____

Exercise 2

Change the subjects (in boldface) below from singular to plural and rewrite the sentences. Be sure to also change the verb to agree with the new subject (all verbs are regular in this exercise). If needed, use a dictionary to determine the appropriate plural ending.

1. Das Buch liegt da drüben.

_____

_____

2. Der Tourist fliegt nach Frankfurt.

_____

_____

3. Der Junge kocht am Wochenende.

_____

_____

4. Die Studentin geht in die Mensa.

_____

_____

5. Der Krankenpfleger bleibt im Zimmer.

_____

_____

Exercise 3

Change the subjects (in boldface) below from plural to singular. Be sure to also change the verb to agree with the new subject (all verbs are regular in this exercise). If needed, use a dictionary to determine the gender of the noun.

1. Die Schüler schreiben heute viel.

_____

_____

2. Die Autoren wohnen hier.

_____

_____

3. Die Sekretärinnen tippen sehr schnell.

_____

_____

4. Die Profis kaufen die Autos.

_____

_____

5. Die Lampen stehen auf dem Tisch.

_____

_____

10

11 Nouns *Compound Nouns*

Compound nouns are the combination of several words to form a single noun with a new meaning.

Compound nouns are formed by combining two nouns, adding the stem of a verb to a noun, or adding an adjective to a noun.

das Bett (the bed) + *die Decke* (the cover) = *die Bettdecke* (the bedcover)

rennen (to race) + *der Wagen* (the car) = der *Rennwagen* (the race car)

schnell (fast) + *der Zug* (the train) = der *Schnellzug* (the express train/fast train)

Die **Bettdecke** *liegt schon auf dem Bett.*
The **bedcover** is already lying on the bed.

Dieser **Rennwagen** *ist am schnellsten.*
This **race car** is the fastest.

Der **Schnellzug** *hält nicht überall.*
The **express train** doesn't stop everywhere.

The last component of a compound noun always determines both its gender and how its plural is formed.

*das Tee**haus*** (the teahouse)
*die Tee**häuser*** (the teahouses)

*das Koch**buch*** (the cookbook)
*die Koch**bücher*** (the cookbooks)

*der Rot**wein*** (the red wine)
*die Rot**weine*** (the red wines)

Achtung!

Occasionally, when two nouns are combined, a so-called *n*-joiner is inserted to between them. There is no set rule for when this occurs. However, *n*-joiners are often added when the first component ends with an *-e*.

die Straße (the street) + *die Lampe* (the light) = *die Straße**n**lampe* (the streetlight)

die Lippe (the lip) + *der Stift* (the stick) = *der Lippe**n**stift* (the lipstick)

die Straße (the street) + *die Bahn* (the train) = *die Straße**n**bahn* (the streetcar)

Exercise 1

Create compound nouns from the nouns below. Indicate the gender of each new compound noun by also including the corresponding nominative case definite article (*der, die*, or *das*).

1. das Haus + der Schlüssel =

_____

2. das Handy + die Nummer =

_____

3. der Tee + der Löffel =

_____

4. die Hand + die Tasche =

_____

5. der Kaffee + der Tisch =

_____

6. die Schreibwaren + das Geschäft =

_____

7. das Telefon + das Buch =

_____

8. der Regen + der Mantel =

_____

9. der Kaffee + die Maschine =

_____

10. der Schnee + der Mann =

_____

Exercise 2

Provide the plural form (along with the definite article) for each compound noun below.

1. das Telefonbuch

_____

2. die Straßenlampe

_____

3. der Studentenausweis

_____

4. der Teeladen

_____

5. der Krankenwagen

_____

Exercise 3

List five other compound nouns in German. Use the nominative definite article for each, and provide its meaning in English.

1. _____

2. _____

3. _____

4. _____

5. _____

Exercise 4

Determine the meanings of each compound noun below based on the components that make them up.

1. der Handschuh

_____

2. das Krankenhaus

_____

3. der Schreibtisch

_____

4. das Esszimmer

_____

5. die Erdbeere

_____

6. der Fingerhut

_____

7. der Waschlappen

_____

8. der Regenschirm

_____

Exercise 5

Use the English definition provided in parentheses to fill in the correct compound noun for each sentence below.

Am (**1.**) _____ (weekend) feiern wir im Dorf.

Jeden Januar haben wir ein großes (**2.**) _____

(winter festival). Die Kinder bauen (**3.**) _____

(snowmen), und sie laufen mit (**4.**) _____

(skates). Dieses Jahr habe ich mir extra ein paar neue (**5.**)

_____ (mittens) dafür gestrickt!

11

Some masculine, singular nouns, called *n-nouns*, take an -*n* or -*en* ending when they are in a case other than the nominative.

N-nouns often refer to people or animals.

*Der **Student** heißt Christian.* (nominative)
The **student** is named Christian.

*Ich kennen den **Studenten** gut.* (accusative)
I know the **student** well.

Ausnahme

Other common *n*-nouns include *der Gedanke* (the thought), *der Glaube* (the belief), and *der Name* (the name). These three nouns take both an -*n* and an -*s* in the genitive case.

der Name (the name) → *des Namens* (of the name; the name's)

N-nouns usually form the plural by adding -*(e)n* to the end of the singular form. The singular and plural form of N-nouns are identical in cases other than the nominative; articles and adjectives can be used to distinguish between them.

*Der **Elefant** ist **groß**.* (nominative)
The elephant is **big**.

*Der Trainer arbeitet mit **dem großen Elefanten**.* (dative)
The trainer is working with **the big elephants**.

Achtung!

Der Herr (the gentleman) is an *n*-noun but takes only -*n* in the singular form. *Der Herr* forms the plural (in all cases) with -*en*.

*Der **Herr** steht an der Ecke.* (nominative)
The **gentleman** is standing on the corner.

*Ist das der Regenschirm des **Herrn**?* (genitive)
Is that the **gentleman**'s umbrella?

*Die **Herren** stehen an der Ecke.* (nominative)
The gentlemen are standing on the corner.

*Siehst du die **Herren** da drüben?* (accusative)
Do you see the **gentlemen** over there?

Exercise 1

Put a checkmark next to the *n*-nouns below. Then rewrite them in the accusative, dative, and genitive cases.

_____ der Professor	_____ der Gedanke
_____ die Straße	_____ die Frau
_____ der Affe	_____ der Wissenschaftler
_____ das Mädchen	_____ das Messer
_____ der Sessel	_____ der Name

_____

_____

_____

_____

_____

_____

Exercise 2

Write the following nominative noun phrases in the accusative, dative, and genitive.

1. der Prinz

_____

_____

_____

2. der Glaube

_____

_____

_____

3. der Herr

_____

_____

_____

4. der Löwe

_____

_____

_____

5. der Tourist

_____

_____

_____

3. Der Fotograph zeigt **dem Mann** sein Werk.

_____

_____

_____

4. Der Tourist gibt **dem Elefanten** den Ball.

_____

_____

_____

5. Der Autor erzählt **dem Mädchen** eine Geschichte.

_____

_____

_____

Exercise 3

Change the two bold noun phrases in each sentence so that the subject (nominative) becomes the indirect object (dative) and vice versa. Be sure to watch for changes in _n_-nouns.

1. Der Journalist schenkt **der Frau** ein Foto.

_____

_____

_____

2. Die Dame kocht **dem Studenten** das Essen.

_____

_____

_____

12

Nominative personal pronouns replace noun phrases and proper nouns as the subject of a sentence.

	Singular		**Plural**	
I	*ich*	we	*wir*
you	*du*	you (plural)	*ihr*
he/she/it	*er/sie/es*	they	*sie*
		you (formal)	*Sie*

Das Handy funktioniert nicht.
The cell phone doesn't work.

Es funktioniert nicht.
It doesn't work.

Matthias arbeitet jeden Tag.
Matthias works every day.

Er arbeitet jeden Tag.
He works every day.

The nominative personal pronouns are most often used in combination with a verb.

	Singular	**Plural**
	ich gehe I go	*wir gehen* we go
gehen (to go)	*du gehst* you go	*ihr geht* you all go
	er/sie/es geht he/she/it/one goes	*sie gehen* they go
		Sie gehen you go (formal)

Achtung!

There are three forms of the pronoun *sie*, which vary in number and capitalization rules.

1. *sie:* she (lowercase, singular)

Ist sie ein hübsches Mädchen?
Is **she** a pretty young girl?

Sie ist ein hübsches Mädchen.
She is a pretty girl.

2. *sie:* they (lowercase, plural)

Sind sie Zwillinge?
Are **they** twins?

Sie sind Zwillinge.
They are twins.

3. *Sie:* you (formal, uppercase, always conjugated in the plural, whether referring to one person or more than one)

Sind Sie Rechtsanwalt?
Are **you** a lawyer?

Sie sind Rechtsanwalt?
You're a lawyer?

Herr und Frau Schiller, folgen Sie mir, bitte.
Mr. and Mrs. Schiller, please follow me.

Achtung!

The pronouns *er*, *sie*, and *es* replace noun phrases beginning with the articles *der*, *die*, and *das*, respectively.

The nominative third-person pronouns er, sie, and es can represent both objects and people. *Er* can mean *he* when referring to a person or *it* when referring to a masculine noun.

Der Lehrer ist nett. Er unterrichtet Mathe.
The teacher is nice. **He** teaches math.

Der Apfel ist süß. Er ist ganz saftig.
The apple is sweet. **It** is really juicy.

The personal pronoun *sie* can mean *she* when referring to a person or *it* when referring to a feminine noun.

Die Kellnerin arbeitet viel. Sie bekommt viel Trinkgeld.
The waitress works a lot. **She** gets a lot of tips.

Die Melone ist rund. Sie ist ganz frisch.
The melon is round. **It** is really fresh.

Achtung!

Sie is also the plural third-person pronoun and can mean *they* when referring to both people and objects.

Die Kinder spielen im Park. Sie haben Spaß.
The children are playing in the park. **They** are having fun.

Die Fischstäbchen kochen schnell. Sie sind lecker.
The fish sticks cook quickly. **They** are delicious.

The personal pronoun *es* can means both *he* or *she* when referring to a neuter noun representing either gender, and can also mean *they* when referring to a collective noun.

> **Das Kind** ist 12 Jahre alt. **Es** ist nett.
> **The child** is 12 years old. **He/She** is nice.

> **Das Fleisch** schmeckt gut. **Es** ist zart.
> **The meat** tastes good. **It** is tender.

> **Das Geschirr** kommt von meiner Oma. **Es** ist alt.
> **The dishes** are from my grandmother. **They** are old.

Alltagssprache

Until the spelling reform at the start of this century, the pronouns *du* and *ihr,* as well as their corresponding accusative and dative case forms, were capitalized throughout personal letters as a sign of respect. Today, only the formal *you* (*Sie*) is still capitalized in all instances.

Exercise 1

Replace the subject in the following sentences with the appropriate nominative personal pronoun.

1. Das Haus ist zu klein.

_____

2. Der Bär schläft im Wald.

_____

3. Eine Brille liegt neben der Lampe.

_____

4. Die Bücher stehen im Regal.

_____

5. Das kleine Kind weint nicht oft.

_____

Exercise 2

Select the most appropriate personal pronoun for the subject of each verb. Use the ending of each verb to determine the correct answer.

1. Was mache _____ hier überhaupt?
   a. ich   b. wir   c. ihr

2. Frau Krüger, möchten _____ ein Glas Wein?
   a. Sie   b. sie   c. du

3. _____, Heinrich und Hannah, ziehen nach Genf um.
   a. Du   b. Ihr   c. Wir

4. Ist es wahr, dass _____ gerne zusammen kocht?
   a. es   b. ich   c. ihr

5. Warum hörst _____ solche Musik nicht?
   a. sie   b. du   c. er

Exercise 3

Decide whether *sie* or *Sie* is the correct answer in each question below.

1. Herr Schneeberger, arbeiten sie/Sie immer noch bei BMW?
2. Hat sie/Sie wirklich zwei Waschmaschinen?
3. Ist sie/Sie deine Großmutter?
4. Entschuldigung, können sie/Sie mir bitte sagen, wo die Toilette ist?

Exercise 4

Use context to determine the appropriate English translation of the boldface pronouns below.

1. Seid **ihr** alle da? _____

2. Der braune Teller liegt auf der Theke. **Er** ist gross genug.

   _____

3. Herr Meier, sind **Sie** bald fertig? _____

4. Hast du das Mädchen gesehen? **Es** ist um die Ecke

   gerannt. _____

5. Wo sind die Stühle? **Sie** waren gestern noch da.

   _____

13

Accusative personal pronouns replace noun phrases or proper nouns as the direct object of a sentence or as the object of prepositions requiring the accusative case.

	Singular		Plural
me	*mich*	us	*uns*
you	*dich*	you (plural)	*euch*
him/her/it	*ihn/sie/es*	them	*sie*
		you (formal)	*Sie*

*Erik will **den Film** auswählen.*
Erik wants to choose

*Erik will **ihn** auswählen.*
Erik wants to choose it.

*Kennst du **Michael**?*
Do you know **Michael**?

*Kennst du **ihn**?*
Do you know **him**?

Similar to nominative personal pronouns, accusative third-person personal pronouns replace both people and objects. *Ihn* can means *him* when referring to a person or *it* when referring to a masculine noun.

*Er ruft **den Arzt** an.*
He is calling **the doctor**.

*Er ruft **ihn** an.*
He is calling **him**.

*Er zerbricht **den Spiegel**.*
He's breaking **the mirror**.

*Er zerbricht **ihn**.*
He's breaking **it**.

The personal pronoun *sie* can mean *she* when referring to a person or *it* when referring to a feminine noun.

*Ich sehe **die Krankenschwester**.*
I see **the nurse**.

*Ich sehe **sie**.*
I see **her**.

*Ich kaufe **die Lampe**.*
I am buying **the lamp**.

*Ich kaufe **sie**.*
I am buying **it**.

The personal pronoun *es* can means both *him* and *her*, when referring to a neuter noun representing either gender, and can also mean *them* when referring to a collective noun such as *das Personal* (personnel/staff).

*Sie repariert **das Bücherregal**. Sie repariert **es**.*
She is fixing **the bookcase**. She is fixing **it**.

*Sie begrüsst **das Personal**. Sie begrüsst **es**.*
She greets **the staff**. She greets **them**.

In sentences with both nominative and accusative pronouns, the nominative pronoun comes first.

*Siehst **du** mich?*
Do **you** see me?

*Kann **sie** sie fragen?*
Can **she** ask her/them?

*Können **Sie** sie fragen?*
Can you (formal) ask her/them?

Exercise 1

Rewrite the following sentences by replacing the direct object with the appropriate accusative personal pronoun.

1. Der Lärm stört die Kinder.

_____

_____

2. Der Räuber versteckt den Schatz.

_____

_____

3. Mutti will eine Reise im Internet buchen.

_____

_____

4. Wir kennen das Spiel schon.

_____

_____

5. Wer hat Rolf gesehen?

_____

_____

Exercise 2

Rewrite the sentences below by replacing the bold noun (direct object) with an accusative personal pronoun. Then ask a question using the nominative personal pronoun given in parentheses and the accusative pronoun used in your original sentence. Be sure to conjugate the verb correctly with the new subject.

Beispiel:
Ich kenne **den Mann.** (du)
Ich kenne ihn. Kennst du ihn auch?

1. Ich kaufe **den Kaffee.** (ihr)

_____

_____

2. Wir singen **das Lied.** (du)

_____

_____

3. Meine Schwester spart **das Geld.** (wir)

_____

_____

4. Du kennst **die Verkäuferin** seit langem. (er)

_____

_____

5. Mein Vater probiert **den Apfelstrudel.** (Sie)

_____

_____

Exercise 3

Rewrite each sentence by making the direct object below the subject and vice versa. Be sure to conjugate the verb correctly with the new subject.

Beispiel:
Er sucht sie seit gestern.
Sie sucht ihn seit gestern.

1. Sie umarmt mich.

_____

2. Er hat sie gestern gesehen.

_____

3. Hat sie euch angerufen?

_____

4. Wo hast du ihn getroffen?

_____

5. Kann ich dich mitnehmen?

_____

14

Dative personal pronouns replace an indirect object (the person or thing to whom or for whom something is being done).

	Singular		Plural
to/for me	*mir*	to/for us	*uns*
to/for you	*dir*	to/for you (plural)	*euch*
to/for him/ her/it	*ihm/ihr/ihm*	to/for them/ you (formal)	*ihnen/Ihnen*

*Der Bauer gibt **mir** die Eier.*
The farmer gives the eggs **to me**/gives **me** the eggs.

*Der Bauer zeigt **uns** seine Tiere.*
The farmer shows his animals **to us**/shows **us** his animals.

*Gehört **dir** diese CD?*
Does this CD belong **to you**?

*Ich kann **euch** diese CD leihen.*
I can lend this CD **to you all**/lend **you all** this CD.

*Besorgst du **ihm** einen Schlafsack?*
Are you providing a sleeping bag **for him**/providing **him** with a sleeping bag?

*Sie kauft **ihnen** einen Schlafsack.*
She is buying a sleeping bag **for them**/buying **them** a sleeping bag.

Achtung!
Even though *ihm* may replace a grammatically neuter noun phrase, such as *dem Mädchen,* it will translate into English based on the gender of the person.

In sentences with both accusative and dative pronouns, the accusative pronoun comes first.

*Ich gebe **dem Mann** das Buch.*
I'm giving the book **to the man.**

*Ich gebe es **ihm.***
I'm giving it **to him.**

*Wir sagen **der Frau** die Wahrheit.*
We're telling **the woman** the truth.

*Wir sagen sie **ihr.***
We're telling it **to her.**

In sentences with both nominative and dative pronouns, the nominative pronoun comes first.

*Hat der Spieler **dem Trainer** den Ball gegeben?*
Did the player give **the trainer** the ball?

*Hat er **ihm** den Ball gegeben?*
Did he give **him** the ball?

*Verspricht die Mutter **dem Mädchen** das Geld?*
Is the mother promising **the girl** the money?

*Verspricht sie **ihm** das Geld?*
Is she promising **her** the money?

In sentences with nominative, accusative, and dative pronouns, the order is nominative, accusative, dative.

*Hat der Spieler **dem Trainer** den Ball gegeben?*
Did the player give **the trainer** the ball?

*Hat er ihn **ihm** gegeben?*
Did he give it **to him**?

*Verspricht die Mutter **dem Mädchen** das Geld?*
Is the mother promising **the girl** the money?

*Verspricht sie es **ihm**?*
Is she promising it **to her**?

Exercise 1
Rewrite each sentence below, replacing the bold indirect object with a dative personal pronoun.

1. Sagen Sie **dem Kunden,** dass er morgen zurückrufen soll.

_____

_____

2. Gibst du **dem Kind** seinen Ball zurück?

_____

_____

3. Kannst du **der Nachbarin** deine Rollschuhe leihen?

_____

_____

4. Was schenkt er **seiner Braut** zur Hochzeit?

_____

_____

5. Rainer hat **seinem Vater** sein neues Handy gezeigt.

_____

_____

Exercise 2

Rewrite each sentence twice. First, replace only the indirect object with a dative personal pronoun. In the second sentence, replace both the direct and indirect objects with accusative and dative personal pronouns respectively. Watch for word order.

1. Ich kaufe meinem Sohn das Wörterbuch.

_____

_____

2. Sie zeigt der Lehrerin ihre Übersetzung.

_____

_____

3. Oliver schenkt seinen Eltern einen Gutschein.

_____

_____

4. Will Maria den Kindern ein Märchen erzählen?

_____

_____

5. Weißt du schon, ob du Thomas den Rasenmäher leihen kannst?

_____

_____

Exercise 3

Translate the following sentences into German using the correct pronouns. Watch for word order.

1. The soccer player is giving his fan a photograph.

_____

_____

2. She is writing a letter to her.

_____

_____

3. I brought him a cold drink.

_____

_____

4. Eva is telling us a story.

_____

_____

5. Doris and Uwe explained it to them.

_____

_____

15

Reflexive verbs indicate actions that a subject takes upon itself. The subject and the object are the same person or thing, as in "I am washing myself."

Since they are objects of verbs, reflexive pronouns are only used in the accusative and dative cases. They usually come immediately after the reflexive verb.

Ich wasche **mich**. (accusative)
I'm washing **myself.**

Ich wasche **mir** *die Hände.* (dative)
I'm washing **my** hands.

The accusative reflexive pronouns are used when there is no direct object in the sentence.

Singular Acc.		Plural Acc.	
myself	*mich*	ourselves	*uns*
yourself	*dich*	yourselves	*euch*
himself/ herself/itself	*sich*	themselves/ yourself (formal)	*sich*

Ich wasche **mich.**	I wash **myself.**
Du wäschst **dich.**	You wash **yourself.**
Er/sie/es wäscht **sich.**	He/she/it washes **his her/itself.**
Wir waschen **uns.**	We wash **ourselves.**
Ihr wascht **euch.**	You all wash **yourselves.**
Sie waschen **sich.**	They wash **themselves.**

The dative reflexive pronouns are the same as the accusative reflexive pronouns except in the first- and second-person singular (*mir* and *dir* rather than *mich* and *dich*). Dative reflexive pronouns are used when a direct object is mentioned in the sentence.

Du wäschst **dir** *die Hände.*	You wash your hands.
Sie wasche **sich** *die Hände.*	They wash their hands.

Achtung!
The reflexive pronouns are nearly identical to the personal pronouns, with the exception of *sich*.

Some common examples of reflexive verbs and other verbs that typically take a reflexive pronoun include:

sich duschen	(to shower)
sich die Nase putzen	(to blow one's nose)

sich entschuldigen	(to excuse oneself)
sich ärgern	(to be or become angry)
sich aufregen	(to get excited)
sich beeilen	(to hurry)
sich beschweren	(to complain)
sich freuen (with *über*)	(to be happy about)
sich freuen (with *auf*)	(to look forward to)
sich bedanken	(to express one's thanks)
sich konzentrieren	(to concentrate)
sich ausziehen	(to get undressed)
sich umziehen	(to change one's clothes)
sich anziehen	(to get dressed)

Exercise 1

Indicate whether the bold pronouns in the following sentences are personal pronouns or reflexive by circling P or R, respectively.

1. Zu eurem Hochzeitstag kaufe ich **euch** eine Kaffeemaschine.   P   R

2. Sobald ich zu Hause bin, ziehe ich **mir** die nassen Socken aus.   P   R

3. Hat er **sich** schon dafür entschuldigt, dass er zu spät gekommen ist?   P   R

4. Ich kenne **mich** in dieser Stadt überhaupt nicht aus.   P   R

5. Obwohl es dunkel ist, kann ich **dich** schon sehen.   P   R

Exercise 2

Indicate whether the reflexive pronouns in the following sentences are in the accusative (direct object) or dative (indirect object) case by circling A or D, respectively.

1. Meine Kinder putzen sich nicht oft genug die Zähne.   A   D

2. Wenn du dich nicht konzentrierst, wirst du nicht gut spielen.   A   D

3 Habt ihr euch auf dem Schützenfest amüsiert?   A   D

4. Du siehst fürchterlich aus. Warum kämmst du dir
die Haare nicht? A D

5. Er geht in die Stadt und kauft sich eine Hose. A D

Exercise 3

**Fill in the blank with the proper reflexive pronoun.
Remember the pronoun should indicate the same person
or thing as the subject.**

1. Die Kinder sind total dreckig. Ich hoffe, sie duschen

_____ bald.

2. Hast du vielleicht ein Taschentuch? Ich möchte

_____ die Nase putzen.

3. Die Spieler ärgern _____ immer wenn

sie verlieren.

4. Wenn wir _____ nicht beeilen, werden

wir unseren Flug verpassen.

5. Ich bin ziemlich sicher, dass du _____

das Bein gebrochen hast.

Exercise 4

Put the sentence elements below in the correct order.

1. Michael / Am Abend / putzt / die Zähne / sich

_____

_____

2. er / hat / das Geschenk / für / sich / bedankt

_____

_____

3. benehmen / du / kannst / nicht / dich / warum

_____

_____

4. beschweren / sich / sie / wird / bei / den Behörden /
sicherlich

_____

_____

5. ins Restaurant / bevor / mich / ziehe / wir / gehen / ich / um

_____

_____

16

Possessive pronouns refer back to a previously mentioned or understood noun while simultaneously indicating ownership or possession of it.

Like their English equivalents, the possessive pronouns replace noun phrases. They agree in number, case, and gender with their antecedents.

mine	*mein-*	ours	*unser-*
yours (fam. sing.)	*dein-*	yours (fam. pl.)	*euer-*
his, hers, its	*sein-, ihr-, sein-*	theirs/yours (formal)	*ihr-/Ihr-*

*Ich habe meine Jacke. Hast du **deine**? (Hast du deine Jacke?)*
I have my jacket. Do you have **yours**? (Do you have your jacket?)

Ausnahme

The possessive pronouns are nearly identical to the possessive adjectives with the exception of the masculine nominative and the neuter nominative and accusative.

	M	**F**	**Neuter**	**Pl.**
Nom.	*meiner*	*meine*	*meins*	*meine*
Acc.	*meinen*	*meine*	*meins*	*meine*
Dat.	*meinem*	*meiner*	*meinem*	*meinen*

*Willst du mit meinem Wagen fahren oder mit **deinem**?*
Do you want to go in my car or in **yours**?

Du hast deinen Bleistift.
You have your pencil.

*Das hier ist **meiner**.*
This (one) here is **mine**.

Wir haben zwei Hefte.
We have two notebooks.

*Das ist **meins** und das ist **deins**.*
This (one) is **mine** and this (one) is **yours**.

The possessive pronouns can be combined with *wegen* (because of/due to) by inserting *-t* or *-et* between the two words. This construction can mean *for one's sake*, *because of him*, or *as far as one's concerned*.

meinetwegen	*unsertwegen*
deinetwegen	*euretwegen*
seinetwegen/ ihretwegen	*ihretwegen/ Ihretwegen*

*Das brauchst du nicht **meinetwegen** zu machen.*
You don't have to do that **for my sake.**

*Das hat sie **deinetwegen** gemacht.*
She did that **because of you.**

***Seinetwegen** kannst du jetzt gehen.*
As far as he's concerned, you can go now.

Exercise 1

Respond negatively to each question below by saying that (A) it is yours, (B) you want to use yours, or (C) you want to drive (with) yours. Follow the model given in each instance.

A. Beispiel: Ist das seine Brille?
Nein, das ist meine.

1. Ist das sein Stuhl?

_____

2. Sind das seine Papiere?

_____

3. Ist das sein Buch?

_____

B. Beispiel: Willst du meinen Kuli benutzen?
Nein, danke. Ich habe meinen.

1. Willst du meine Kreide benutzen?

_____

2. Willst du mein Heft benutzen?

_____

3. Willst du meine Karten benutzen?

_____

C. Beispiel: Willst du mit meinem Auto fahren?
Nein, ich fahre mit meinem.

1. Willst du mit meiner Ente fahren?

_____

2. Willst du mit meinem Wagen fahren?

_____

3. Willst du mit meinen Skis fahren?

_____

Exercise 2

Fill in each blank with the appropriate personal pronoun indicated in parentheses.

1. Du hast deine Tasche, und ich habe _____.
(mine)

2. Er schreibt seinen Aufsatz, und sie schreibt _____.
(hers)

3. Wir kaufen ihren Wagen, und sie kaufen _____.
(ours)

4. Ich lese ihr Buch, und sie liest _____. (yours)

5. Doris kocht ihr Essen und auch _____. (his)

Exercise 3

Fill in the blank with the translation of the English phrase in parentheses.

1. Tu das nicht _____. (because of me)

2. _____ will sie kein Fleisch kochen. (for your sake)

3. _____ kannst du morgen kommen. (as far as she's concerned)

4. Das brauchst du nicht _____ zu machen. (for our sake)

5. _____ mussten wir noch einen Tag warten. (because of them)

Exercise 4

Translate the following sentences using the correct possessive pronoun.

1. This is my backpack. Where is yours?

_____

_____

2. As far as I am concerned, he can start on Wednesday.

_____

_____

3. Their papers are lying on the table. Do you have ours?

_____

_____

4. Excuse me! My suitcase is also black. Is this yours (formal)?

_____

_____

17

Demonstrative pronouns point out a particular object or person. They may be translated just as a personal pronoun or for additional emphasis, similar to *that one, these, those*, etc.

The demonstrative pronouns are identical to the definite articles, with the exception of the dative plural form.

	M	F	Neuter	Pl.
Nom.	*der:* it/that one	*die:* it/that one	*das:* it/that one	*die:* they/these
Acc.	*den:* it/that one	*die:* it/that one	*das:* it/that one	*die:* them/those
Dat.	*dem:* (to/for) it/that	*der:* (to/for) it/that	*dem:* (to/for) it/that	*denen:* (to/for) them/those

*Hast du meinen Rucksack gesehen? Ja, **der** liegt auf dem Tisch.*
Have you seen my backpack? Yes, **it's** lying on the table.

*Hast du noch deine alte Brille? Nein, **die** hab' ich nicht mehr.*
Do you still have your old glasses? No, I don't have **them** anymore.
Note: *Brille* (glasses) is singular in German.

*Warum wirfst du diese Tomaten weg? **Die** sind schon alt. Mit **denen** kann man nichts anfangen.*
Why are you throwing these tomatoes away? **These/ They** are already old. You can't do a thing with **them/ those.**

Alltagssprache

Referring to people using the demonstrative pronouns is more common in speech than in writing. It usually implies a strong sense of familiarity between the speaker and the subject.

„Wo ist Erik?"   *„**Der** ist wohl draußen."*
"Where is Eric?"   "**He's** probably outside."

In formal situations or when discussing someone not familiar to the speaker, the personal pronoun *er* is used instead.

Exercise 1

Fill in each blank with the appropriate demonstrative pronoun.

1. Ist das deine neue Kamera? Ja, mit _____ will ich die nächsten Fotos machen.

2. Wo ist die Kleine? _____ habe ich lange nicht mehr gesehen.

3. Das ist der Thomas. Von _____ haben wir die Karten bekommen.

4. Das war der Jürgen. _____ haben wir letztes Wochenende besucht.

5. Hast du das Buch gekauft? _____ will ich auch lesen.

Exercise 2

Create four exchanges between you and a friend about the classmates described in the table below. Express what you like about them using a demonstrative pronoun.

Tobias	hat Talent
Claudia	ist intelligent
Bertram	ist hilfreich
Berndt	ist großzügig
Sabina	ist lustig

Beispiel: <u>Magst du Bertram?</u>
<u>Ja, **der** ist ja hilfreich!</u>

1. _____

_____

_____

2. _____

_____

_____

3. _____

_____

_____

4. _____

_____

_____

Exercise 3

Use the demonstrative adjectives to translate the following discussion between two people who are waiting for a friend.

Wilhelm: Have you seen Markus?
Ute: No, where is he? We always have to wait for him!
Wilhelm: Well, he does have a long way. He lives in Littenweiler, after all.
Ute: That's true . . . but all the same . . .

_____

_____

_____

_____

_____

_____

_____

_____

_____

_____

_____

_____

18

A relative pronoun refers to a noun that appears in a main (independent) clause. Relative pronouns start a relative (dependent) clause that provides more information about the preceding noun.

Relative pronouns agree in number and gender with the noun they refer to/replace. Their case, however, is determined by their use within the relative clause.

	M	F	Neuter	Pl.
Nom.	der	die	das	die
Acc.	den	die	das	die
Dat.	dem	der	dem	denen
Gen.	dessen	deren	dessen	deren

Das ist der Mann, den ich gestern gesehen habe.
(direct object, accusative)
That is **the man (that/whom)** I saw yesterday.

Achtung!

Relative pronouns are identical to the definite articles except in the dative plural and all forms of the genitive case.

Relative pronouns always follow a comma and are usually the first word in the relative (dependent) clause.

Das ist die Kollegin, der ich das Geschenk gegeben habe. (indirect object, dative)
That is **the coworker to whom** I gave the present.

Ausnahme

If a relative pronoun is the object of a preposition within the relative clause, the relative pronoun follows the preposition. The preposition determines the case of the relative pronoun.

Kennst du die Frau, mit der ich gerade gesprochen habe? (mit + dative)
Do you know the woman **with whom** I was just speaking?

Achtung!

Within a relative (dependent) clause, the conjugated verb goes to the end.

Das ist die Professorin, die Englisch unterrichtet.
That is the (female) professor **who teaches** English.

Relative pronouns in the genitive case essentially replace possessive adjectives. However, they agree in number and gender with the noun that they refer to, not the noun that they precede.

Das ist der Schauspieler. Seine (possessive adjective) Frau ist Olympiasiegerin.
That is the actor. **His wife** is an Olympic champion.

Das ist der Schauspieler, dessen (relative pronoun) Frau Olympiasiegerin ist.
That is **the actor whose** wife is an Olympic champion.

Achtung!

In long sentences, a relative clause may come between two parts of the independent clause. In these cases, the relative clause is also followed by a comma.

Der Schauspieler, den Julia geheiratet hat, ist sehr erfolgreich.
The actor **who Julia married** is very successful.

Exercise 1

Fill in the blanks with the correct relative pronoun. Be sure to use the correct case.

1. Der Mann, _____ neben mir steht, heißt Wilhelm.

2. Der Mann, _____ ich gerade begrüsst habe, heißt Wolfgang.

3. Der Mann, durch_____ ich meine Frau kennen gelernt habe, heißt Rolf.

4. Der Mann, mit_____ ich mich unterhalte, heißt Werner.

5. Der Mann, _____ Frau Valerie heißt, heißt Walter.

Exercise 2

Fill in the blanks with the correct genitive relative pronoun.

1. Das ist der Mann, _____ Kinder heute Geburtstag feiern.

2. Das ist die Frau, _____ Sohn Soldat ist.

3. Das sind die Spieler, _____ Trainer ehemaliger Profi ist.

4. Das ist der Marathonläufer, _____ Bestzeit überboten werden sollte.

5. Das ist der Tisch, _____ Herstellerin reich geworden ist.

Exercise 3

Use the relative pronouns and the elements provided to write definitions for the words in bold.

Beispiel: **eine Geige**   eine Musikinstrument   man spielt
Eine Geige ist eine Musikinstrument, die man spielt.

1. eine Banane   eine Frucht   man schält

_____

_____

2. ein Roman   ein Buch   man liest

_____

_____

3. eine Universität   ein Institut   man studiert an

_____

_____

Exercise 4

Use the information in each sentence below to create two different sentences with relative clauses describing the antecedent noun.

Beispiel:
Das Café ist 50 Jahre alt. Es ist fünf Minuten zu Fuß von hier.
Das Café, das 50 Jahre alt ist, ist fünf Minuten zu Fuß von hier.
Das Café, das fünf Minuten zu Fuß von hier ist, ist 50 Jahre alt.

1. Das Restaurant heißt „Zum Goldenen Löwen". Es bietet Platz für 150 Gäste.

_____

_____

2. Die Speisekarte wird jeden Monat verändert. Sie hat 10 Seiten.

_____

_____

3. Die Hauptspeisen kosten zwischen 12,00 und 18,00 Euro. Sie sind hervorragend.

_____

_____

Exercise 5

First, remove the relative pronouns from the sentences below and rewrite each as two individual sentences. Then combine the new sentence pairs in a new way, again using a relative pronoun.

Beispiel:
Die Katzen, mit denen ich wohne, spielen gerne draußen.
Die Katzen spielen gerne draußen. Ich wohne mit ihnen.
Ich wohne mit den Katzen, die gerne draußen spielen.

1. Meine Mitbewohner, mit denen ich Urlaub mache, rauchen zu viel.

_____

_____

2. Das Haus, in dem wir seit drei Jahren wohnen, ist sehr preiswert.

_____

_____

19

Question words (interrogatives) can be used to refer back to things previously mentioned, similar to the relative pronouns.

Was can be used as a relative pronoun when referring back to the indefinite pronouns alles (everything), etwas (something), nichts (nothing), vieles (many things), or das (that).

*Es gibt **nichts, was** ich noch brauche.*
There is **nothing that** I still need.

***Das, was** du machen willst, ist mir auch wichtig.*
That which (what) you want to do is important to me too.

Was can be used as a relative pronoun when referring to an idea.

***Er hat sich nur leicht verletzt, was** eine große Erleichterung für uns alle war.*
He was only slightly injured, which was a huge relief for us all.

Was can be used as a relative pronoun when referring back to a noun that has been formed from a superlative adjective.

*Das ist sicherlich **das Schlimmste, was** uns passieren konnte.*
That is surely **the worst thing that** could have happened to us.

Achtung!

The group of interrogatives referred to as *wo*-compounds begin with *wo(r)*—(**wo**mit, **wor**an, **wor**auf, **wor**über, etc.). The *wo*-compounds are used instead of *was* when the question word itself is the object of a preposition within a dependent clause.

*Alles, **wovon** ich dir erzählt habe, ist wirklich passiert.*
Everything **that** I told you about really happened.

*Er hat sich ziemlich schlecht benommen, **wofür** er sich entschuldigt hat.*
He behaved rather poorly, **for which** he apologized.

*Das Beste, **worüber** sie erzählt hat, war ihre Reise nach Thailand.*
The best thing **that** she talked about was her trip to Thailand.

The interrogative wo (where) can be used instead of the preposition + relative pronoun when referring to places.

*Das ist die Stadt, **in der** ich wohne. Das ist die Stadt, **wo** ich wohne.*
That is the city **in which** I live. That is the city **where** I live.

*Das ist das Feld, **auf dem** wir oft spielen. Das ist das Feld, **wo** wir oft spielen.*
That is the field **on which** we often play. That is the field **where** we often play.

The interrogatives wohin (where to) and woher (where from) can also be used when referring to places if a change of location is involved.

*We fahren mit dem Zug nach Ulm, **wohin** wir auch mit dem Bus fahren können.*
We are taking the train to Ulm, **to where** we can also take the bus.

*Ich komme aus Osnabrück, **woher** meine Frau auch kommt.*
I am from Osnabrück, **the place from which** my wife also comes.

Exercise 1

Unscramble the following sentences. Be sure the interrogative pronoun is in the right place.

Beispiel: alles / Hast / was / gefunden / gesucht / hast / du
Hast du alles gefunden, was du gesucht hast?

1. alles / du / gegessen / gekocht / dein Freund / Hast / was / hat

_____

_____

2. Habt / gekauft / was / sich wünschen / zu Weihnachten / er / ihr / nichts

_____

_____

3. Fernseher / Ein / ist / was / etwas / nicht / brauche / ich

_____

_____

40

Exercise 2

Rewrite the following sentences using a noun formed from a superlative adjective.

Beispiel:
Das ist das bequemste T-Shirt, das ich jemals getragen habe.
Das ist **das Bequemste, was** ich jemals getragen habe.

1. Das ist das schönste Geschenk, das ich jemals bekommen habe.

_____

_____

2. Das ist die beste Nachricht, die wir seit langem gehört haben.

_____

_____

3. Das ist das schlimmste Gericht, das man hier essen kann.

_____

_____

Exercise 3

Combine the following sentences using the *wo(r)*-words, as shown in the example.

Beispiel: Er will unbedingt sein Auto verkaufen. Dagegen kann ich nichts machen.
Er will unbedingt sein Auto verkaufen, wogegen ich nichts machen kann.

1. Gestern hat sie mich beleidigt. Heute hat sie sich aber dafür entschuldigt.

_____

_____

2. Im Winter fahren wir in die Berge. Wir freuen uns sehr darauf.

_____

_____

Exercise 4

Combine the following sentences using *wo, wohin,* or *woher.*

1. Ich komme aus Bregenz. Bregenz liegt im Vorarlberg.

_____

_____

2. Meine Schwester fährt heute nach Basel. Basel liegt an der Grenze zu Deutschland.

_____

_____

3. Ihre Vorfahren stammen aus Biel. Ihr Großvater wohnt noch dort.

_____

_____

Exercise 5

Translate the following sentences into German using the information given to create two different relative clauses.

Beispiel: The museum in which I work is very old.
Das Museum, in dem ich arbeite, ist sehr alt.
Das Museum, wo ich arbeite, ist sehr alt.

1. The building in which I work is very big.

_____

2. I live on an island on which there are no cats.

_____

3. The gas station at which I work is open every day.

_____

20

Indefinite pronouns refer to nonspecific, generic objects or people. They are often used to make broad generalizations.

Some of the more common indefinite pronouns include:

alles	everything
etwas	something
nichts	nothing
viel	much/many things (for non-countable things)
vieles	much/many things (for non-countable things)
wenig	little

Nichts *ist wichtiger als die Liebe.*
Nothing is more important than love.

> ## *Achtung!*
>
> If an indefinite pronoun is an antecedent, *was* (that) is used as the relative pronoun to refer back to it.
>
> *Es gibt **wenig**, **was** er nicht weiß.*
> There is **little that** he doesn't know.

The indefinite pronoun *man* **is used when referring to people.** *Man* **can be translated as** *one, you, we, they,* **or** *people.*

> *Das muss **man** einfach machen.*
> **One** simply has to do that.
>
> **Man** *soll mit ihm langsam reden.*
> **You** should speak slowly with him.
>
> *Heutzutage tanzt **man** anders.*
> Nowadays **we/they/people** dance differently.

Man **can also be used in passive voice constructions, where English would not mention an agent.**

> *Hier spricht **man** Deutsch.*
> German is spoken here.

> ## *Achtung!*
>
> In the accusative and dative cases, *man* becomes *einen* and *einem* respectively.
>
> *Wenn **man einen** schnell erreichen will, sollte man das Handy benutzen.*
> If **you** want to reach **people** quickly, you should use the cell phone.
>
> **Man** *muss mit **einem** über so etwas reden.*
> **You** have to talk to **people** about things like that.

Exercise 1

Replace the bold phrase with the most appropriate indefinite pronoun.

1. Ich habe **den ganzen Text** gelesen.

_____

_____

2. Wir haben **viel Obst und Käse** zum Nachtisch gegessen.

_____

_____

3. Sofia hat **keine Post** bekommen.

_____

_____

4. Georg will **einige Gedichte** schreiben.

_____

_____

5. David kauft nur **wenige Sachen** ein.

_____

_____

Exercise 2

Your friend is telling you about a problem. In each instance give her advice, using the indefinite pronoun *man* to express what you think anyone in her situation should do.

1. Ich will ein paar Kilo abnehmen.

_____

_____

_____

2. Ich will gesünder essen.

_____

_____

_____

3. Ich will mehr Zeit für mich haben.

_____

_____

_____

4. Ich will eine bessere Stelle bekommen.

_____

_____

_____

5. Ich will öfters in Urlaub fahren.

_____

_____

_____

Exercise 3

Use the indefinite pronouns to translate the following discussion between two managers regarding a prospective employee:

Hans: Mr. Schmidt seems to know a lot about the topic. Do we have a better candidate?
Helga: Actually, no, but I think one ought to know something about the technical side of our work as well, and unfortunately he knows little about it.
Hans: Well, a little is better than nothing, isn't it?
Helga: Of course one can learn the technical things on the job as well, after one is employed; as long as one is given the chance and the right training.

_____

_____

_____

_____

_____

_____

_____

_____

_____

_____

_____

21

The subject pronoun *es* most commonly translates as *it*. Several expressions in German use *es* as an impersonal subject. Many of these uses must be memorized as they do not always translate word for word in English.

The pronoun *es* is used to discuss present weather conditions in expressions such as *es regnet* (it's raining) or *es schneit* (it's snowing).

> *Heute **schneit es** wieder.*
> **It's snowing** again today.

The expression *es gibt* (there is/there are) is used with the accusative case to state the existence of something.

> ***Es gibt** wenig, was er nicht weiß.*
> **There is** little that he doesn't know.

> ***Es gibt** viele Blätter auf dem Boden.*
> **There are** a lot of leaves on the ground.

The expression *es geht* expresses a temporary state of being. This expression can be used with the dative to indicate *for whom* things are going.

> ***Es geht mir** gut, und **dir**?*
> **I'm doing** well, and (how are) **you** (doing)?
> > or, **It's going** well **for me,** and (how is it going) **for you**?

Achtung!

Es geht can also be used with the question word *wie* to ask how things are going for someone. In these instances, the question word *wie* comes first, followed by the verb and the subject *es* directly after.

> *Wie **geht es ihm**?*
> How **is he doing**?
> > or, How **is it going for him**?

Alltagssprache

In everyday conversation, the expression *Geht's?* (short for *Geht es?*) is often used to simply ask, *Are things okay?* (literally: *Is it going?*).

> *Geht's?*
> Are things okay? (Is it going?)

> *Ja, es geht.*
> Yeah, they're fine. (Yes, it's going.)

The expression *es tut (mir) Leid* means *I'm sorry.* Literally, it translates as *it does me sorrow.* The person who is sorry is the indirect object and is therefore in the dative case.

> ***Es tut deiner Mutter** echt **Leid,** dass du nicht kommen kannst.*
> **Your mother is** really **sorry** that you can't come.

The impersonal *es* is used as the subject when expressing whether someone or something is hot or cold. The person who is feeling hot or cold is in the dative case.

> ***Es** ist kalt.*
> **It** is cold.

> ***Es ist mir** kalt/warm.*
> **I'm** cold/warm.

Achtung!

In order to ask someone if they are feeling cold or hot, simply invert the word order: Put the verb *is* first position in order to form a yes/no question.

> ***Ist es dir** kalt/warm?*
> **Are you** cold/warm?

Exercise 1

Fill in an appropriate verb for the subject *es*.

1. Wir wollten ein Picknick machen, aber es _____.

2. Wie _____ es deiner Großmutter?

3. Was _____ es heute in der Mensa zu essen?

4. Meinst du, dass es am kommenden Wochenende

_____? Wir wollen nämlich Ski fahren.

5. Ich muss diesen Brief abschicken. Weißt du, wo es

Briefmarken _____?

Exercise 2

Your friend needs the items below. Use *es gibt* and the accusative case to indicate that the things your friend needs are right here.

Beispiel: Ich brauche einen Stuhl.
<u>Hier gibt es einen Stuhl.</u>

1. Ich brauche einen Bleistift.

_____

_____

2. Ich brauche eine Taschenlampe.

_____

_____

3. Ich brauche ein Wörterbuch.

_____

_____

4. Ich brauche ein Pflaster.

_____

_____

5. Ich brauche eine Haarbürste.

_____

_____

Exercise 3

Write a brief email to a friend. Use the pronoun *es* to say you are sorry you haven't written for so long. Then talk about how you are doing, what the weather is like, and how you're feeling.

_____

_____

_____

_____

_____

_____

_____

_____

_____

_____

_____

_____

_____

_____

22

Prepositions indicate the location of people or objects, when things happen, the direction in which people or objects are moving, or the logical relationship of one person or object to another. Prepositions can take the accusative, dative, or genitive case.

The following German prepositions require the accusative case. Prepositions usually precede the noun, pronoun, or noun phrase that make up the prepositional phrase.

bis: until	*Ich wohne hier **bis** nächsten Januar.* I'll be living here **until** next January.
durch: through, by means of	*Wir fahren **durch** den Tunnel.* We are driving **through** the tunnel. ***Durch** die Explosion wurde das Haus zerstört.* The house was destroyed **by** the explosion.
entlang: along	*Sie spaziert den Fluss **entlang.*** She is walking **along** the river.
für: for, pro/ in favor of	*Dieser Brief ist **für** dich.* This letter is **for** you. *Die Mehrzahl ist **für** eine stärkere EU.* The majority **favors/is in favor of/is for** a stronger EU.
gegen: against, into, anti, (in exchange) for, around (with a time expression)	*Hast du etwas **gegen** mich?* Do you have something **against** me? *Das Auto ist **gegen** die Mauer geprallt.* The car crashed **into** the wall. *Wieso bist du **gegen** diese Idee?* Why are you **against** this idea? *Möchte jemand diese Robbie Williams Karte **gegen** eine Tina Turner Karte tauschen?* Would anyone like to trade this Robbie Williams (concert) ticket **for** a Tina Turner (concert) ticket? *Der Präsident kommt **gegen** 10.00 Uhr an.* The president is arriving **around** 10:00 A.M.
ohne: without	*Er geht immer **ohne** mich.* He always goes **without** me.

um: around, at (exactly, with a time expression)	*Die Bank ist **um** die Ecke.* The bank is **around** the corner. *Der Zug kommt **um** 10.17 an.* The train arrives **at** 10:17 A.M.
wider: contrary to, against	***Wider** alle Erwartungen haben anscheinend alle Passagiere den Flugzeugabsturz überlebt.* **Contrary to** expectations, it appears that everyone on board has survived the plane crash. *Ich musste **wider** meinen Willen ins Krankenhaus.* I was forced to go to the hospital **against** my will.

Ausnahme

The accusative preposition *entlang* (along) always comes at the end of a prepositional phrase.

Achtung!

The structure *Um . . . herum* means *around*, in the sense of surrounding or circumnavigating.

*Wir joggen **um** den Park **herum.***
We are jogging (**completely**) **around** the park.

*Wir saßen **um** den Tisch **herum.***
We were sitting (**completely**) **around** the table.

Alltagssprache

As with other prepositions, contractions with the definite articles are used regularly in everyday speech. These contractions are not considered informal in German.

durch + das = durchs	through the
für + das = fürs	for the
um + das = ums	around the

Exercise 1

The following paragraph describes your birthday morning. Circle all of the accusative prepositions.

Gestern stand ich gegen 8.30 Uhr auf. Als ich durch die Küchentür kam, sagte meine Mutter: „Schau was ich für dich gebacken habe!" Ich sah eine wunderschöne Sachertorte mit dreizehn Kerzen. Es war nämlich mein Geburtstag. Um den Tisch herum stand meine Familie mit vielen Geschenken für mich. Unter anderem bekam ich neue Schuhe, eine CD von meiner Lieblingsband, ein Computerspiel und 50 Euro von meiner Oma, doch am besten gefällt mir meine neue Uhr. Ohne sie werde ich das Haus nie wieder verlassen.

Exercise 2

Fill in the appropriate accusative case preposition for each sentence below.

1. Bist du mal _____ den Gotthard-Tunnel gefahren?

2. _____ den Ball können wir nicht weiter spielen.

3. Hast du schon einen DJ _____ die Party?

4. Dieser Weg geht den Fluß _____.

5. Ist dieses Geschenk wirklich _____ mich?

6. Hans trinkt seinen Kaffee schwarz, also _____ Milch.

7. Wie fährt man am besten _____ die Stadt?

8. In Graz spaziere ich oft den Franz-Josef-Kai

_____.

9. Am Freitag nach dem Unterricht sagt uns der Lehrer

immer: „Tschüß, _____ nächste Woche."

Exercise 3

Translate each sentence below into German using the appropriate accusative preposition.

1. The train from Vienna arrives at 10:23 A.M.

_____

2. These flowers are for my wife.

_____

3. I don't go anywhere without my MP3 player.

_____

4. He has no chance against the world champion.

_____

Exercise 4

Your friend Monica is having a birthday party. Write a paragraph using the accusative prepositions to explain what time the party is to begin (*um*), approximately when the guests arrive (*gegen*), for whom the party is held (*für*), and any other relevant details. Use as many of the prepositions as possible, but more importantly, tell a cohesive and concise story

_____

_____

_____

_____

_____

_____

_____

_____

_____

23

24 Prepositions *Dative Prepositions*

The most common German prepositions that take the dative case are *aus, außer, bei, mit, nach, seit, von,* and *zu.* Dative prepositions usually precede the noun, pronoun, or noun phrase that makes up the prepositional phrase.

aus: from, out of	*Er kommt **aus** einer schönen Gegend.* He comes **from** a nice area. *Sie ist schnell **aus** dem Haus gerannt.* She quickly ran **out of** the house.
außer: besides	***Außer** ihm hat kein Schwimmer drei Medaillen gewonnen.* No swimmer **besides** him won three medals.
bei: at/at the office of, near, at the house of, while, with (you)/on (you)	*Er arbeitet **bei** der ÖMV Tankstelle.* He works **at** the ÖMV gas station. *Der Supermarkt ist **bei**m (bei dem) Bahnhof.* The supermarket is **near** the train station. *Mein Bruder wohnt immer noch **bei** der Mutter.* My brother still lives **at** our mother's **house.** *Ich habe mich **bei**m (bei dem) Fußball verletzt.* I hurt myself **while** playing soccer. *Hast du Geld **bei** dir?* Do you have money **on you**?
mit: with, by	*Einen Hamburger **mit** Pommes, bitte.* A hamburger **with** french fries, please. *Ich fahre jeden Tag **mit** dem Zug.* I travel **by** train every day.
nach: after, to, according to, in	***Nach** der Pause geht es gleich weiter.* We'll continue right **after** the break. *Wir fahren **nach** Kroatien.* We are driving **to** Croatia. *Sortieren Sie diese Briefe bitte **nach** dem Eingangsdatum.* Please sort these letters **according to** their arrival date. *Meiner Meinung **nach** hast du Recht.* (comes after the noun in this expression) **In** my opinion, you're right.

seit: for, since	***Seit** einem Jahr wohne ich in Innsbruck.* I've been living in Innsbruck **for** a year. *Es geht ihm **seit** Anfang Oktober viel besser.* He's been feeling a lot better **since** the beginning of October.
von: from, of, by, about	*Dieses Geschenk ist **von** meinem Bruder.* This present is **from** my brother. *Haben Sie eine Karte **von** der Innenstadt?* Do you have a map **of** the downtown area? *Dieses Gebäude wurde **von** unserer Firma renoviert.* This building was renovated **by** our company. *Das ist eine Geschichte **von** Liebe und Hass.* That is a story **about** love and hate.
zu: to, for, to the house/office of	*Wir fahren jetzt **zu**r (zu der) Bank.* Now we're going **to** the bank. *Das habe ich **zu**m (zu dem) Geburtstag bekommen.* I got that **for** my birthday. *Heute Abend fahre ich **zu** Oma und Opa.* Tonight I'm driving **to** Grandma and Grandpa's **house.**

Alltagssprache

As with other prepositions, contractions with the definite articles are used regularly in everyday speech. These contractions are not considered informal in German.

bei + dem = beim	at the
von + dem = vom	from the
zu + dem = zum	to the
zu + der = zur	to the

Exercise 1

Fill in the correct form of the noun phrase provided in parentheses.

1. Peter wohnt bei (seine Eltern) _____

2. Wir stehen schon seit (eine Stunde) _____

_____ im Stau.

3. Sie trinkt gerne einen Kaffee nach (das Mittagessen)

_____.

4. Außer (ich) _____ spricht hier keiner Japanisch.

Exercise 2

Match the prepositional phrase in column A with the most appropriate noun phrase from column B.

A	B
_____ **1.** Ich komme gerade von	a. den Sommerferien
_____ **2.** Geh bitte aus	b. der Arbeit
_____ **3.** Das besprechen wir erst nach	c. Flughafen
_____ **4.** Feierst du wirklich mit	d. dem Weg
_____ **5.** Schnell! Wir müssen zum	e. deinem Ex-Freund?

Exercise 3

Complete the paragraph by inserting the appropriate dative case preposition in the blanks.

Ich studiere (**1.**) _____ einem Jahr hier in Graz.

Ich wohne nicht alleine, sondern (**2.**) _____

meiner besten Freundin. Sie heißt Jasmin und kommt

(**3.**) _____ der Hauptstadt von Tirol, Innsbruck.

Eines Tages wollen Jasmin und ich (**4.**) _____

einer großen Firma arbeiten. (**5.**) _____ dem

Studium muss das wohl möglich sein. Also, ciao derweil. Ich

gehe jetzt (**6.**) _____ Uni, denn ich muss lernen!

Exercise 4

Answer the questions below in complete sentences using the information provided in parentheses. Include the most appropriate preposition in the dative case.

Beispiel: Wo gehst du jetzt hin? (der Bahnhof)
<u>Ich gehe jetzt zum Bahnhof.</u>

1. Sind Sie alleine nach Mallorca geflogen? (meine Schwester)

_____

_____

2. Wann kommt ihr? (die Arbeit)

_____

_____

3. Wo arbeitest du? (der Supermarkt)

_____

_____

4. Wie lange studiert er schon in Bern? (ein Jahr)

_____

_____

5. Woher kommt sie? (ein Dorf)

_____

_____

Two-way prepositions take either the accusative or the dative case, depending on the context. There are nine two-way prepositions.

Two-way prepositions take the accusative case when they indicate motion (*wohin?*): something that is going into or being placed into a location. Two-way prepositions take the dative case when they indicate location (*wo?*): where someone or something is or the area or location where an activity is taking place.

	Wohin? (Acc.)	Wo? (Dat.)
an: (up) against; on (vertical)	*Ich lehne die Matratze **an** die Wand.* I'm leaning the mattress **against** the wall.	*Die Matratze lehnt **an** der Wand.* The mattress is leaning **against** the wall.
auf: on (top of; horizontal)	*Er legt den Schlüssel **auf** den Stuhl.* He is placing the key **on** the chair.	*Der Schlüssel liegt **auf** dem Stuhl.* The key is **on** the chair.
hinter: behind	*Stell das Sofa **hinter** den Tisch.* Put the sofa **behind** the table.	*Das Sofa ist **hinter** dem Tisch.* The sofa is **behind** the table.
in: into (inside of)	*Geben Sie die Kartoffeln **in** einen Topf.* Put the potatoes **in** a pot.	*Die Kartoffeln sind **in** einem Topf.* The potatoes are **in** a pot.
neben: next to	*Ich setze mich **neben** das Boot hin.* I'm going to sit down **next to** the boat.	*Ich sitze **neben** dem Boot.* I'm sitting **next to** the boat.
über: above/ over	*Sie hängt ihre Jacke **über** den Stuhl.* She's hanging her jacket **over** the back of the chair.	*Ihre Jacke hängt **über** dem Stuhl.* Her jacket is hanging **over** the back of the chair.
unter: below	*Der Ball rollt **unter** das Auto.* The ball is rolling **under** the car.	*Der Ball ist **unter** dem Auto.* The ball is **under** the car.
vor: in front of	*Tu das Schild **vor** den Baum.* Move the sign **in front of** the tree.	*Das Schild ist **vor** dem Baum.* The sign is **in front of** the tree.
zwischen: between	*Ich stell' den Sessel **zwischen** die Pflanzen.* I'm putting the armchair **between** the plants.	*Der Sessel ist **zwischen** den Pflanzen.* The armchair is **between** the plants.

Achtung!

An easy way to remember the two-way prepositions is to picture a box that opens and think of their meaning in relation to the box as you recite them.

Alltagssprache

As with other prepositions, contractions with the following definite articles are used regularly in everyday speech. These contractions are not considered informal in German.

an + das = ans	on the
an + dem = am	on the
auf + das = aufs	on the
hinter + das = hinters	behind the
hinter + dem = hinterm	behind the
in + das = ins	in the
in + dem = im	in the
über + das = übers	above the
über + dem = überm	above the
vor + das = vors	in front of the
vor + dem = vorm	in front of the

Exercise 1

Decide if the preposition in each sentence below is used in the accusative or the dative and circle the corresponding letter (A for accusative, D for dative).

1. Das Poster hängt an der Wand.   A   D

2. Der Mann steht neben einem Baum   A   D

3. Ich gehe morgen ins Kino.   A   D

4. Hinter dem Haus befindet sich die Garage.   A   D

5. Stell' bitte den Tisch vor das Fenster.   A   D

Exercise 2

Identify the correct prepositional phrase to complete each sentence below.

1. Der Dieb versuchte zwei Stunden lang _____ Haus einzubrechen.
   a. über das   b. zwischen das   c. in das

2. Wie heißt das Café, das _____ Restaurant ist?
   a. neben dem   b. auf dem   c. am

3. Der Kerzenständer steht _____ Fenstersims.
   a. hinter dem   b. auf dem   c. über dem

4. _____ Bett habe ich viele Sachen versteckt.
   a. Auf dem   b. Unter dem   c. Neben dem

Exercise 3

Read the following sentences and decide if the prepositions take the accusative or the dative. Circle the article that is based on the correct case.

1. Bernd stellt die Bücher wieder in das/dem Regal.

2. Geben Sie mir bitte die Zeitung, die hinter Sie/Ihnen liegt.

3. Sie bauen das neue Fußballstadion neben die/der Schule.

4. Mein Hund Rex legt sich gerne unter den/dem Tisch.

5. Die Buchhandlung ist zwischen den/dem Supermarkt und die/der Apotheke.

Exercise 4

The following statements indicate the motion or location of some nouns. Use the prepositional phrases to answer the questions that follow.

Beispiel: Ich stelle die Gläser in den Schrank.Wo sind die Gläser?
             Die Gläser sind im Schrank.

1. Ich schütte das Wasser ins Glas. Wo ist das Wasser?

   _____

   _____

2. Der Mann legt die Kamera auf den Tisch. Wo ist die Kamera?

   _____

   _____

3. Sie schiebt die Schubkarre hinter die Scheune. Wo ist die Schubkarre?

   _____

   _____

4. Harold stellt die Tastatur vor den Monitor. Wo ist die Tastatur?

   _____

   _____

25

Most prepositions take either the accusative and/or the dative case, but there are a few that take the genitive case.

The most common German prepositions that take the genitive case are *(an)statt, trotz, während,* and *wegen*.

(an)statt: instead of	**Anstatt/Statt** *ihrer Schwester hat sie ihre Freundin eingeladen.* **Instead** of (inviting) her sister, she invited her friend.
trotz: in spite of	**Trotz** *des Schmerz hat sie die schwere Übung gemacht.* **In spite** of the pain, she completed the difficult exercise.
während: during	**Während** *des Semesters hat er immer wenig Freizeit.* He always has little free time **during** the semester.
wegen: due to/ because of	**Wegen** *des Wetters bleiben wir heute zu Hause.* We're staying home today **because of** the weather.

Alltagssprache

The genitive case is slowly giving way to the dative case, and in everyday speech, you will often hear the dative used.

Wegen des Regens *wollen wir heute nicht spazieren gehen.* (genitive)
Wegen dem Regen *wollen wir heute nicht spazieren gehen.* (dative)
Because of/due to the rain, we don't want to go for a walk today.

Other common prepositions that take the genitive case are used to indicate the relationship between two objects with respect to their location.

außerhalb: outside (of)	**Außerhalb** *des Hauses sprechen die Eltern nur Deutsch mit den Kindern.* **Outside** of the house, the parents speak only German with their children.
diesseits: this side (of)	**Diesseits** *des Zauns müssen wir mähen.* We have to mow **on this side of** the fence.
innerhalb: inside/ within (of)	**Innerhalb** *der Firma benutzt man einen anderen Ausdruck dafür.* Another expression is used for that **within** the company.
jenseits beyond/the other side (of)	**Jenseits** *der alten Stadtmauer sind die Wohnungen moderner.* **On the other side of** the old city wall, the apartments are more modern.
oberhalb: above	**Oberhalb** *dieser Höhe wird es schwerer, Luft zu kriegen.* **Above** this elevation, it becomes more difficult to breathe.
unterhalb: below/ beneath	*Unterschreiben Sie bitte* **unterhalb** *dieser Zeile.* Please sign **below** this line.

Exercise 1

Fill in the correct form of the nominative case phrase provided in parentheses. Remember: The prepositions in these sentences take the genitive.

1. Lutz schreibt immer schöne Briefe trotz (seine Handschrift)

   _____.

2. Thomas und Jutta kaufen ein Motorrad statt (ein Wagen)

   _____.

3. Während (der Urlaub)

   _____ ruft Kerstin nie an.

4. Wegen (ihre Arbeit) _____

   hat Lena kaum Zeit.

5. Wenn die Kinder größer werden, will sie außerhalb (das

   Haus) _____ arbeiten.

Exercise 2

Complete the following sentences with the appropriate genitive case preposition.

1. _____ des vielen Regens gibt es keine Überschwemmungen.

2. _____ des Sommers spielen die Kinder immer lieber draußen.

3. Pius will mit der Achterbahn fahren, aber _____ seiner Größe darf er nicht.

4. _____ der Äpfel, kauft der sich die Orangen.

5. Wo warst du _____ der Pause?

Exercise 3

Change of plans: Write five sentences using prepositions that require the genitive case. Tell why you did not do what you planned (*wegen*), what you did in spite of something (*trotz*), and what you did either instead of something else (*statt*) or while something else was going on (*während*).

1. _____

   _____

   _____

2. _____

   _____

   _____

3. _____

   _____

   _____

4. _____

   _____

   _____

5. _____

   _____

   _____

26

53

Prepositions *Prepositions Used with Certain Verbs*

The combination of specific prepositions with a given verb often varies from one language to another. The meanings of some verbs may even vary depending on the preposition that is used.

Some common verb + preposition pairings in German require the use of the accusative case.

bitten + um: to ask for/request	*Herr Meier **bittet um** ein Wort mit Ihnen.* Mr. Meier **would like** a word with you.
denken + an: to think about/of	*Er **denkt** oft **an** dich.* He often **thinks of** you.
lachen + über: to laugh about	*Sie **lacht über** alles.* She **laughs about** everything.
lächeln + über: to smile about	*Das Kind **lächelt über** die lustigsten Sachen.* The child **smiles about** the funniest things.
nachdenken + über: to think about/ponder	*Simon **denkt über** seine Zeit in Paris **nach.*** Simon **is thinking about** his time in Paris.
schicken + an: to send to	***An** wen soll ich das Paket **schicken?*** **To** whom should I **send** this package?
schreiben + an: to write to	*Er hat einen Brief **an** Herrn Braun **geschrieben.*** He **wrote** a letter **to** Mr. Braun.
sprechen + über: to talk/speak about	*Der Professor **spricht über** die Ökologie.* The professor **is talking about** the ecology.

Some common verb + preposition pairings require the use of the dative case.

anfangen mit: to start with	*Sie **fangen** immer da**mit an.*** They always **start with** that.
fragen + nach: to ask for	*Sie hat **nach** meiner Kollegin **gefragt.*** She **asked for** my (female) colleague.
halten + von: to think of (opinion)	*Was **halten** Sie **vom** Film?* What do you **think of** the movie?
leiden + an: to suffer from	*Herr Schmidt **leidet an** einer schweren Krankheit.* Mr. Schmidt **is suffering from** a serious disease.
sprechen + mit: to talk to/with	*Wir **sprechen** oft **mit** unseren Freunden.* We **talk** a lot **with** our friends.
telefonieren + mit: to talk to (on the phone)	***Mit** wem **telefonierst** du?* Who are you **talking to (on the phone)?**

Exercise 1

Fill in each blank by conjugating the verb in parentheses to agree with the subject of the sentence.

1. Ich _____ an dich. (denken)

2. Sie _____ mit ihrem Freund. (telefonieren)

3. Er _____ an einer schweren Erkältung. (leiden)

4. Sie _____ den Kellner um ein Glas Wasser. (bitten)

5. Worüber _____ wir? (sprechen)

Exercise 2

Fill in the appropriate preposition in each sentence below, paying close attention to the verb being used.

1. Sie lächelt immer _____ seine Witze.

2. Denkst du _____ ihre Frage nach?

3. Frangen wir _____ dem nächsten Kapitel an.

4. Was hältst du _____ dem neuen Freund deiner Schwester?

5. _____ wen schreibt er?

Exercise 3

Translate the following questions into German using the correct verb + preposition pair.

1. Are you laughing about her?

_____

_____

2. He's asking for you.

_____

_____

3. I'm thinking of a story.

_____

_____

4. What are they writing about?

_____

_____

5. What do you think about that?

_____

_____

27

Some common reflexive verb + preposition pairings in German require the use of the accusative case.

sich beklagen + über: to complain about
Die Touristen **beklagen sich** *ständig* **über** *die Hitze.*
The tourists **complain** constantly **about** the heat.

sich einsetzen + für: to put oneself out (in regard to effort)
Er **setzt sich** *jeden Tag* **für** *sie ein.*
He **gives his all for** her every day.

sich interessieren + für: to be interested in
Kirstin **interessiert sich für** *Medizin.*
Kirstin **is interested in** medicine.

sich freuen + auf: to look forward to
Wir **freuen uns** *schon* **auf** *die Party.*
We **are** already **looking forward to** the party.

sich freuen + über: to be happy about
Der Kandidat **freut sich über** *die Ergebnisse der letzten Umfrage.*
The candidate **is happy about** the results of the last poll.

sich kümmern + um: to care for/take care of/
to look after
Wer **kümmert sich um** *das Kind?*
Who **is looking after** the child?

sich lustig machen + über: to make fun of
Sabina **macht sich über** *ihren kleinen Bruder lustig.*
Sabina **makes fun of** her little brother.

sich vorbereiten + auf: to prepare for
Sie **bereitet sich** *auf die Prüfung* **vor**.
She **is preparing for** the test.

Achtung!

Note the change in meaning that can occur when a verb is paired with a specific preposition, for example, *sich freuen.*

Sich beschäftigen mit (to be occupied/to busy oneself with/to concern oneself with) is a common reflexive verb + preposition pairing that requires the use of the dative case.

Er **beschäftigt sich** *nicht* **mit** *ihren Sorgen.*
He **does**n't **concern himself with** her worries.

Exercise 1

Fill in the blanks below by conjugating the verb given in parentheses to agree with the subject of the sentence. Add the appropriate reflexive pronoun to complete each sentence.

1. _____ du _____ über mich lustig?
(sich lustig machen)

2. Wir _____ _____ aufs
Wochenende. (sich freuen)

3. Die Schüler _____ _____ über die
Hausaufgaben. (sich beklagen)

4. Heinz _____ _____ für Musik.
(sich interessieren)

5. Womit _____ er _____? (sich
beschäftigen)

Exercise 2

Fill in the appropriate preposition in each sentence below, paying close attention to the verb being used.

1. Die Krankenschwester kümmert sich _____
den Kranken.

2. Die neuen Eltern freuen sich _____ das Kind.

3. Andrea bereitet sich _____ das Essen vor.

4. Jutta setzt sich immer _____ ihn ein.

5. Claudia interessiert sich _____ alles.

Exercise 3

Translate the following sentences into German using the appropriate verb + preposition pairings.

1. Little Thomas is occupying himself with his toys.

_____

_____

2. We are looking forward to vacation.

_____

_____

3. She is making fun of me.

_____

_____

4. What are you interested in?

_____

_____

5. He's complaining about that.

_____

_____

28

Adjectives in German can come either before or after the noun they modify. Adjectives that precede the noun almost always take an ending that agrees in gender, case, and number. These endings also vary depending on the word that the adjective follows.

Adjectives that directly follow the definite articles (*der, die, das,* and so on) end in either *-e* or *-en,* depending on case, gender, and number.

	M	F	Neuter	Pl.
Nom.	*-e*	*-e*	*-e*	*-en*
Acc.	*-en*	*-e*	*-e*	*-en*
Dat.	*-en*	*-en*	*-en*	*-en*
Gen.	*-en*	*-en*	*-en*	*-en*

Achtung!

The adjective *hoch* (tall) drops the *-c-* when an ending is added.

*Wo ist der **hohe** Berg?*
Where is the **tall** mountain?

This ending change also takes place when adjectives follow any of the so-called *der-*words: words that take similar endings to the definite articles, such as *dies-, jed-, jen-, manch-,* and *welch-,* as well as *alle, beide, sämtliche,* and *solche.*

Alle roten *T-Shirts gehören ihm.*
All red T-shirts belong to him.

Ausnahme

Some color words, such as *lila* (purple) and *rosa* (pink), as well as the adjective *prima* (excellent) never change.

Wo ist die rosa Jacke?
Where is the pink jacket?

When adding endings to adjectives that follow the *der-*words, the adjective will end with *-en* if the noun is in the dative or genitive case.

*Mit **welcher netten** Schauspielerin will er tanzen?* (dative)
With which **nice actress** does he want to dance?

*Kennst du den Namen **dieses kleinen** Kindes?*
(genitive)
Do you know this **small child**'s name?

When adding endings to adjectives that follow the *der-*words, the adjective will end with *-en* if the noun is masculine accusative, so that there is repetition of the *-n.*

*Hast du **den neuen** Wagen gesehen?*
Did you see the **new car**?

Ausnahme

Predicate adjectives do not precede the noun they modify and typically follow the verbs *sein* or *werden* in German. These adjectives do not take an ending.

*Der Mann **ist nett.***
The man **is nice.**

*Der **nette Mann** wohnt nebenan.*
The **nice man** lives next door.

When two or more adjectives appear in a series, they all take the same ending.

*Die **schöne, intelligente** Frau hat vier Kinder.*
The **beautiful, intelligent** woman has four children.

Ausnahme

Some adjectives that end in *-el, -auer,* or *–euer,* such as *dunkel* (dark), *sauer* (sour), and *teuer* (expensive), drop the *e* before their final consonant when an adjective ending is added.

*Gefallen dir die **dunklen** Farben?*
Do you like the **dark** colors?

Ausnahme

Many adjectives representing place names end in *-er* and are capitalized. These adjectives do not take adjective endings.

*In den **Frankfurter Vororten** sind die Wohnungen immer noch teuer.*
The apartments **in the suburbs of Frankfurt** are still expensive.

Exercise 1

Fill in the blank with the nominative case form of the adjective given in parentheses.

1. das _____ Programm (blöd)

2. der _____ Fernseher (billig)

3. die _____ Banane (gelb)

4. das _____ Handy (neu)

5. die _____ Schauspieler (komisch)

6. das _____ Hemd (kariert)

Exercise 2

Each sentence below uses an adjective to describe a noun. Compose new sentences for each noun using the new noun and the verb in parentheses. In the new sentence, the item from the original sentence should be the direct object.

Beispiel: Der Ball ist rot. (Der Mann/werfen)
Der Mann wirft den roten Ball.

1. Dieser Bildschirm ist hell. (Ein Kunde/kaufen)

_____

_____

2. Solche Bücher sind interessant. (Eine Dame/lesen)

_____

_____

3. Der Lehrer ist intelligent. (Mein Nachbar/kennen)

_____

_____

4. Beide Kinder sind lustig. (Ein Fotograph/fotographieren)

_____

_____

5. Die Braut ist wunderschön. (Ein Gast/umarmen)

_____

_____

Exercise 3

Rearrange the sentence elements below using the best phrase from the options given. Note: Each sentence includes a preposition requiring the use of the dative case.

die blaue Brücke   das kleine Loch   der schwarze Hund   das weiche Taschentuch   die große Pause

1. Ich putze mir die Nase mit

_____

2. Christian paddelt das Kanu bis zu

_____

3. Robert hat erst nach . . . Religion.

_____

4. Das ist der Maulkorb von

_____

5. Es kommen viele Ameisen aus . . . heraus.

_____

Exercise 4

Fill in the blanks below with the proper adjective ending. Watch for agreement in gender, case, and number.

1. Dieses teur_____ Buch wurde von dem reich_____ Mann ersteigert.

2. Die schwarz_____ Katze des einsam_____ Hausmeisters isst viel zu viel.

3. Ich habe alle warm_____ Brötchen mit dem frisch_____ Aufstich bestrichen.

4. Hat das warm_____ Haus den heftig_____ Sturm ohne Schäden überstanden?

5. Hans steigt in das weiß_____ Auto seiner neu_____ Freundin ein

29

Adjectives that follow the indefinite articles (*ein, eine,* and so on) and other words with similar endings (so-called *ein*-words), such as *kein* (no/not a) and the possessive adjectives (*mein, dein, sein, unser, ihr, Ihr,* and *euer*) take the following endings depending on the number, gender, and case of the noun the adjective modifies.

	M	F	Neuter	Pl.
Nom.	-er	-e	-es	-en
Acc.	-en	-e	-es	-en
Dat.	-en	-en	-en	-en
Gen.	-en	-en	-en	-en

Achtung!

Although there is no plural of *ein*, other *ein*-words do have a plural form.

When following an *ein*-word that has no ending itself, adjectives end in either *-er* (masculine) or *-es* (neuter) depending on the gender of the noun they modify.

> *Ein reicher Mann gibt viel Geld aus.*
> **A rich** man spends a lot of money.

> *Ihr großes Haus kostet ein Vermögen.*
> **Her big** house costs a fortune.

Adjectives following the indefinite article *eine* and other *ein*-words ending in *-e* always end in *-e* as well.

> *Meine frische Semmel riecht super.*
> **My fresh** roll smells great.

Adjectives in the dative and genitive cases always end in *-en.*

> *Wir fahren mit unserem neuen Auto.*
> We're driving/going with **our new** car.

> *Der Mann seiner älteren Schwester heißt Johann.*
> **His older** sister's husband is called Johann.

Adjectives following a plural possessive adjective or *kein* in the plural (*keine*) always end in *-en.*

> *Keine jüngeren Studenten studieren hier.*
> **No younger** students attend the university/study here.

Exercise 1

Fill in the blank with the correct nominative form of the adjective given in parentheses.

1. eine _____ Antwort (schlau)

2. ein _____ Grund (dumm)

3. eine _____ Orange (frisch)

4. ein _____ System (altmodisch)

5. eine _____ Batterie (alte)

6. ein _____ Käse (weich)

Exercise 2

Rewrite the following sentences twice according to the information in parentheses. In the first sentence, use the accusative case. In the second sentence, use the dative case with the preposition *mit*.

Beispiel: Martin hat einen Salamander.   (Der Junge/rot)
<u>Der Junge hat einen roten Salamander.</u>
<u>Der Junge mit einem roten Salamander heißt</u>
<u>Martin.</u>

1. Peter hat eine Katze. (Der Mann/weiß)

_____

_____

2. Julia hat einen Hund. (Die Frau/schwarz)

_____

_____

3. Ernst hat ein Pferd. (Das Kind/braun)

_____

_____

4. Andrea hat keine Frösche. (Das Mädchen/grün)

_____

_____

Exercise 3

Translate the following sentences into German using the genitive case. Pay close attention to the use of the possessive adjectives and the endings on the adjectives that follow them.

1. They are the teachers of our best students.

_____

_____

2. That is a picture of our old friend.

_____

_____

3. She is the sister of my wonderful wife.

_____

_____

4. That is the address of his first house.

_____

_____

5. This is a sample of her best paintings.

_____

_____

Exercise 4

Fill in the blanks below with the proper endings for adjectives following the *ein*-words.

1. Ich kenne einen nette_____ Mann, der ein rot_____ Auto

hat.

2. Sein_____ Vater sagt, dass die Simpsons eine lustig_____

Sendung ist.

3. Mein komisch_____ Schwager hat ein groß_____ und

schnell_____ Pferd.

4. Katrin ist eine schön_____ Frau und hat ein zauberhaft___

Lächeln.

5. Mein_____ Mutter hat mir gesagt, dass ich mein_____

dreckig_____ Socken waschen muß.

Exercise 5

Describe your room, apartment, or house using the *ein*-words followed by adjectives. Do you live with any relatives or friends? If so, you can comment on their things using the possessive adjectives (*sein, ihr, Ihr*).

_____

_____

_____

_____

_____

_____

_____

_____

_____

_____

_____

_____

_____

_____

_____

_____

30

When an adjective does not follow a *der*-word or *ein*-word, the adjective takes what is called a *strong* ending to signal the number, gender, and case of the noun it modifies.

Strong endings, except for the masculine and neuter genitive endings, are similar in form to the *der*-word endings.

	M Ending	F Ending	Neuter Ending	Pl. Ending
Nom.	-er	-e	-es	-e
Acc.	-en	-e	-es	-e
Dat.	-em	-er	-em	-en
Gen.	-en	-er	-en	-er

Grüner Tee schmeckt ihm. (nominative, masculine)
He likes **green** tea.

*Sie isst **gern** pikante Wurst.* (accusative, feminine)
She likes to eat **spicy** sausage.

*Wasch diese Bluse mit **kaltem** Wasser.* (dative, neuter)
Wash this blouse with **cold** water.

*Der Geruch **frischer** Fische hängt am Markt in der Luft.*
(genitive, plural)
The smell of **fresh** fish hangs in the air at the market.

The strong endings are also used for adjectives that follow cardinal numbers.

*von drei **guten** Freunden*
from three **good** friends

*wegen zwei **grober** Fehler*
on account of two **bad** mistakes

Achtung!

When a noun is followed by two or more adjectives, all adjectives take the same ending.

*mit kalt**em**, grün**em** Tee*
with cold, green tea

*trotz wunderbar**en**, sonnig**en** Wetters*
despite wonderful, sunny weather

Exercise 1

Complete the table with the correct endings for each adjective.

	M	F	Neuter	Pl.
Nom.	exzellent__ Wein	bittere Schokolade	zäh___ Fleisch	streng__ Gesetze
Acc.	exzellent__ Wein	bitter___ Schokolade	zähes Fleisch	streng__ Gesetze
Dat.	exzellent__ Wein	bitter___ Schokolade	zäh___ Fleisch	strengen Gesetzen
Gen.	exzellenten Weines	bitter___ Schokolade	zäh___ Fleisch__	streng__ Gesetze

Exercise 2

Combine the adjectives below with the given noun using the proper adjective ending in the nominative case.

Beispiel: sauer, die Gurken → <u>saure Gurken</u>

1. gelb   der Senf _____

2. salzig   die Brezeln _____

3. grün   die Äpfel _____

4. frisch   die Milch _____

5. alkoholfrei das Bier _____

6. lecker   der Kuchen _____

7. gebraten   die Nudeln _____

8. bitter   die Schokolade _____

9. süß   die Erdbeeren _____

10. gesund   das Müsli _____

Exercise 3

Fill in the blanks in the sentences below with the correct adjective ending.

1. Romantisch_____ Mann sucht seine Traumfrau.

2. Er verbrachte drei lang_____ Jahre im Dschungel.

3. Die Gardinen sind aus durchsichtig_____ Material gefertigt.

4. Wir werden das Problem mit einfach_____ Methoden lösen.

5. Trotz sein_____ Probleme ist Gerhard meistens gut gelaunt.

6. Gut_____ Freunde schätze ich wie hartverdient_____ Geld.

7. Weil stressig_____ Situationen mir nicht gefallen, bewundere ich ruhig_____ Menschen.

8. Weiß_____ Spargel schmeckt mir besser als grün_____ Spargel, aber grün_____ Äpfel schmecken mir besser als rot_____ Äpfel.

9. Langweilig_____ Zimmer kann man einfach mit schön_____ Blumen auffrischen.

10. Weil ich groß_____ Hunger habe, werde ich jetzt zwei riesig_____ Portionen köstlich_____ Pfannkuchen essen.

Exercise 4

Rewrite the sentences below using the adjectives in parentheses. Be sure to use the proper adjective ending.

Beispiel: Er isst gern Käse. (weich)
    Er isst gern weichen Käse.

1. Er trinkt gern Kaffee. (heiß)

_____

_____

2. Ich höre gern Musik. (klassisch)

_____

_____

3. Sie sitzen gern auf Hockern. (hoch)

_____

_____

4. Wir essen heute Lasagne statt Pizza (kalt, frisch)

_____

_____

5. Was kostet mehr? Eine Kiste Wein oder zwei Kisten Bier? (gut, schlecht)

_____

_____

31

Some adjectives in German do not take the regular adjective endings. In some cases, position and function in the sentence determine whether an adjective takes an ending. Other adjectives never take endings regardless of how they are used.

Predicate adjectives follow the linking verbs *sein* or *werden* and directly modify the subject of the sentence. Predicate adjectives do not precede the noun they modify and do not take endings.

>*Dieses Auto ist **rot.***
>This car ist **red.**

>*Die Frau wird **alt.***
>The woman is getting **old.**

The adjectives *viel* (much, a lot of) and *wenig* (little) do not take adjective endings in the singular. They do take endings in the plural, and their meanings change slightly, as they refer to things that are countable: *viele* (many) and *wenige* (few).

>*Er hat **viel** Brot gegessen.*
>He ate **a lot of** bread.

>*Sie hat **viele** Fische gesehen.*
>She saw **many** fish.

>*Wir sind mit **wenig** Geld zufrieden.*
>We are satisfied with **little** money.

>*Sie wollen **wenige** Fehler sehen.*
>They want to see **few** mistakes.

Some color words that end in *-a* or *-e* do not change form to agree with the nouns they modify.

>*Sie hat eine neue **lila** Bluse.*
>She has a new **lilac-colored** blouse.

>*Karl trägt immer einen **beige** Mantel.*
>Karl always wears a **beige** coat.

Adjectives formed from place names + the ending *-er* (these adjectives are most often derived from cities) are capitalized and do not change.

*Der **Kölner** Dom steht fast direkt am Bahnhof.*
The Cathedral **of Cologne** is almost right next to the train station.

Ausnahme

One country, Switzerland (*die Schweiz*), has two adjective forms. One form ends in *-er* and is uninflected (*Schweizer*). The other adjective form is *schweizerisch*, which does take an adjective ending.

*Die **Schweizer** Armee ist gut vorbereitet.*
The **Swiss** army is well prepared.

*Die **schweizerischen** Städte sind relativ klein.*
The **Swiss** cities are relatively small.

Within Switzerland, the adjective *eidgenössisch* is often used for *Swiss*. This adjective refers to the *Eidgenossenschaft*, short for *die schweizerische Eidgenossenschaft*, literally *Swiss oath fellowship*, a term that refers back to the original oaths out of which the Swiss Confederation grew. The adjective *eidgenössisch*, like *schweizerisch*, is inflected to agree with the noun it modifies when preceding the noun.

*Viele **eidgenössische** Autoren werden auch dabei sein.*
Many **Swiss** authors will also be there.

Some adjectives that never take endings must simply be memorized. The most common include *mehr* (more), *lauter* (sheer, pure), and *prima* (excellent).

>*Vor **lauter** Freude hat sie geweint.*
>She cried out of **pure** joy.

Exercise 1

Place a checkmark next to those adjectives below that do not agree with the noun they modify.

_____	**1.** blau	_____	**5.** Münchner
_____	**2.** rosa	_____	**6.** orange
_____	**3.** teuer	_____	**7.** schlau
_____	**4.** schwarz	_____	**8.** Tiroler

Exercise 2

Fill in the blanks below with the appropriate adjective endings. If no ending is required, place an *x* in the blank.

1. Liest du *Die Frankfurter_____ Allgemein_____ Zeitung*?

2. Ihre Lieblingsfarbe ist lila, aber sie trägt gern orange_____ Kleider.

3. Was mir an Berlin gefallen hat, waren die Berliner_____ Theater. Wir haben jeden Abend ein anderes Theater besucht.

4. Mit dem groß_____ beige_____ Stuhl will ich nichts machen.

5. Die schön_____ Tiroler_____ Landschaft ist nicht zu vergleichen.

Exercise 3

Translate the following sentences into German. Watching for the correct use (or omission of) the adjective endings.

1. This lilac-colored sweater is beautiful!

_____

_____

2. Did you visit the port in Hamburg?

_____

_____

3. Are you going on the orange or the black ship?

_____

_____

4. Have you ever had marzipan from Lübeck?

_____

_____

5. His small beige pants don't fit him anymore.

_____

_____

Exercise 4

You're signing into a new social networking website. Complete the profile below by describing yourself, your friends, where you are from, and the things you like. Include as many adjectives as possible, and think carefully about whether or not they require endings.

Name: _____

Alter: _____

Hobbies: _____

_____

Heimat: _____

_____

Ich über mich: _____

_____

_____

_____

_____

_____

_____

_____

32

Adjectives *Comparatives and Superlatives*

The comparative form of an adjective allows comparisons between the qualities of two nouns (for example, higher or lower). The superlative form of an adjective allows for comparisons to the greatest degree (highest, lowest).

Most German adjectives add the *-er* suffix to form the comparative.

klein/kleiner (small/smaller)
interessant/interessanter (interesting/more interesting)

Like other adjectives, comparative forms take no additional endings if they are predicate adjectives or if they are used as adverbs.

*Dieses Bild ist **schön**.*
This picture is **beautiful.**

*Dieses Bild ist **schöner**.*
This picture is **more beautiful.** (predicate adjective)

*Diese Kiste ist **schwer**.*
This crate is **heavy.**

*Diese Kiste ist **schwerer**.*
This crate is **heavier.** (predicate adjective)

*Sie kleidet sich **elegant**.*
She dresses **elegantly.**

*Sie kleidet sich **eleganter**.*
She dresses **more elegantly.** (adverb)

If a comparative form precedes the noun it modifies, the appropriate adjective ending is added to the comparative form.

*Das ist das **schöne** Bild.*
This is the **beautiful** picture.

*Das ist das **schönere** Bild.*
This is the **more beautiful** picture.

To form the superlative, most German adjectives add *am* plus the suffix *-sten* when used as a predicate adjective or as an adverb.

*Dieses Auto ist **teuer**.*
This car is **expensive.**

*Dieses Auto ist **am teuersten**.*
This car is **the most expensive.**

*Dieser Fahrer fährt **schnell**.*
This driver drives **fast.**

*Dieser Fahrer fährt **am schnellsten**.*
This driver drives **the fastest.**

If a superlative form precedes the noun it modifies, the appropriate adjective ending is added to the superlative form and no *am* is included.

*Das ist das **teuere** Auto.*
This is the **expensive** car.

*Das ist das **teuerste** Auto.*
This is the **most expensive** car.

Ausnahme

Many one-syllable words add an umlaut to the vowel (*ä, ö,* and *ü*) in both the comparative and the superlative.

stark (strong)
stärker (stronger)
am stärksten (strongest)

alt (old)
älter (older)
am ältesten (oldest)

oft (often)
öfter (more often)
am öftesten (most often)

jung (young)
jünger (younger)
am jüngsten (youngest)

Ausnahme

For adjectives ending in *-d, -t, -s, -sk, -ss, -ß, -sch, -tz, -x,* or *-z,* the superlative suffix is *-esten.*

schlecht (bad)	*am schlecht**esten*** (worst)
kurz (short)	*am kürz**esten*** (shortest)
gesund (healthy)	*am gesünd**esten*** (healthiest)

There are several irregular comparatives and superlatives. Some of the more common examples include:

gut (good)	*besser* (better)	*am besten* (best)
gern (gladly)	*lieber* (more gladly)	*am liebsten* (most gladly)
hoch (high)	*höher* (higher)	*am höchsten* (highest)
nah (near)	*näher* (nearer)	*am nächsten* (nearest)
viel (much)	*mehr* (more)	*am meisten* (most)

Exercise 1

Fill in the comparative and superlative forms of the adjectives below.

	Comparative	Superlative
1. nett	_____	_____
2. klein	_____	_____
3. bequem	_____	_____
4. hübsch	_____	_____

Exercise 2

Fill in the blank using the most appropriate adjective from the choices in parentheses. Decide if it should be in the comparative or superlative form, and add an adjective ending as necessary.

Beispiel: Superman ist der <u>stärkste</u> Mensch auf der Erde. (schwach, stark)

1. Ich habe einen Ford, aber ein Ferrari ist _____. (langsam, schnell)

2. Mein Haus ist teuer, aber sein Schloss ist _____. (billig, teuer)

3. Zur Zeit ist es warm in Schweden, aber in Griechenland hat

man _____ Wetter. (kalt, warm)

4. Jeder kennt sie. Sie ist wahrscheinlich die

_____ Schauspielerin. (unbekannt, bekannt)

5. Von all den Bergen in Deutschland ist die Zugspitze

_____. (niedrig, hoch)

Exercise 3

Use the comparative and superlative forms of the adjectives *alt* (old) and *jung* (young) to create meaningful comparisons between Thomas, Jochen, and Kurt using the prompts below.

Thomas ist 66 Jahre alt.
Jochen ist 44 Jahre alt.
Kurt ist 22 Jahre alt.

Beispiel: Kurt → <u>Kurt ist am jüngsten.</u>

1. Thomas → _____

2. Jochen vs. Kurt → _____

3. Jochen vs. Thomas → _____

Exercise 4

Use at least five of the following phrases in comparative and superlative forms to compare and contrast three people you know.

ist klein	spricht schnell	tanzt gut
lächelt oft	spielt gern Fussball	ist freundlich
ist lustig	ist fleißig	ist sportlich ist brav

_____

_____

_____

_____

_____

_____

_____

_____

33

There are several common German expressions that use adjectives to compare two or more nouns.

So + adjective + wie is used when comparing two things that are the same in some respect. This expression is equivalent to the English expression as . . . as.

*Diese Suppe ist **so dünn wie** die andere.*
This soup is **as watery as** the other one.

Als follows a comparative form to express the equivalent of than when comparing two items that are unequal in some respect.

*Ich finde diesen Pulli **schöner als** den anderen.*
I think this pullover is **prettier than** the other one.

Immer is used with a comparative form to express the equivalent of the English more and more.

*Es wird **immer kälter.***
It's getting **colder and colder.**

The expression Je + comparative adjective, desto + comparative adjective is used with two different comparative forms to express the equivalent of English the . . . , the . . .

Je schneller, desto besser meint er!
He thinks **the quicker, the better!**

Exercise 1

Fill in the blank with the correct form of the adjective in parentheses. Determine if it should remain as is or be presented in the comparative form.

1. Je _____ (schnell) man fährt, desto

_____ (hoch) ist die Strafe.

2. Meine Schwester ist vier Jahre _____

(jung) als ich.

3. Das mexikanische Essen schmeckt mir genau so

_____ (gut) wie das italienische Essen.

4. Mein Opa ist so _____ (gesund) wie ein

40-jähriger Mann.

5. Je _____ (viel) er arbeitet, desto

_____ (müde) wird er.

Exercise 2

Express the following comparisons in German.

1. Gasoline is getting more and more expensive.

_____

_____

_____

2. This skirt is as long as the other one.

_____

_____

_____

3. The more I practice, the better I understand.

_____

_____

_____

4. Our cat is as big as our dog.

_____

_____

_____

5. This movie is funnier than the other one.

_____

_____

_____

Exercise 3

The information below describes two trips: one to Berlin and one to Munich. Compare these trips using the comparative expressions with the adjectives given.

Adjectives: billig, teuer, interessant, amüsant, unterhaltsam, erholsam, lang, kurz

	Trip 1	Trip 2
Wohin?	nach Berlin	nach München
Wie lange?	ein langes Wochenende	eine Woche
Wie?	mit dem Flugzeug	mit dem Zug
Wie viel?	2.500 Euro	2.500 Euro
Was?	2× Abendessen	Besuch der Kunstmuseen
	1× Theater	Besuch der Schlößer in Füssen
	1× Tanzen	im Nachtklub
		Wanderung oder Radtour in den Voralpen, je nach Wunsch
		Segeln am Starnberger See

_____

_____

_____

_____

_____

_____

_____

_____

_____

_____

_____

34

35 Adjectives *Adjectival Nouns*

In German, adjectives can also be used as nouns. As nouns, adjectives are capitalized, but their endings vary according to the standard adjective-ending rules.

When referring to people, adjectival nouns are either masculine or feminine based on the gender of the person to whom they refer.

*Wo ist der **alte Mann**?* (nom., following a *der*-word)
→ *Wo ist der **Alte**?*
Where is the **old man**? Where is the **old man/one**?

*Kennst du den **neuen Kollegen**?* (acc., following a *der*-word)
→ *Kennst du den **Neuen**?*
Do you know our **new colleague**? Do you know the **new man/one**?

*Er hat mit einer **jungen Frau** getanzt.* (dat., following an *ein*-word)
→ *Er hat mit einer **Jungen** getanzt.*
He danced with a **young woman.**
He danced with a **young woman/one.**

*Sind das die Werke der **modernen Autoren**?* (gen., following a *der*-word)
→ *Sind das die Werke der **Modernen**?*
Are these the works of the **modern authors**?
Are these the works of the **modern authors/ones**?

When referring to an object, adjectival nouns are neuter.

*Das ist wirklich das **Beste**.*
That is really the **best (thing).**

*Das **Neue** dran ist das Design.*
The **new (thing)** about it is the design.

Exercise 1

Replace each adjective and noun phrase below with an appropriate adjectival noun. Keep your answer in the nominative case.

1. die schlaue Frau

2. der große Mann

3. die blonde Frau

4. das gute Ding

5. die talentierte Frau

6. der schwache Mann

7. das lustigste Ding

8. der großzügige Mann

Exercise 2

Fill in the blanks with an appropriate adjectival noun based on the adjective in parentheses. Note: Pay attention to gender, number, and case in your answer.

1. Ein _____ hätte ohne Mühe durchs kleine Loch kriechen können. (klein)

2. Die _____ kennen wir schon. (neu)

3. Das _____ dabei war ihr Lebenslauf. (interessant)

4. Eine _____ lag im nächsten Bett. (krank)

5. Mit diesen _____ reist sie nächstes Jahr nach Amerika. (deutsch)

6. Kennst du den Bruder des _____? (alt)

7. Weißt du, was das _____ ist? (best)

8. Der _____ gewinnt den Preis. (besser)

Exercise 3

Translate the following sentences using adjectival nouns.

1. The poor man was hungry.

_____

_____

_____

2. Do you know the nice woman over there?

_____

_____

_____

3. He always finds the good.

_____

_____

_____

4. She explained it to the new folks.

_____

_____

_____

5. The most expensive thing is always the drinks.

_____

_____

_____

35

36 Adjectives *Participles as Adjectives*

Present and past participles can also act as adjectives to modify nouns.

Present participles acting as adjectives take the regular adjective endings to agree with the noun the present participle modifies when preceding the noun.

kochen (to cook)
*Das **kochende** Wasser muss abgekühlt werden.*
The **boiling** water has to be cooled down.

fliehen (to escape)
*Hast du den **fliehenden** Mann gesehen?*
Did you see the **fleeing** man?

Past participles acting as adjectives also take the regular adjective endings to agree with the noun the past participle modifies when preceding the noun.

gesperrt (blocked)
*Sie wollte die **gesperrte** Straße überqueren.*
She wanted to walk across the **blocked-off** street.

zerbrochen (broken)
*Er hat die **zerbrochene** Vase repariert.*
He repaired the **broken** vase.

Adjectival participles can also be extended with information that would typically be given in a separate clause. If the activity described in the dependent clause is ongoing, a present participle is used. If the activity described in the dependent clause was completed, a past participle is used.

*Kennst du den Studenten, **der Gitarre spielt**? =*
*Kennst du den **Gitarre spielenden** (present participle) Studenten?*
Do you know the student **who is playing guitar**? =
Do you know the **guitar-playing** student?

Achtung!

Nearly any information that would be included in a relative clause can be used to extend an adjective in German. The equivalent of these constructions can sometimes translate awkwardly in English.

*Wo sind die Texte, die wir im Dezember ausgewält haben? = Wo sind die von uns im **Dezember ausgewählten** (past participle) Texte?*

Where are the lyrics we picked out in December? =
Where are the **December-selected** lyrics?

Exercise 1

Combine the verbs and nouns below to create noun phrases using present participles as adjectives.

Beispiel: reisen, der Kaufmann: <u>der reisende Kaufmann</u>

1. spielen, das Kind:

_____

2. brechen, das Glas:

_____

3. zu schnell fahren, das Auto:

_____

4. bellen, der Hund:

_____

5. lachen, die Frau:

_____

Exercise 2

Combine the verbs and nouns below to create noun phrases using past participles as adjectives.

1. schließen, die Tür:

_____

2. backen, der Fisch:

_____

3. grillen, das Gemüse:

_____

4. sprechen, das Wort:

_____

5. sparen, das Geld:

_____

Exercise 3

Respond in the affirmative to each question below using either a present or past participle as an adjective.

1. Haben Sie die Kinder gesehen, die tanzen?

_____

_____

_____

2. Haben Sie den Brief gelesen, den sie getippt hat?

_____

_____

_____

3. Haben Sie die Verwandten kennen gelernt, die in München wohnen?

_____

_____

_____

4. Kennen Sie den Musiker, der Jazz singt?

_____

_____

_____

5. Essen Sie die Kekse, die Ingrid gebacken hat?

_____

_____

_____

Exercise 4

Translate the following sentences using extended adjectives.

1. We ate the meat that was grilled by my father.

_____

_____

2. He saw the girl who was singing in the bar.

_____

_____

3. This is a sweater that was handmade by my grandmother.

_____

_____

_____

4. She knows the boy who is playing baseball.

_____

_____

_____

37 Adverbs *Temporal*

Adverbs modify adjectives or verbs and provide information about time, manner, and place. In most cases, German adverbs follow the subject, conjugated verb, or object they modify. When multiple adverbs are present, a strict (time-manner-place word) order is followed.

Temporal adverbs describe the time at which something occurs. They can answer the questions *When? (Wann?)*, *How often? (Wie oft?)*, or *How long? (Wie lange?)*

> Ich bin **gestern** angekommen.
> I arrived **yesterday.**

> Er liest **manchmal** auf Deutsch.
> He **sometimes** reads in German.

> Sie ist **schon lange** bei uns.
> She has been with us **for a long time.**

Achtung!

Temporal adverbs are often found in first position in a sentence, with the conjugated verb in the second position.

Morgens muss er zur Arbeit.
Mornings he has to go to work.

Some common temporal adverbs that answer the question *Wann?* include:

vorgestern	the day before yesterday
gestern	yesterday
heute	today
morgen	tomorrow
übermorgen	the day after tomorrow
jetzt	now
nun	now
gerade	just (in the process of)
bald	soon
später	later
früher	earlier, sooner
vorher	before(hand)
nachher	afterward

> Willst du **später** zusammen einen Kaffe trinken?
> Do you want to have a coffee together **later**?

The adverbs *morgens* (mornings), *nachmittags* (afternoons), *abends* (evenings), and *nachts* (nights) are used to describe events that are repeated or habitual.

> **Abends** geht er immer spazieren.
> He always goes for a walk in **the evening.**

Some common temporal adverbs that answer the question *Wie oft?* include:

nie	never
selten	seldom, rarely
manchmal	sometimes
oft	often, frequently
immer	always
täglich	daily
wöchentlich	weekly
monatlich	monthly
jährlich	annually

> Die Medikamente musst du zweimal **täglich** nehmen.
> You have to take the medicine twice **daily.**

Some common temporal adverbs that answer the question *Wie lange?* include:

lang	for a long time
kurz	for a brief period; briefly

> Kannst du **kurz** mit ihm reden?
> Can you talk to him **for a moment**?

Achtung!

Lang can also be added to the ending of other time expressions to indicate duration.

jahre**lang**	for years
monate**lang**	for months

*Er hat **jahrelang** versucht, Sänger zu werden.*
He tried **for years** to become a singer.

Exercise 1

Fill in the blanks below with the appropriate temporal adverb based on the English clue in parentheses.

1. Wir gehen _____ einkaufen. (now)

2. _____ oder _____

   lernt man das. (sooner or later)

3. Gehst du _____ nach Hause? (soon)

4. Er nimmt die Medikamente drei Mal _____

   _____ . (daily)

5. Sie gehen nur _____ spazieren. (rarely)

6. Ich habe das echt _____ gesagt! (never)

7. Wir haben uns _____ nicht mehr

   gesehen. (for a long time)

8. Sie wollte Ski laufen gehen, aber _____

   musste sie sich warm anziehen. (beforehand)

9. _____ spricht er mit seiner

   Großmutter auf Deutsch. (sometimes)

10. Sie hat _____ mit dem Arzt

    telefoniert. (briefly)

Exercise 2

Wann machen Sie das? Answer the following questions by choosing the most appropriate response from the choices below.

morgens   nachmittags   abends   nachts

1. Wann machen Sie eine Pause?

   _____

2. Wann treffen Sie sich mit Freunden?

   _____

3. Wann gehen Sie zur Arbeit?

   _____

4. Wann schlafen Sie?

   _____

5. Wann trinken Sie einen Kaffee?

   _____

6. Wann sehen Sie fern?

   _____

Exercise 3

Match each verb phrase in column A to a time when you did it or will do it from the options in column B. Then, for each temporal adverb, create one sentence using either the present perfect tense or the future tense. Begin each sentence with the temporal adverb and be sure to keep your conjugated verb (in these instances your helping verb) in second position.

A	B
eine DVD ausleihen	vorgestern
ins Kino gehen	gestern
im Café sitzen	heute
Deutsch lernen	morgen
Familie besuchen	uebermorgen
am Computer sitzen	
spazieren gehen	

_____

_____

_____

_____

_____

_____

38 Adverbs *Modal and Causal*

Modal adverbs describe the manner in which something occurs or to what extent something exhibits a certain quality. Causal adverbs describe why something occurs. When multiple adverbs are present, a strict time-manner-place word order is followed.

Modal adverbs can answer the questions How? (Wie?) and How much? (Wie sehr?).

> Ich fahre **allein** nach Koblenz.
> I am going **alone** to Koblenz.

> Er kann ja **kaum** warten.
> He can **hardly** wait.

Some common modal adverbs that answer the questions Wie? and Wie sehr? include:

sehr	very
fast	almost
kaum	hardly
teilweise	partially, in part, to some *extent*
schrittweise	little by little, step by step
allmählich	gradually
langsam	slowly, gradually
schnell	quickly
gern	gladly
leider	unfortunately
zusammen	together
alleine	alone, independently
unabhängig von	independently of

> Wir liefen **schnell** nach Hause.
> We ran home **quickly.**

> Sie ist **sehr** müde.
> She is **very** tired.

Where in English, adverbs take an -ly ending or have an entirely different form from the adjective, many modal adverbs in German share the adjective form.

> Das ist **perfekt**! Das hast du **perfekt** gemacht!
> That is **perfect**! You did that **perfectly**!

> Das ist **gut**! Das hast du **gut** gemacht!
> That is **good**! You did that **well**!

Causal adverbs can answer the question Why? (Warum? or Wieso?).

> Sie trinken nur selten, **deshalb** haben sie so viel Durst.
> The don't drink very often; **that is why** they are so thirsty.

Some common causal adverbs that answer the questions Warum? and Wieso? include:

deshalb	therefore, that is why
deswegen	because of that, for that reason
daher	that's why, therefore
darum	because, therefore, so

> Wir wohnen nicht hier, **darum** wissen wir nicht, wo die Stadtbibliothek ist.
> We don't live here, **so** we don't know where the public library is.

Alltagssprache

Several of the causal adverbs can stand alone in everyday speech to give a curt response to the certain questions. Similar to English, this use is a means of avoiding details about why something did or did not happen.

Weshalb? Deshalb.	Why? Because.
Weswegen? Deswegen.	Why? Because.
Warum? Darum.	Why? Because.

Achtung!

The adverb ending -*weise* is generally attached to nouns and occasionally adjectives to make them into adverbs.

> Was tust du **normalerweise**?
> What do you **usually** do?

> **Teilweise** kann ich ihn schon verstehen.
> I can understand him **to some extent**.

Exercise 1

Fill in the blanks below based on the English cues in parentheses and the context of each sentence.

1. Der Inspektor muss _____ feststellen, was der Verbrecher gemacht hat. (step by step)

2. Katrina arbeitet lieber _____. Sie mag die Gruppenarbeit nicht so sehr. (independently)

3. _____ ist er nicht mein Typ. (unfortunately)

4. _____ müssen wir unsere Koffer etwas früher aufgeben. (therefore)

5. _____ kann ich das schon verstehen. (in part)

6. Wir gehen morgen _____ ins italienische Restaurant. (together)

7. _____ wollte sie die Reise umbuchen. (because of that)

8. _____ bringt er dir Blumen. (that's why)

9. Er spielt _____ am Computer. (gladly)

10. Es wird _____ kalt. (slowly)

Exercise 2

Fill in the blanks below with the most appropriate modal adverb from the choices below.

sehr   fast   kaum

1. Wenn er leise spricht, kann ich ihn

_____ hören.

2. Wilhelm erzählt viele Witze. Doris findet ihn

_____ lustig.

3. Ich brauche nur noch eine Minute. Ich bin

_____ fertig.

4. Sie hat zwei Stücke Kuchen gegessen. Sie kann

_____ noch was essen.

5. Die neueste Technologie ist

_____ teuer.

Exercise 3

Respond to the questions below in complete sentences using the appropriate modal or causal adverbs in your answers.

1. Gehst du heute Abend mit uns ins Konzert?

_____

_____

_____

2. Hörst du oft Rockmusik?

_____

_____

_____

3. Wie soll ich das Projekt durchführen?

_____

_____

_____

4. Soll ich immer laut schreien?

_____

_____

_____

5. Muss ich alleine arbeiten?

_____

_____

_____

38

39 Adverbs *Local and Directional*

Local and directional adverbs describe where something occurs or the direction to or from which something travels. When multiple adverbs are present, a strict time-manner-place word order is followed.

Local adverbs can answer the question *Where?* (*Wo?*) Directional adverbs can answer the questions *To where?* (*Wohin?*) and *from where*? (*Woher?*).

*Was machst du **hier**?*
What are you doing **here**?

*Gehst du **hinein**?*
Are you going **in**?

*Er kam langsam **heraus**.*
He came **out** slowly.

Some common local adverbs that answer the question *Wo?* include:

hier	here
dort	there (farther away)
da	there (closer by)
weg	away
drinnen	inside
draußen	outside, outdoors
oben	upstairs, above
unten	downstairs, below
vorne	in front
hinten	in the back

Achtung!

The adverbial phrase *mitten in* + a dative noun or noun phrase includes a preposition (*in*) and means *in the middle of*.

*Er wohnt **mitten im** Wald.*
He lives **in the middle of** the woods.

Some common directional adverbs that answer the questions *Wohin?* and *Woher?* include:

geradeaus	straight ahead
weg	away
vorwärts	forward
rückwärts	backward
rechts	to the right
links	to the left
dahin	(to) there
daher	(from) there

hinein	into
hinaus	out of
herein	into
heraus	out of

Achtung!

The use of *hinein, hinaus, herein,* and *heraus* depends on the location of the speaker in relation to the object or area being discussed.

hinein: used when going from where the speaker is to another place

hinaus: used when going out from where the speaker is

herein: used when coming from another place into the location where the speaker is

heraus: used when coming out from another place to the location where the speaker is

*Geh **hinein**! Komm **herein**!*
Go **inside**! Come **inside**!

*Das Kind geht in das Haus **hinein**. Das Kind kommt in das Haus **herein**.*
The child goes **inside** the house. The child comes **inside** the house.

*Geh **hinaus**! Komm **heraus**!*
Go **outside**! Come **outside**!

*Das Kind geht aus dem Haus **hinaus**.*
The child goes **out** of the house.

*Das Kind kommt aus dem Haus **heraus**.*
The child comes **out** of the house.

Exercise 1

Fill in the blanks based on the English cues in parentheses and the context of each sentence.

1. Ist der Hund _____? (inside)

2. Seit wann ist Herr Schmidt _____? (away)

3. Bist du noch _____? (here)

4. Fahren Sie _____! (straight ahead)

5. Der Weinkeller ist _____, damit der Wein kühl bleibt. (downstairs)

6. Wenn du jetzt _____ abbiegst, bist du schon da! (to the left)

7. Kannst du auch _____ Schlittschuh laufen? (backward)

8. Die Toiletten sind _____ neben der Rezeption. (in front)

Exercise 2

In the pictures below, picture yourself as the speaker in the dark shirt. Use the *Sie* form of the imperative to give commands to the other person in each picture using *hinein*, *hinaus*, *herein*, and *heraus* based on the verbs provided.

Beispiel: kommen

Kommen Sie heraus!

1. gehen _____

_____

2. Kommen _____

_____

3. Gehen _____

_____

Exercise 3

You forgot your notebook in your dorm room and need your roommate to bring it to you. Write a paragraph explaining where your notebook is in your room and where your class is on campus. Use local and directional adverbs with the *du* imperative to instruct your roommate.

_____

_____

_____

_____

_____

39

Most German verbs end in *-en* in their infinitive form, as in *backen* (to bake), *hören* (to hear), *joggen* (to jog), and *kaufen* (to buy).

In the present tense, regular German verbs are conjugated by dropping their ending (*-en*) and adding the following endings based on the subject.

Singular		Plural	
ich (I)	**-e**	*wir* (we)	**-en**
du (you)	**-st**	*ihr* (you)	**-t**
er/sie/es (he/she/it)	**-t**	*sie/Sie* (they/you, formal)	**-en**

Achtung!

While English has three present tense forms, German has only one. The one present tense form in German translates all three English present tenses.

backen   (to bake)
*ich back**e***   I bake/I do bake/I am baking

Verbs ending in *-den* or *-ten* (such as *antworten*), a consonant + *-men* (such as *atmen*), or a consonant + *-nen* (such as *öffnen*) follow special conjugation rules in order to ease pronunciation.

Singular		Plural	
ich (I)	*-e*	*wir* (we)	*-en*
du (you)	**-e**st	*ihr* (you)	**-e**t
er/sie/es (he/she/it)	**-e**t	*sie/Sie* (they/you, formal)	*-en*

	Singular	Plural
antworten (to answer)	*ich antwort**e*** I answer	*wir antwort**en*** we answer
	*du antwort**est*** you answer	*ihr antwort**et*** you all answer
	*er/sie/es antwort**et*** he/she/it answers	*sie/Sie antwort**en*** they/you answer

Verbs that end in *-eln* (such as *klingeln*) and *-ern* (such as *wandern*) drop only the *-n* and add the following endings:

Singular		Plural	
ich (I)	*-e*	*wir* (we)	**-n**
du (you)	*-st*	*ihr* (you)	*-t*
er/sie/es (he/she/it)	*-t*	*sie/Sie* (they/you, formal)	**-n**

	Singular	Plural
wandern (to hike/wander)	*ich wander**e*** I hike	*wir wander**n*** we hike
	*du wander**st*** you hike	*ihr wander**t*** you all hike
	*er/sie/es wander**t*** he/she/it hikes	*sie/Sie wander**n*** they/you hike

Ausnahme

Verbs that already end in *-sen* (such as *reisen*) or an *s* sound such as *-ßen* (*heißen*) or *-zen* (*tanzen*) add only a *-t* in the *du* form.

reisen (to travel)   *du reis**t*** (you travel)

tanzen (to dance)   *du tanz**t*** (you dance)

Alltagssprache

In colloquial speech and in the transcription of oral text, the *-e* ending is often dropped in the *ich* form of the regular verbs and replaced with an apostrophe, as in *ich back'*, *ich kauf'*, *ich geh'*, or *ich wander'*. In written German, however, the endings are always retained.

Exercise 1

Fill in each blank below by conjugating the infinitive form of the regular verb in parentheses.

1. Was _____ Sie, Herr Schmidt? (schreiben)

2. Heute _____ ich gegen 10.00 Uhr. (kommen)

3. Nächstes Jahr _____ wir ein Wohnmobil. (kaufen)

4. Was _____ er in der Stadt? (machen)

5. _____ ihr morgen zum Strand? (gehen)

6. Martha und ich _____ heute das Abendessen. (kochen)

7. Wo _____ du jetzt, Andreas? (arbeiten)

8. Die Kinder _____ Briefmarken. (sammeln)

Exercise 2

Choose the appropriate subject from those provided to fill in the subject of each sentence below. Use each subject only once.

ich   dein Vater   ihr   du   die Kinder

1. Wo spielen _____ heute?

2. Spart _____ viel Geld, Peter und Sabina?

3. _____ arbeite seit gestern Abend am Computer.

4. Lächelt _____ oft?

5. Was suchst _____?

Exercise 3

Translate the following sentences into German.

1. He is buying a book.

_____

_____

2. She jogs often.

_____

_____

3. The children are cooking the soup.

_____

_____

4. They are answering you.

_____

_____

5. I do hike on the weekend.

_____

_____

Exercise 4

Choose an appropriate answer for each question below from the choices given.

Beispiel: Guten Tag, Josef. Was machst du?
                 (mein Geld zählen)
                 <u>Ich zähle mein Geld.</u>

nach Salzburg fahren   eine Lehre machen
einen Kuchen backen   einen Job suchen   im Park joggen

1. Hi, Ralf! Was machst du?

_____

_____

2. Hallo, Steffi! Hallo, Fritz! Was macht ihr?

_____

_____

3. Servus, Flo! Was macht eigentlich dein Bruder hier?

_____

_____

4. Ciao, Jochen! Was machen deine Schwestern gerade?

_____

_____

5. Grüß dich, Stefan! Was macht deine Mutter in der Küche?

_____

_____

40

Not all German verbs follow the standard conjugation pattern in the present tense.

Irregular verbs (also known as *strong* verbs) have a vowel-stem change in the second- and third-person singular (*du* and *er/sie/es*). Some of the most common vowel-stem changes include:

a → ä	*fahren:* to go (by vehicle) *ich fahre, du fährst, er/sie/es fährt* *schlafen* to sleep *ich schlafe, du schläfst, er/sie/es schläft*
au → äu	*laufen:* to run; to walk *ich laufe, du läufst, er/sie/es läuft*
e → i	*helfen:* to help *ich helfe, du hilfst, er/sie/es hilft* *geben:* to give *ich gebe, du gibst, er/sie/es gibt*
e → ie	*lesen:* to read *ich lese, du liest, er/sie/es liest* *stehlen:* to steal *ich stehle, du stiehlst, er/sie/es stiehlt*
o → ö	*stoßen:* to push *ich stoße, du stößt, er/sie/es stößt*

Ausnahme

The verb *nehmen* has more than just a vowel-stem change.

e → i *nehmen:* to take
ich nehme, du nimmst, er/sie/es nimmt

Ausnahme

The verb *wissen* has a more drastic stem change and changes in the first-person singular as well as the second- and third-person singular.

i → ei *wissen:* to know
ich weiß, du weißt, er/sie/es weiß

Irregular verbs that end in *-ten* do not add an *-e-* in the second person and have no additional ending in the third person singular.

a → ä *halten:* to stop; to hold
ich halte, du hältst, er/sie/es hält

Exercise 1
Complete the following chart with the correct conjugations for each irregular verb.

	sprechen (to speak)	braten (to roast)	nehmen (to take)
ich	spreche		
du		brätst	
er/sie/es	spricht		nimmt
wir	sprechen		nehmen

Exercise 2
Complete the following sentences using the correct form of the infinitive in parentheses.

1. _____ (wissen) du, wie spät es ist?

2. Wenn ich den Stein loslasse, _____ (fallen) er sicherlich ins Wasser.

3. Hey, wo _____ (laufen) er hin?

4. Was _____ (halten) du von dem Film?

5. Von wem ist der Brief, den sie gerade _____ (lesen)?

6. _____ (geben) du ihr die Ohrringe, obwohl sie mit dir nicht mehr _____ (sprechen)?

7. Wenn du den Ball zu mir _____ (werfen), fange ich ihn auf jeden Fall. Aber was ist wenn ich den Ball zu dir zurückwerfe? _____ (fangen) du ihn auch?

8. Auch wenn er mir die tropische Frucht _____ (empfehlen), esse ich sie nicht. Aber was ist wenn ich ihm eine tropische Frucht empfehle? _____ (essen) er sie?

9. Wenn du die Diamanten _____ (stehlen), werde ich dir nicht helfen. Und auch wenn du mir _____ (helfen), werde ich ich die Gemälde nicht stehlen.

10. Wenn du den ganzen Tag _____ (schlafen), kannst du das Buch nicht lesen. Aber wenn du das Buch den ganzen Tag _____ (lesen), kannst du wahrscheinlich nicht schlafen.

Exercise 3

Create an appropriate question for each of the answers provided below. Be sure to include the bold verb in either use the second or third person singular in the question.

1. Ich **weiß** absolut nichts über die Geschichte Deutschlands.

_____

_____

_____

2. Ich glaube nicht, weil er immer vorsichtig ist. Aber ich **zerbreche** sie bestimmt!

_____

_____

_____

3. Was meinst du? Ich **fahre** überhaupt nicht schnell.

_____

_____

_____

4. Nein, sie kann ganz schlecht **sehen**.

_____

_____

_____

5. Ja, klar! Alle Hunde **fressen** Fleisch.

_____

_____

41

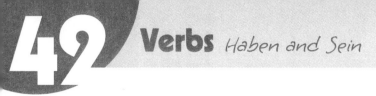

Verbs *Haben and Sein*

Two important verbs in the German language are *haben* (to have) and *sein* (to be).

Both *haben* and *sein* have irregular conjugations.

	Singular	Plural
haben (to have)	*ich habe* I have	*wir haben* we have
	du hast you have	*ihr habt* you (plural) have
	er/sie/es hat he/she/it has	*sie/Sie haben* they/you (formal) have
sein (to be)	*ich bin* I am	*wir sind* we are
	du bist you are	*ihr seid* you (plural) are
	er/sie/es ist he/she/it is	*sie/Sie sind* they/you (formal) are

In the present tense, *haben* is usually used in conjunction with an accusative noun (the direct object of the verb).

> *Ich **habe einen Computer**.*
> I **have a computer.**

> *Du **hast eine Freundin**.*
> You **have a girlfriend.**

> *Sie **hat ein Auto**.*
> She **has a car.**

> *Wir **haben keinen Fernseher**.*
> We don't **have a television.**

> *Ihr **habt keine Ahnung**.*
> You all **have no idea.**

> *Sie **haben kein Geld**.*
> They don't **have any money.**

***Sein* is a linking verb used to describe qualities of the subject and does not take a direct object. In the present tense, *sein* is usually used together with adjectives or nouns in the nominative case.**

> *Ich **bin müde**.*
> I **am tired.**

> *Du **bist ein lustiger Kerl**.*
> You **are a funny guy.**

> *Es ist **ein schönes, weißes Haus**.*
> It **is a pretty, white house.**

> *Wir **sind stark**.*
> We **are strong.**

> *Ihr **seid höflich**.*
> You all **are polite.**

> *Sie **sind zweisprachig**.*
> They/you (formal) **are bilingual.**

Exercise 1

Choose whether *haben* or *sein* is appropriate to use in each sentence below.

1. Ich bin/habe müde.

2. Sie ist/hat eine Schwester.

3. Er ist/hat Rettungsschwimmer.

4. Meine Freunde sind/haben sehr konservativ.

5. Ihr seid/habt keine Ahnung.

Exercise 2

Fill in each blank with the appropriate form of the verb *haben*.

1. Ich _____ zwei Brüder. Und du? Wie viele

Brüder _____ du?

2. Meine Kusine _____ vier Radios. Und deine

Kusinen? Wie viele Radios _____ sie?

3. Unser Onkel _____ drei Häuser. Und ihr? Wie

viele Häuser _____ ihr?

4. Ihre Tanten _____ sieben Katzen. Und wir?

Wie viele Katzen _____ wir?

5. Ich _____ zehn Euro. Und Sie? Wie viele Euro

_____ Sie?

Exercise 3

Fill in each blank with the appropriate form of the verb *sein*.

1. Claudia _____ Sportlerin. Was _____

du von Beruf?

2. Wie alt _____ dein Vetter? Er _____

dreißig Jahre alt.

3. Wir _____ geschieden, aber unsere _____

_____ noch verheiratet.

4. Ich _____ Studentin an einer amerikanischen

Uni.

5. Wo _____ ihr, denn? Ich habe euch überall

gesucht.

Exercise 4

Translate the following sentences into German using the correct form of *haben* and *sein*.

1. She has a cell phone in her purse.

_____

_____

2. Are you a lawyer? (formal)

_____

_____

3. The children are tired.

_____

_____

4. Elke and Rainer, are you ready?

_____

_____

5. I have a computer at home.

_____

_____

42

Some verbs have separable prefixes, which are prefixes that are separated from the stem when the verb is conjugated.

The prefix of a verb with a separable prefix is always stressed.

weitersuchen (prefix is stressed and separable)
ich suche weiter (I continue looking)

versuchen (prefix is unstressed and inseparable)
ich versuche (I try)

When the verb is conjugated, the separable prefix is placed at the end of the clause or sentence. The stem of the verb that remains is conjugated to agree with the subject and follows the normal verb placement rules.

Ich stehe um 7.00 Uhr auf, aber er steht um 4.00 Uhr auf.
I **get up** at 7:00, but he **gets up** at 4:00.

The stems of verbs with separable prefixes are verbs in their own right and have meanings that may be different from their prefix form. Prefixes do not alter the conjugation of the verb stem.

	Singular	Plural
no prefix: *fahren* (to drive)	*ich fahre* I drive	*wir fahren* we drive
	du fährst you drive	*ihr fahrt* you (plural) drive
	er/sie/es fährt he/she/it drives	*sie/Sie fahren* they/you (formal) drive
separable prefix: *abfahren* (to depart)	*ich fahre ab* I depart	*wir fahren ab* we depart
	du fährst ab you depart	*ihr fahrt ab* you (plural) depart
	er/sie/es fährt ab he/she/it departss	*sie/Sie fahren ab* they/you (formal) depart

Some common separable prefixes include

ab-	*abfahren* (to depart) *Wann fährt der Zug ab?* When does the train **depart**?
an-	*anfangen* (to begin) *Wir fangen morgen um 10.00 Uhr an.* We are **starting** tomorrow at 10 A.M.
auf-	*aufstehen* (to get up) *Steh schon auf! Es wird spät.* **Get up** already! It's getting late.
aus-	*ausgehen* (to go out) *Gehst du mit uns aus?* Are you **going out** with us?
bei-	*beibringen* (to teach) *Wann bringst du mir bei, auf Italienisch zu zählen?* When are you going to **teach** me how to count in Italian?
ein-	*einkaufen* (to go shopping) *Wo kauft sie am liebsten ein?* Where does she prefer to **shop**?

her-	herschauen (to look towards) **Schau her!** Ein Alligator! **Look over here!** An alligator!
hin-	hinfahren (to go by vehicle) Das Konzert ist morgen. **Fahren** wir **hin**? The concert is tomorrow. Are we **going to go (from here)**?
los-	losfliegen (to take off/depart by plane) Wann **fliegen** wir endlich **los**? When are we finally going to **take off**?
mit-	mitkommen (to come with/along) Ich fahre nach Berlin. **Kommt** ihr **mit**? I'm driving to Berlin. Are you guys **coming along**?
nach	nachsprechen (to repeat) Die Schüler **sprechen** der Lehrerin **nach**. The pupils **repeat** what the teacher says.
raus-	rauswerfen (to throw out) Wir **werfen** morgen unsere alten Sachen **raus**. Tomorrow we are going to **throw out** our old things.
rein-	reinlassen (to let in) **Lass** ihn bitte **rein**. Please **let** him **in**.
vor-	vorschlagen (to recommend) Was **schlägst** du **vor**? What do you **suggest**?
weg-	wegziehen (to move away) Ich **ziehe weg**. I'm **moving away**.
zu-	zuhören (to listen to) **Hör** ihm **zu**. **Listen to** him.
zurück-	zurückrufen (to call back) **Rufen** Sie mich bitte in einer Stunde **zurück**. Please **call** me **back** in an hour.

Achtung!

Just as with woher (where from, whence) and wohin (where to, whither), her indicates motion toward someone or something and hin indicates motion away from someone or something.

Exercise 1

Indicate whether the verbs in the sentences below have separable prefixes. Circle SEP for separable prefixes and INSEP for inseparable prefixes.

1. Wann will er aufstehen?   SEP   INSEP

2. Morgen werden wir unsere Freunde besuchen.   SEP   INSEP

3. Solche Sachen können schon vorkommen.   SEP   INSEP

4. Wenn du so weiter isst, wirst du sicherlich zunehmen.   SEP   INSEP

5. Ihr habt den Pokal auf alle Fälle verdient.   SEP   INSEP

Exercise 2

Underline the verbs and their prefixes in the following sentences.

1. Wie siehst du denn aus?
2. Rufen wir bei ihr nochmal an?
3. Ich räume mein Zimmer erst morgen auf.
4. Es fällt mir nicht auf, dass du größer geworden bist.
5. Sie bringt ihrer Tochter langsam bei, wie man Schach spielt.

Exercise 3

Place the sentence fragments below in the proper order.

1. man / aufgeben / wo / das Gepäck / ?

_____

_____

2. zuhören / die Spieler / dem Trainer / immer

_____

_____

3. du / dass / stimmt / mitbringen / kein Geld / es / ?

_____

_____

43

The prefix of a verb with an inseparable prefix is always unstressed.

*aúf*stehen (prefix is stressed and separable)
ich stehe **auf** (I get up)

*ver*stéhen (prefix is unstressed and inseparable)
ich **ver**stehe (I understand)

*weíter*suchen (prefix is stressed and separable)
ich suche **weiter** (I continue looking)

*ver*súchen (prefix is unstressed and inseparable)
ich **ver**suche (I try)

The stems of verbs with inseparable prefixes are verbs in their own right and have meanings that may be different from their inseparable prefix forms. Prefixes do not alter the conjugation of the verb stem.

	Singular	Plural
no prefix: *fahren* (to drive)	*ich fahre* I drive	*wir fahren* we drive
	du fährst you drive	*ihr fahrt* you (plural) drive
	er/sie/es fährt he/she/it drives	*sie/Sie fahren* they/you (formal) drive
inseparable prefix: *erfahren* (to experience)	*ich erfahre* I experience	*wir erfahren* we experience
	du erfährst you experience	*ihr erfahrt* you (plural) experience
	er/sie/es erfährt he/she/it experiences	*sie/Sie erfahren* they/you (formal) experience

If the stem of the verb is strong, it is also strong with a prefix. Likewise, if the verb stem is weak, it is also weak with a prefix. However, the *ge-* prefix found on most past participles is not included for verbs with inseparable prefixes.

fahren (to drive)	*ist* **ge**fahren (has driven)
erfahren (to experience)	*hat* **er**fahren (has experienced)
suchen (to look for)	*hat* **ge**sucht (has looked for)
besuchen (to visit)	*hat* **be**sucht (has visited)

The prefixes **be-, emp-, ent-, er-, ge-, mis-, ver-,** and **zer-** are always inseparable.

Was **besprechen** *wir heute?*
What are we going **to discuss** today?

Was **empfehlen** *Sie?*
What do you **recommend**?

Wofür haben Sie sich **entschieden***?*
What did you **decide on**?

Erklären *Sie das, bitte!*
Please **explain**!

Das **gefällt** *mir.*
I **like** that.

Das hat er **missverstanden.**
He **misunderstood** that.

Sie hat das Haus **verlassen.**
She **left** the house.

Das Feuer **zerstörte** *fast alles.*
The fire **destroyed** almost everything.

Exercise 1

Put a checkmark next to the verbs that contain inseparable prefixes.

_____ **1.** umsteigen

_____ **2.** bestellen

_____ **3.** entfernen

_____ **4.** überreden

_____ **5.** mitkommen

_____ **6.** zerbrechen

_____ **7.** verzeihen

_____ **8.** umziehen

Exercise 2

Fill in each blank below by conjugating the infinitive form of the regular verb in parentheses. If the verb has an inseparable prefix, put an *x* in the second blank.

1. Sie _____ ihr Haus

_____. (verkaufen)

2. Das Metal _____

das Auto _____. (zerkratzen)

3. Wie _____ man sowas

_____? (erfahren)

4. _____ Sie hier

_____! (umkehren)

5. Wie _____ das der

Wissenschaftler _____?

(beweisen)

6. Martha und ich _____ uns die Jacken

_____. (ausziehen)

7. Der Journalist _____ den Text

_____. (bearbeiten)

8. Der Spion _____ die Nachrichten

_____. (entziffern)

Exercise 3

Translate the following sentences into German.

1. I am ordering the books online.

_____

_____

2. Excuse me!

_____

_____

3. He hugs his dog every day.

_____

_____

4. Are you selling that at the flea market?

_____

_____

5. Does she like the house?

_____

_____

Verbs *Reflexive Verbs*

Reflexive verbs are used to indicate that the subject is doing something to or for himself/herself. They can also indicate a reciprocal action. Generally, pronouns that accompany reflexive verbs are in the accusative case, though some reflexive verbs require the dative case.

Each reflexive verb is conjugated to agree with is subject. The reflexive pronoun also agrees with the subject.

*Wir **schreiben uns** oft.*
We **write each other** often.

Achtung!

Reflexive verbs may have separable or inseparable prefixes.

*Das Mädchen **sieht sich** im Spiegel **an**.*
The girl **is looking at herself** in the mirror.

Many reflexive verbs in German are also reflexive in English, such as *sich waschen* (to wash oneself). However, some verbs that are reflexive in German are not reflexive in English. Some of the more common reflexive verbs that are not easily recognizable include:

sich ärgern	to get angry
sich freuen	to be happy about (with über), look forward to (with auf)
sich fühlen	to feel
sich interessieren	to be interested in (with für)
sich überlegen	to consider
sich wundern	to be surprised, to wonder

Many reflexive verbs that refer to body parts and articles of clothing take a dative reflexive pronoun to refer back to the subject (the person) and the accusative definite article to refer to the direct object (the body part or article of clothing).

*Ich wasche **mir** (dat.) **das Gesicht** (acc.).*
I am washing **my face.**

*Ziehst du **dir** (dat.) **die Schuhe** (acc.) an?*
Are you putting on **your shoes**?

*Er hat **sich** (dat.) **das Bein** (acc.) verletzt.*
He injured **his leg.**

Exercise 1

Fill in each blank below by conjugating the infinitive form of the verb in parentheses. Include the appropriate form of the reflexive pronoun.

1. Sie _____ _____ im Juni.
   (sich heiraten)

2. Die alten Freunde _____ _____
   ein gutes Neues Jahr. (sich wünschen)

3. Wie oft _____ du _____ die
   Zähne am Tag? (sich die Zähne putzen)

4. _____ _____ das Kind jeden
   Abend? (sich waschen)

5. Wir _____ _____ auch bei der
   Arbeit. (sich amüsieren)

6. Viele Leute _____ _____
   am Flughafen zum Abschied. (sich umarmen)

7. _____ Sie _____!
   (sich hinsetzen)

8. Ich _____ _____ , dass er
   nichts gesagt hat. (sich wundern)

Exercise 2

Answer the following questions in complete sentences.

1. Kämmst du dir die Haare am Morgen?

   _____

   _____

2. Rasierst du dich jeden Tag?

   _____

   _____

3. Wie oft wäscht du dir die Haare in der Woche?

_____

_____

4. Was ziehst du dir zur Arbeit an?

_____

_____

5. Was ziehst du dir am Wochenende an?

_____

_____

Exercise 3

Translate the following dialogue between Beate and Berndt into German using the reflexive verbs.

Beate: Do you talk to Katrin often?
Berndt: No, but we write each other emails frequently. Or sometimes we exchange text messages. But that costs extra.
Beate: When did you see each other last?
Berndt: Well, that was already two weeks ago, but we're meeting each other this weekend at her place.

_____

_____

_____

_____

_____

_____

_____

_____

Exercise 4

Write a short paragraph describing how you get ready in the morning. Use at least three of the reflexive phrases below. Do not use a phrase more than once.

sich duschen   sich die Zähne putzen   sich die Haare waschen   sich rasieren

_____

_____

_____

_____

_____

_____

_____

_____

_____

_____

_____

_____

45

Modals verbs are usually combined with another verb and provide additional information about that main verb. Modal verbs describe whether an action *can* be done, *ought to* be done, or *must* be done. The German modals include *können* (to be able to), *dürfen* (to be allowed to), *wollen* (to want to), *sollen* (to ought to), *mögen* (to like to), and *müssen* (to have to).

In the present tense, modal verbs are always conjugated to agree with the subject of the sentence. The main verb in the clause or sentence is presented in the infinitive (full) form.

Er **kann** mich gut **verstehen.**
He **can understand** me well.

Wir **dürfen** nicht hier **bleiben.**
We **are** not **allowed to stay** here.

Although the modal verbs are irregular, their conjugation is fairly easy to memorize. The plural forms follow the pattern of regular verbs. All singular forms contain the same vowel change, and the *ich* and *er/sie/es* forms are identical and have no ending.

	Singular	Plural
könnnen (to be able to, can)	*ich kann* I can	*wir können* we can
	du kannst you can	*ihr könnt* you (plural) can
	er/sie/es kann he/she/it can	*sie/Sie können* they/you (formal) can
dürfen (to be allowed to, may)	*ich darf* I may	*wir dürfen* we may
	du darfst you may	*ihr dürft* you (plural) may
	er/sie/es darf he/she/it may	*ssie/Sie dürfen* they/you (formal) may

Können and dürfen both express a request, *can* or *may*, but have very distinct uses. The verb *können* expresses the ability to do something.

Ich **kann** schwimmen.
I **can/am able to** swim.

Morgen **können** wir schwimmen gehen.
We **can go/will be able to** swimming tomorrow.

Entschuldigung, **können** Sie mir bitte sagen, wo der Bahnhof ist?
Excuse me, **can** you/are you **able to** tell me where the train station is?

The verb *dürfen* expresses the granting or denial of permission.

Ich **darf** nicht spielen.
I am not **allowed to/must** not play.

Darf ich dich bitte etwas fragen?
May I/am I permitted to ask you something?

Alltagssprache

In order to make a request more polite, *dürfen* is often used instead of *können*.

Kann ich bitte einen Vorschlag machen?
Can I please make a suggestion?

Darf ich bitte einen Vorschlag machen?
May I please make a suggestion?

Achtung!

When the action is understood through context, the infinitive is sometimes left out of a modal construction in both written as well as spoken German. This is often the case when a modal is used with the verb *machen* (to make); verbs showing motion toward, such as *gehen* (to go); and the verb *sprechen* (to speak), when a language is mentioned.

Schau, das **kann** ich auch **machen!**
    = Schau, das **kann** ich auch!
Look, I **can do** that too!
    = Look, I **can** (do) that too!

Darfst du ins Kino **gehen**?
    = **Darfst** du ins Kino?
Are you **allowed to go to** the movies?
    = Are you **allowed** (to go) to the movies?

Ich **kann** Deutsch **sprechen.**
    = Ich **kann** Deutsch.
I **can speak** German.
    = I **can** (speak) German.

Exercise 1

Circle the correct modal verb to complete each sentence.

1. Durch Spazierengehen darf/kann man abnehmen.

2. Hier darf/kann ich singen. Das ist mir erlaubt.

3. Darf/kann man im Restaurant rauchen?

4. Hier darfst/kannst du nicht parken. Es gibt keinen Platz mehr.

5. Die Arbeit am PC darf/kann die Augen anstrengen.

Exercise 2

Fill in the blanks with the correct form of the modal verb in parentheses.

1. Ich _____ nur Deutsch, aber meine Freundin

spricht Deutsch, Englisch und Italienisch. Und du? Wie

viele Sprachen _____ du? (können/ können)

2. Sie weiß, dass sie Fußball spielen _____,

aber der Arzt hat ihr gesagt, dass sie noch drei Wochen

keinen Sport treiben _____. (können/dürfen)

3. Papa, _____ wir bitte am Wochenende

Videospiele spielen? (dürfen)

4. Wie ist es eigentlich? _____ man hier im

Restaurant rauchen? (dürfen)

5. Hier _____ man super Ski fahren. (können)

Exercise 3

Write a question using either *dürfen* or *können* appropriate to elicit the answers given below.

1. Nein, du musst zu Hause bleiben.

_____

_____

2. Es tut mir Leid, ich habe kein Geld.

_____

_____

3. Weil ich meine Hausaufgaben noch machen muss.

_____

_____

Exercise 4

Translate the following sentences into German using either *können* or *dürfen* in each sentence.

1. He knows how to cook.

_____

_____

2. May I please have a piece of cake?

_____

_____

3. She can do that for you.

_____

_____

4. Can you please tell me what time it is?

_____

_____

5. My brother speaks French very well.

_____

_____

46

93

Verbs *Mögen, Müssen, Sollen, and Wollen*

Modal verbs describe whether an action *can* be done, *ought to* be done, or *must* be done. The other four German modal verbs are *mögen* (to like to), *müssen* (to have to), *sollen* (to ought to), and *wollen* (to want to).

Although the modal verbs are irregular, their conjugation is fairly easy to memorize. The plural forms follow the pattern of regular verbs. All singular forms contain the same vowel change, and the *ich* and *er/sie/es* forms are identical and have no ending.

	Singular	Plural
mögen (to like)	*ich mag* I like	*wir mögen* we like
	du magst you like	*ihr mögt* you (plural) like
	er/sie/es mag he/she/it likes	*sie/Sie mögen* they/you (formal) like
müssen (to have to, must)	*ich muss* I have to	*wir müssen* we have to
	du musst you have to	*ihr müsst* you (plural) have to
	er/sie/es muss he/she/it has to	*sie/Sie müssen* they/you (formal) have to
sollen (to be supposed to, ought to, should)	*ich soll* I should	*wir sollen* we should
	du sollst you should	*ihr sollt* you (plural) should
	er/sie/es soll he/she/it should	*sie/Sie sollen* they/you (formal) should
wollen (to want to)	*ich will* I want to	*wir wollen* we want to
	du willst you want to	*ihr wollt* you (plural) want to
	er/sie/es will he/she/it wants to	*sie/Sie wollen* they/you (formal) want to

Achtung!

Ich will indicates that one *wants* to do something, *not* that one *will* do it.

*Ich **will** nach Europa fliegen.*
I **want** to fly to Europe.

Modals have idiomatic uses that are common in contemporary written and spoken German. The verb *mögen* can also express a momentary offer or request.

***Magst** du mir bitte die Butter geben?*
Can you please pass (me) the butter?

***Magst** du einen Kaffee?*
Do you care for a (cup of) coffee?

The verb *sollen* can express an impersonal plan.

*Hier **sollen** neue Häuser entstehen.*
Supposedly, they **are going to** build new houses here.

The verb *wollen* can express a plan or intention.

*Sie **wollen** bald ein Café aufmachen.*
They **plan to** open a café soon.

*Ich **will** unbedingt nach Heidelberg umziehen.*
I definitely **intend to** move to Heidelberg.

Ausnahme

The subjunctive form of *mögen* is *möchten*. It is used to make formal or polite requests. In the subjunctive, the conjugation varies from the typical modal pattern.

	Singular	Plural
möchten	*ich möchte* I would like	*wir möchten* we would like
	du möchtest you would like	*ihr möchtet* you (plural) would like
	er/sie/es möchte he/she/it would like	*sie/Sie möchten* they/you (formal) would like

*Ich **möchte** ein Bier, einen Salat und einen Wienerschnitzel (haben), bitte.*
I **would like** a beer, a salad, and a Wiener schnitzel, please.

Alltagssprache

Note that *wollen* is not as polite as *möchten*.

*Ich **will** noch eine Kugel Eis (haben).*
I **want** another scoop of ice cream.

*Ich **möchte** noch eine Kugel Eis (haben).*
I **would like** another scoop of ice cream.

Achtung!

As with *können* and *dürfen*, the other modals can be used without another verb when the meaning is implicit.

*Ich **muss** nach Hause (gehen).*
I **have to** go home.

***Kommst** du? Nein, ich **will** nicht!*
Are you **coming**? No, I don't **want to**.

Exercise 1

Rewrite the following sentences using the modal verbs in parentheses in the correct conjugated form.

1. Er bedankt sich bei seiner Freundin. (sollen)

_____

2. Wir arbeiten. (müssen)

_____

3. Nein, danke, ich trinke keinen Kaffee. (möchten)

_____

4. Ich ziehe von hier weg. (wollen)

_____

Exercise 2

Complete each sentence two times by conjugating the modal verb in parentheses using different subjects from the choices below. Be sure to watch word order.

Erich   meine Freunde und ich   du   ihr   Sie
Linda   ich   sie

Beispiel: (wollen)
Um mehr über die Welt zu wissen, <u>will er jeden Tag die Zeitung lesen</u>.

1. (sollen)   Um gesünder zu werden,

_____

2. (müssen)   Um erfolgreich in der Schule zu sein,

_____

3. (wollen)   Um die Wohnung schöner zu machen,

_____

4. (möchten)   Um Erfahrung im Ausland zu sammeln,

_____

Exercise 3

Translate the following sentences into German using appropriate modal verbs.

1. He does not like this city.

_____

_____

2. I have to go to bed. I want to get up early tomorrow.

_____

_____

3. We should go home now.

_____

_____

47

For general negation, *nicht* is placed before the infinitive accompanying a modal.

> *Ich kann die **Kiste nicht tragen**.*
> I **can't/am not able to carry** the box.

Nicht also precedes elements such as prepositional phrases and nonspecific expressions of time and quantity, which may precede the infinitive that accompanies a modal.

> *Er will nicht **in Bonn** wohnen.*
> He doesn't want to live **in Bonn.**

> *Man soll das nicht **immer** machen.*
> You shouldn't **always** do that.

Although *müssen* often translates as *must,* the negation of *must* (*must not*) is formed with *nicht* + the modal verb *dürfen.*

> *Man **darf nicht** zu viel trinken.*
> You're **not allowed** to/**mustn't** drink too much.

The negation of *müssen* translates as *does not* and is formed with either *müssen* + *nicht* or *brauchen nicht . . . zu.*

> *Andreas **muss** heute **nicht** arbeiten.*
> *Andreas **braucht** heute **nicht zu** arebeiten.*
> Andreas **doesn't have** to work today.

3. Der Schauspieler muss morgen anfangen.

_____

4. Der Autor will seinen nächsten Roman schreiben.

_____

_____

5. Das Kind muss das Eis essen.

_____

_____

6. Karolina möchte ihren Großvater besuchen.

_____

_____

7. Das Radio kann ich hören.

_____

_____

8. Helena soll die Medikamente nehmen.

_____

_____

Exercise 1

Negate the following sentences that contain modals.

1. Martin will im Lebensmittelgeschäft arbeiten.

_____

_____

2. Wilhelm soll mit ihr singen.

_____

_____

Exercise 2

A friend is helping you decide what to do on vacation. She asks you a series of questions. Respond to her questions in the negative.

1. Willst du Ski fahren?

_____

_____

2. Willst du fliegen?

_____

_____

3. Kannst du Französisch sprechen?

_____

_____

4. Kannst du Auto fahren?

_____

_____

5. Willst du erreichbar sein?

_____

_____

Exercise 3

Translate the following sentences into German using the proper modal negation.

1. The children mustn't play in the street.

_____

_____

2. She can't read yet.

_____

_____

3. He doesn't want to eat his vegetables.

_____

_____

4. We shouldn't wait too long.

_____

_____

5. I don't have to go to school today.

_____

_____

Exercise 4

Create an exchange between a parent and child. Use at least three modals negated correctly as they respond negatively to each other.

_____

_____

_____

_____

_____

_____

_____

_____

_____

_____

_____

_____

_____

_____

_____

_____

_____

_____

_____

48

In the present perfect tense, *haben* (to have) is always used as the helping verb with a modal, regardless of the main verb. A double-infinitive construction of the modal and main verbs follows the conjugated form of *haben*.

Ich **muss gehen.** (present tense)
I **have to go.**

Ich **habe gehen müssen.** (present perfect)
I **have had to go.** (I had to go.)

Er **darf essen.** (present tense)
He **is allowed to eat.**

Er **hat essen dürfen.** (present perfect
He **has been allowed to eat.** (He was allowed to eat.)

Ausnahme

If the main verb is not stated, but implied, the past tense is typically formed by putting the modal into the simple past.

Ich **muss** nach Hause. (*gehen* is implied)
I **have to (go)** home.

Ich **musste** nach Hause. (simple past)
I **had to (go)** home.

In the simple past, the modal verb is placed where the conjugated verb is typically positioned. The main verb in the infinitive form is placed at the end of the construction.

Ich **habe gehen müssen.** (present perfect)
I **have had to go.** (I had to go.)

Ich **musste gehen.** (imperfect or simple past)
I **had to go.**

Er **hat essen dürfen.** (present perfect)
He **has been allowed to eat.** (He was allowed to eat.)

Er **durfte essen.** (imperfect or simple past)
He **was allowed to eat.**

The modals do not take umlauts in the simple past. All modals use the simple past *-t-* before the verb ending.

	Singular	**Plural**
dürfen (to like)	*ich durfte* I was allowed	*wir durften* we were allowed
	dudurftest you were allowed	*ihr durftet* you all were allowed
	er/sie/es durfte he/she/it was allowed	*sie/Sie durften* they/you (formal) were allowed

ich konnte	I was able to
ich mochte	I liked to
ich musste	I had to
ich wollte	I wanted to
ich sollte	I was supposed to

Als Kind **durfte** ich nicht durchs Haus **rennen.**
As a child, I was not **allowed/permitted to run** through the house.

Alltagssprache

The present perfect construction is often avoided by using the modals in the simple past (or imperfect tense), especially in conversation. Although translated literally there is a slight difference between the two forms, there is no difference in meaning between the two past tense constructions in German.

Exercise 1

Fill in each blank with the simple past form by conjugating the infinitive form of the modal and placing the main verb in its proper position.

1. Was _____ Sie _____, Herr Schmidt? (wollen/schreiben)

2. Gestern _____ ich nicht _____. (können/kommen)

3. Moritz _____ nicht verspätet _____. (dürfen/sein)

4. Was _____ Maria _____? (sollen/mitbringen)

5. Was _____ du zu Weihnachten _____? (wollen/bekommen)

6. Martha und ich _____ das Abendessen _____. (müssen/kochen)

7. _____ ihr als Kinder im See _____? (dürfen/schwimmen)

8. Ich _____ Futter für den Hund _____. (sollen/einkaufen)

Exercise 2

Change the following sentences from the present perfect tense to the simple past.

1. Ich habe gestern arbeiten müssen.

_____

_____

2. Er hat uns letzte Woche besuchen sollen.

_____

_____

3. Wir haben letzten Sommer eine Afrikareise machen wollen.

_____

_____

4. Sie haben als Kinder nicht ohne Mantel nach draußen gehen dürfen.

_____

_____

5. Als Junge hat er nicht Rad fahren können.

_____

_____

Exercise 3

Translate the following sentences into German using the simple past form of the modals.

1. Erik was supposed to buy a notebook.

_____

_____

2. Kerstin was not able to come to our house this evening.

_____

_____

3. The children wanted to drink hot chocolate.

_____

_____

4. We were not allowed to follow them.

_____

_____

5. Did you all have to take the train?

_____

_____

49

 **Verbs** *Verbs That Require the Dative Case*

Several German verbs require the use of the dative case.

Nouns in the dative in German are generally the subject in the English translation. Some of the common verbs that require the dative include:

antworten (to answer)	*Sie antwortet **euch**.* She is answering **you all**.
danken (to thank)	*Ich danke **euch**.* I thank **you all**.
fehlen (to be lacking)	*Du fehlst **mir**.* **I** miss you.
folgen (to follow)	*Folgen Sie **mir**, bitte.* Please follow **me**.
gefallen (to please)	*Das Buch gefällt **ihm**.* **He** likes the book.
gehören (to belong to)	***Wem** gehört das?* **To whom** does this belong?
gelingen (to succeed)	*Es gelingt **ihm** jedes Mal.* **He** succeeds every time.
glauben (to believe)	*Er glaubt **uns** nicht.* He does not believe **us**.
gratulieren (to congratulate)	*Ich gratuliere **dir**.* I congratulate **you**.
helfen (to help)	*Helfen Sie **mir**!* Help **me**!
Leid tun (to do one sorrow)	*Das tut **mir** Leid.* **I'm** sorry.
passen (to fit, to suit)	*Die Hose passt **dir** gut.* The pants fit/suit **you** well.
passieren (to happen)	*Was ist **dir** passiert?* What happened **to you**?
schmecken (to taste)	*Reis schmeckt **mir** nicht.* **I** don't like rice.
versprechen (to promise)	*Das verspreche ich **dir**.* I promise **you** that.
wehtun (to hurt)	*Das Bein tut **mir** weh.* **My** leg hurts.
zuhören (to listen)	*Hör **mir** jetzt zu!* Listen **to me** now!

Exercise 1

Complete each sentence below using the conjugated form of one of the verbs below. Use the past participle if the context of the sentence requires it.

fehlen   gelingen   gratulieren
passieren   schmecken

1. Die Suppe _____ meiner Arbeitskollegin nicht.

2. Jedes Mal wenn er weggeht, _____ er uns sehr.

3. Was ist dir und deinem Mitbewohner _____?

4. Wir _____ dir zum Geburtstag!

5. Es ist ihr endlich _____, dass sie ihre Traumstelle bekommen hat.

Exercise 2

Circle the appropriate dative personal pronoun based on the context given in each sentence pair.

1. Er mag Blumen. Blumen gefallen ihm/Ihnen sehr.

2. Ich kaufe das Auto eines Tages. Glauben Sie mir/ihr!

3. Vielen Dank für das Geschenk. Ich danke ihm/dir.

4. Brauchen Sie Hilfe? Kann ich ihnen/Ihnen helfen?

5. Ihr kennt den Weg besser als ich. Ich folge uns/euch.

6. Es tut mir/dir mächtig Leid, dass ich mich verspätet habe.

Exercise 3

Use the options below to create the most appropriate response for each question. Use a dative personal pronoun in your response.

Beispiel: Was gehört dir? das lustige Poster
Mir gehört das lustige Poster.

der rechte Arm
ein Stück Linzer Torte
weil er zu lange gebraucht hat
die Musik der Fantastischen Vier
eine Reise nach Leipzig
das kleine, schwarze Kleid

1. Was für Musik gefällt dir?

_____

_____

2. Was schmeckt Ihnen am besten?

_____

_____

3. Warum ist es ihm nicht gelungen?

_____

_____

4. Was habe ich euch versprochen?

_____

_____

_____

5. Was tut Ihnen weh?

_____

_____

_____

6. Was passt ihr am besten?

_____

_____

50

51 Verbs *Kennen and Wissen*

In German, there are two verbs that roughly translate as *to know*: *kennen* and *wissen*. These verbs are not interchangeable, and each has its own unique usage.

Kennen indicates familiarity or acquaintance with people, places, and things. *Kennen* always takes a direct object.

> *Kennen Sie den Mann dort drüben?*
> Do you **know** that man over there?

> *Ich kenne dieses Lied.*
> I **know** this song.

> *Wie gut kennst du Wien?*
> How **familiar** are you with Vienna?

Wissen indicates knowledge of facts and information.

> *Weiß er, dass Wien in Österreich ist?*
> Does he **know** that Vienna is in Austria?

Sentences containing *wissen* typically include a clause beginning with a question word, such as *wer* (who), *was* (what), *warum* (why), *wo* (where), or *wann* (when), or the conjunction *dass* (that). This construction is used to ask or state whether someone knows a particular bit of information.

> *Wissen Sie, wo der Mann wohnt?*
> Do you **know where** the man lives?

> *Ich weiß, dass das Lied neu ist.*
> I **know that** the song is new.

Kennen follows regular conjugation rules. However, *wissen* is an irregular verb.

	Singular	**Plural**
kennen (to know)	*ich kenne* I know	*wir kennen* we know
	du kennst you know	*ihr kennt* you all know
	er/sie/es kennt he/she/it knows	*sie/Sie kennen* they/you (forma)l know
wissen (to know)	*ich weiß* I know	*wir wissen* we know
	du weißt you know	*ihr wisst* you all know
	er/sie/es weiß he/she/it knows	*sie/Sie erfahren* they/you (formal) know

Exercise 1

Use context to determine whether *kennen* or *wissen* should be used in each sentence below. Circle the correct verb.

1. Kennst/Weißt du meinen Bruder?

2. Wir kennen/wissen nicht, warum Hans kein Auto hat.

3. Ich kenne/weiß, dass SF1 ein Schweizer Fernsehsender ist.

4. Weißt/Kennst du was? Ich kenne/weiß ein gutes Restaurant nicht weit von hier.

5. Wie viele Leute kennst/weißt du auf dieser Party? Ich kenne/weiß es nicht genau.

Exercise 2

Identify the correct response to each question.

1. Magst du Stollen?
   a. Ich weiß nicht. Ich habe Stollen noch nie gegessen.
   b. Ja, sie kennt Stollen.
   c. Ja, ich weiß, dass du Stollen magst.

2. Weißt du, wann Franz Geburtstag hat?
   a. Nein, ich weiß nicht, wann er Geburtstag hat.
   b. Nein, Franz kennt mich nicht.
   c. Sicher weiß ich das. Er steht um 8.00 Uhr auf.

3. Welche Haarfarbe hat Jutta?
   a. Frag mich nicht. Sie kennt mich nicht.
   b. Jeder weiß, dass sie rotes Haar hat.
   c. Jutta weiß, dass ich braunes Haar habe.

Exercise 3

Use the prompts below to create questions using the correct conjugate of *kennen* or *wissen* according to the pronoun in parentheses.

Beispiel: wie spät es ist (ihr)   Wisst ihr, wie spät es ist?
           den alten Mann (du)   Kennst du den alten Mann?

1. was Jutta studiert (er)

_____

_____

2. den Weg nach Hause (du)

_____

_____

3. meine Frau (du)

_____

_____

4. dass Harald Rechtsanwalt ist (ihr)

_____

_____

5. wo der Bahnhof ist (Sie)

_____

_____

Exercise 4

Translate the following dialog into German using the correct German verb for *to know*.

Maria: Do you know why Jürgen is not here?
Berndt: No. Should we call him?
Maria: Do you know his phone number?
Berndt: No. And I don't know his father's name.
Maria: I know his sister. I know where they live. It's not far.
Berndt: Let's go to his house!

_____

_____

_____

_____

_____

_____

_____

_____

_____

_____

_____

_____

_____

_____

_____

_____

_____

51

Verbs *Lassen*

The verb *lassen* (to let) is an irregular verb.

	Singular	Plural
lassen (to let)	*ich lasse* I let	*wir lassen* we let
	du lässt you let	*ihr lasst* you all let
	er/sie/es lässt he/she/it lets	*sie/Sie lassen* they/you (forma)l let

Lassen also has an irregular imperative form.

du form	*Lass . . . !* Leave/Let . . . !
ihr form	*Lasst . . . !* Leave/Let . . . !
Sie form	*Lassen Sie . . . !* Leave/Let . . . !

Lassen has several specific uses beyond its English equivalent. **Lassen** can mean *to leave* so*mething somewhere.*

Tina **lässt** ihren Regenschirm immer im Auto.
Tina always **leaves** her umbrella in the car.

Wilhelm hat sein Handy zu Hause **gelassen.**
(present perfect tense)
Wilhelm **left** his cell phone at home.

Achtung!

To leave is also expressed with the verbs *verlassen* (when a specific place is indicated) or *abfahren* (when no place is indicated). *Abfahren* can also mean *to depart.*

Doris **verlässt** das Haus.
Doris **is leaving** the house.

Wir sind schon **abgefahren.**
We already **left.**

Lassen can also mean *to permit* or *to allow* someone to do something when combined with another verb in the infinitive form. The infinitive in this construction is placed at the end of the clause or sentence.

Lassen Sie mich behilflich **sein.**
Allow me to be of help to you./**Allow me** to help you.

When combined with the pronoun *uns* (us), **lassen** can translate as *let us* or *let's.*

Lass uns zusammen arbeiten.
Let's coorperate.

Lassen can also mean *stop* when referring to a stop in action.

Lasst das.
Stop (doing) that.

Lassen can be used together with an infinitive to mean *to have* an activity *done* by someone else. In these constructions, the infinitive is placed at the end of the clause or sentence.

Sie **lässt** ihr Auto **reparieren.**
She's **having** her car **repaired.**

Exercise 1

Fill in each blank below with the correct conjugated form of *lassen*. Some blanks may call for the infinitive or past participle.

1. Wo hat er seine Schuhe _____?

2. _____ du dir die Haare schneiden?

3. Sigrid _____ ihre Schlüssel nie im Auto.

4. Manfred will den Regenschirm im Auto

_____.

5. Ich _____ meine Sachen einfach auf dem Tisch.

Exercise 2

Use the imperative forms of *lassen* to complete the following sentences as indicated by the pronoun in parentheses.

1. _____ das! (Sie)

2. _____ uns alle offen miteinander reden! (ihr)

3. _____ mich dir helfen! (du)

4. _____ uns nach Hause fahren! (du)

5. _____ uns etwas engagierter werden! (du)

Exercise 3

You are fixing up your new home. What are you having done and by whom? Write a paragraph matching the following professionals and their tasks.

der Maler	Wände anstreichen
der Zimmermann	die neuen Möbel installieren
der Schreiner	Zimmer renovieren
der Designer	neue Schränke bauen

_____

_____

_____

_____

_____

_____

_____

_____

_____

_____

_____

_____

_____

_____

_____

_____

_____

_____

52

53 Verbs *Verb + Infinitive*

Modal verbs are often used with the infinitive to describe conditions, such as whether the action *can* be done, or *ought to* be done, or *must* be done. Other auxiliary verbs in German also take infinitives to express conditions about certain actions.

Some common auxiliary verbs used with the infinitives include:

sehen	to see (something being done)
hören	to hear (something being done)
lassen	to have something done (by someone else)
bleiben	to remain in the act; to continue to do something
gehen	to go (to do something)
fahren	to go (by car) (to do something)

In present tense auxiliary verb + infinitive constructions, the infinitive is placed at the end of the clause or sentence.

Ich **sah** ihn den Fluss entlang **laufen.**
I **saw** him **walking** along the river.

Wir **hören** ihn oft **schnarchen.**
We often **hear** him **snoring.**

Er **lässt** sich ein neues Haus **bauen.**
He's **having** a new house **built** for himself.

Sebastian **bleibt** den ganzen Tag **stehen.**
Sebastian **remains standing** all day.

Wann **gehst** du **einkaufen?**
When are you **going shopping?**

Fahrt ihr am Sonntag **spazieren?**
Do you all **go for a drive** on Sunday?

In the present perfect tense, the past participle of the auxiliary verb follows the infinitive of the main verb at the end of the clause or sentence.

Wann **bist** du **einkaufen gegangen?** (past participle of *gehen*)
When **did** you **go shopping?**

Ausnahme

The auxiliary verbs *sehen* (to see), *hören* (to hear), and *lassen* (to leave) are not used in the past participle form in the present perfect tense. Instead, a double-infinitive construction is used, with the construction infinitive + auxiliary infinitive.

Wir **haben** ihn **schnarchen hören.**
We **heard** him **snoring.**

Exercise 1

Fill in each blank with the correctly conjugated present tense form of the auxiliary verb and infinitive in parentheses.

1. Warum _____ er sich die Haare

_____? (schneiden lassen)

2. _____ du sie _____? (kommen hören)

3. Ich _____ dich am Computer

_____. (arbeiten sehen)

4. _____ Sie bitte _____. (stehen bleiben)

5. Willst du heute Abend _____

_____? (essen gehen)

Exercise 2

Fill in each blank with the correct present perfect tense for of the auxiliary verb and infinitive in parentheses.

1. Die Hausfrau hat das Haus _____

_____. (putzen lassen)

2. Wir sind schon eine Stunde dort _____

_____. (sitzen bleiben)

3. Bist du schon _____

_____? (schwimmen gehen)

4. Hat der Hausbesitzer den Dieb das Geld _____

_____? (stehlen sehen)

5. Wir sind _____

_____. (spazieren fahren)

Exercise 3

There was a break-in in your neighborhood. Report what you heard and saw using the auxiliary verb indicated along with an infinitive.

Beispiel: Der Nachbar stand draußen vor dem Haus. (sehen)
Ich habe den Nachbarn draußen vor dem Haus stehen sehen.

1. Jemand hat das Fenster hinten kaputt gemacht. (hören)

_____

_____

2. Claudia rief die Polizei auf ihrem Handy an. (hören)

_____

_____

3. Der Nachbar ist nach hinten gelaufen. (sehen)

_____

_____

4. Der Nachbar hat jemanden laut angeschrieen. (hören)

_____

_____

5. Der Verbrecher ist weg gerannt. (sehen)

_____

_____

Exercise 4

Translate the following sentences into German using the correct form of the auxiliary verb and the infinitive.

1. She saw the children playing.

_____

_____

2. We went out drinking last night.

_____

_____

3. You (familiar, singular) should go jogging.

_____

_____

4. They remained seated on the plane.

_____

_____

5. I had my shoes shined (cleaned).

_____

_____

53

In some cases where German uses an auxiliary verb + infinitive construction, the word *zu* (to) is not stated, as it would be in English. However, in most instances *zu* (to) is stated together with the infinitive in these constructions.

In most instances when the infinitive of a verb is combined with an auxiliary verb, *zu* precedes the infinitive.

> *Sie versucht, Tennis **zu spielen**.*
> She is trying **to play** tennis.

Achtung!

Zu is never used in constructions that include modal verbs.

When a verb has a separable prefix, *zu* is placed between the prefix and the stem of the infinitive.

> *Er hat vergessen, mich **abzuholen**.*
> He forgot **to pick** me **up**.

Some common expressions that use *zu* include:

> *Lust haben, . . . zu* + infinitive (to want to)
> *Ich **habe** keine **Lust**, ins Kino **zu gehen**.*
> I **do**n't **feel like going to** the movies.

> *Zeit haben, . . . zu* + infinitive (to have time to)
> *Er **hat** nicht viel **Zeit**, zum Bahnhof **zu rennen**.*
> He **doesn't have time to run to** the train station.

> *versuchen, . . . zu* + infinitive (to try to)
> *Wir werden **versuchen**, ihn **zu erreichen**.*
> We will **try to reach** him.

> *vergessen, . . . zu* + infinitive (to forget to)
> *Sie hat **vergessen**, ihn **anzurufen**.*
> She **forgot to call** him.

> *anfangen/beginnen, . . . zu* + infinitive (to start to)
> *Hast du schon **angefangen**, das Buch **zu lesen**?*
> Did you already **start reading** the book?

> *aufhören, . . . zu* + infinitive (to quit/stop)
> *Jasmin und Daniela haben **aufgehört zu rauchen**.*
> Jasmin and Daniela **quit smoking**.

The *zu* + infinitive construction can be *extended* to include more information about an action. In German, this information precedes *zu* + infinitive and is generally set off by a comma for clarity. This is referred to as an *extended infinitive*.

> *Jasmin und Daniela haben **aufgehört zu rauchen**.*
> Jasmin and Daniela **quit smoking**.

> *Jasmin und Daniela haben **aufgehört**, Zigaretten **zu rauchen**.*
> Jasmin and Daniela **quit smoking** cigarettes.

> *Jasmin und Daniela haben **aufgehört**, morgens Zigaretten **zu rauchen**.*
> Jasmin and Daniela **quit smoking** cigarettes in the morning.

> *Jasmin und Daniela haben **aufgehört**, morgens nach dem Frühstück Zigaretten **zu rauchen**.*
> Jasmin and Daniela **quit smoking** cigarettes in the morning after breakfast.

Other common *zu* + infinitive constructions include:

> *ohne . . . zu* + infinitive (without doing)
> *Sie hat angerufen, **ohne** ihn **zu fragen**.*
> She called **without asking** him.

> *statt . . . zu* + infinitive (instead of doing)
> *Sie hat eine E-Mail geschickt, **statt** ihn **anzurufen**.*
> She sent an email **instead of calling** him.

> *um . . . zu* + infinitive ([in order] to do)
> *Sie hat ihn angerufen, **um** ihn zum Essen **einzuladen**.*
> She called him **in order to invite** him to dinner.

Exercise 1

Use the verb phrases below to complete each sentence below. Conjugate the verb in each expression to agree with the subject of the clause or sentence, and place *zu* before the infinitive.

Lust haben . . . zu
versuchen . . . zu
aufhören . . . zu
ohne . . . zu
um . . . zu

1. Wir _____, die Umwelt sauber

_____ halten, da wir umweltfreundlich sein

wollen.

2. _____ ein Wort _____

sagen, stieg er leise ins Auto.

3. Der Patient _____ nicht

_____, seine Medikamente

_____ nehmen.

4. _____ du _____,

übermorgen bei uns Kaffee und Kuchen _____ haben?

5. Ich bin nach Deutschland geflogen, _____

mein Deutsch _____ verbessern.

Exercise 2

Answer the following questions using the *zu* + infinitive construction.

1. Hast du Zeit, mich abzuholen?

_____

_____

2. Hat dein Mitarbeiter vergessen, etwas zu machen?

_____

_____

3. Ich wollte ins Konzert gehen. Was willst du stattdessen machen?

_____

_____

4. Warum bist du in die Stadt gefahren?

_____

_____

5. Ich möchte heute Abend etwas unternehmen. Worauf hättest du Lust?

_____

_____

Exercise 3

Translate the following sentences into German using the proper *zu* + infinitive construction.

1. I am trying to lose weight.

_____

_____

2. Are you (familiar, singular) starting to learn German?

_____

_____

3. Do you (formal) know if he has time to go to the bookstore?

_____

_____

4. She can drive to his house without looking at the map.

_____

_____

5. I went to the grocery store to buy milk.

_____

_____

54

The past participle of regular (*weak*) verbs is formed by taking the verb stem (the infinitive without the *-en* ending) and adding a *ge-* prefix and a *-t* suffix.

Infinitive	Prefix	Stem	Suffix	Past Participle
haben (to have)	ge-	hab	-t	gehabt
machen (to make/do)	ge-	mach	-t	gemacht
sagen (to say)	ge-	sag	-t	gesagt
suchen (to lwwok)	ge-	such	-t	gesucht

*Was **hat** er zum Mittagessen **gehabt**?*
What **did** he **have** for lunch?

*Ich habe lange **gesucht**.*
I **looked** for a long time.

Alltagssprache

In many cases, if a verb in English forms its past participle with *-ed*, it is weak in German.

*Sie haben lange **gespielt**.*
They **played** for a long time.

*Ich habe viel Geld **gespart**.*
I **saved** a lot of money.

If the verb stem ends in either *-d* or *-t,* or in *-m* or *-n* preceded by a consonant other than *l* or *r,* the past participle takes the suffix *-et.*

Infinitive	Prefix	Stem	Suffix	Past Participle
en**den** (to end)	ge-	end	-et	geendet
arbei**ten** (to work)	ge-	arbeit	-et	gearbeitet
at**men** (to breathe)	ge-	atm	-et	geatmet
reg**nen** (to rain)	ge-	regn	-et	geregnet

*Wie lange **hat** es gestern **geregnet**?*
How long **did** it **rain** yesterday?

Achtung!

Verbs that end in *-ieren,* such as *adoptieren* (to adopt), *passieren* (to happen), *probieren* (to try), *studieren* (to attend a university; to major in), and *telefonieren* (to call), form the past participle without the *ge-* prefix. They typically take the *-t* ending.

*Ich **habe** ein Kind **adoptiert**.*
I **have adopted** a child.

The past participle of irregular (*strong*) verbs is formed by adding the *ge-* prefix and an *-en* suffix. The verb stem itself, however, can change in a variety of ways. Some of common irregular verbs include:

Infinitive	Past Participle
gehen (to go)	ge**gang**en
helfen (to help)	ge**holf**en
lesen (to help)	ge**les**en
schreiben (to help)	ge**schrieb**en
singen (to help)	ge**sung**en
treffen (to help)	ge**troff**en

*Wohin sind Sie **gegangen**?*
Where did you **go** (to)?

The past participle of *mixed* verbs, those that combine elements of both weak and strong verbs, is usually formed by adding the *ge-* prefix and *-t* suffix to the irregular verb stems. Some of common mixed verbs include:

Infinitive	Past Participle
brennen (to burn)	ge**brann**t
bringen (to bring)	ge**brach**t
denken (to think)	ge**dach**t
kennen (to know; to be acquainted with)	ge**kann**t
nennen (to name)	ge**nann**t
rennen (to run)	ge**rann**t
senden (to send)	ge**sand**t
wissen (to know, as a fact)	ge**wuss**t

*Roland **hat** ein großes Geschenk **gebracht.***
Roland **has brought** a large gift.

***Hast** du das **gewusst**?*
Did you **know** that?

Exercise 1

Give the past participles for the following weak and mixed verbs.

1. kaufen _____

2. fragen _____

3. spielen _____

4. tanzen _____

5. hören _____

6. machen _____

7. kehren _____

8. heiraten _____

9. öffnen _____

10. regnen _____

11. nennen _____

12. tippen _____

13. wissen _____

14. legen _____

15. denken _____

Exercise 2

Indicate whether the following verbs are weak (W) or strong (S). Then give the proper past participle form. Use the past participle in English as a clue.

1. kochen (cooked)   W   S _____

2. lernen (learned)   W   S _____

3. treffen (met)   W   S _____

4. merken (noticed)   W   S _____

5. singen (sung)   W   S _____

6. feiern (celebrated)   W   S _____

7. schreiben (written)   W   S _____

8. lesen (read)   W   S _____

Exercise 3

Provide the infinitives from which these strong past participles likely stem.

1. gefunden _____

2. gesunken _____

3. geschrieben _____

4. gefahren _____

5. zurückgefahren _____

6. empfangen _____

7. eingeladen _____

8. gelesen _____

9. genommen _____

10. gestiegen _____

11. geholfen _____

12. missverstanden _____

13. abgefahren _____

14. zerbrochen _____

55

The present perfect tense is the past tense form most commonly used in conversation to describe events that have happened. The present perfect is formed with an auxiliary verb (*haben* or *sein*) + past participle.

Just as the present tense in German has several translations in English, so does the past tense.

> *Er **hat gekocht.***
> He **cooked**/He **did cook**/He was **cooking**/He has **cooked**.

Most verbs form the present perfect tense with the verb *haben* (to have) conjugated to agree with the subject. The past participle is placed at the end of the sentence.

> *Wir **haben** Suppe **gegessen.***
> We **have eaten** soup.

Achtung!

The verb *haben* has an irregular conjugation.

ich habe	I have	*wir haben*	we have
du hast	you have	*ihr habt*	you (plural) have
er/sie/es hat	he/she/it has	*sie/Sie haben*	they/you (formal) have

All reflexive verbs take *haben* in the present perfect tense.

> *sich beeilen* (to hurry)
> *Du **hast** dich beeilt.*
> You hurried.

> *sich anziehen* (to get dressed)
> *Er **hat** sich angezogen.*
> He got dressed.

Exercise 1

Complete each sentence by filling in the blank with the correct past participle for the word in parentheses.

1. Am Samstag habe ich stundenlang mit meinem Freund

   _____ (telefonieren).

2. Hast du wirklich _____ (wissen), dass

   ich den Kuchen gebacken habe?

3. Wie lange hat er an der Universität in Stuttgart

   _____ (studieren)?

4. Sie hat _____ (denken), dass ich mit ihr

   ins Kino gehen würde.

5. Sie hat schon _____ (probieren),

   ihre Mutter zu erreichen, aber dabei hat sie keinen Glück

   gehabt.

Exercise 2

Complete each sentence with the past participle from the pool.

geschnitten	geschlagen	gestohlen
getan	gesehen	genommen
geschält	geholfen	

1. Was habt ihr in Krefeld _____?

2. Warum hast du ihr nicht _____, ihre

   Koffer zu tragen?

3. Ich habe die Avocados zuerst _____

   und dann in Scheiben _____.

4. Hast du _____, wie weit er den Ball

   _____ hat?

5. Wie viele Sachen hat der Dieb _____?

   Oder hat er doch nichts _____?

Exercise 3

Rewrite the following sentences in the present perfect tense. Note: The first five sentences contain weak verbs.

1. Ich baue mit meinen Freunden ein Gartenhaus.

_____

_____

2. Martin kauft die Werkzeuge.

_____

_____

3. Astrid und Ursula bohren Löcher in die Wand.

_____

_____

4. Moritz sägt das Brett in zwei Stücke.

_____

_____

5. Wir schrauben viel an diesem Tag.

_____

_____

6. Was bringen sie zur Party?

_____

_____

7. Mathias schreibt jede Woche eine E-Mail an seine Mutter.

_____

_____

8. Erika hilft sehr mit den Kindern.

_____

_____

56

57 Verbs *Present Perfect Tense with Sein*

Some verbs form the present perfect tense using the auxiliary verb *sein* (to be) + past participle.

> *Ich **bin** nicht weit **gelaufen**.*
> I **did**n't **walk/run** far.

The auxiliary verb *sein* is used with the past participle instead of *haben* (to have) in the following situations:

to express motion from one place to another (change of location)	*Ich **bin** nach Rostock **gefahren**.* I **drove** to Rostock. *Sie **ist** nach Hause **gegangen**.* She **went** home.
to express a change of condition	*Die Pflanzen **sind gewachsen**.* The plants **have grown**. *Wann **ist** er **gestorben**?* When **did** he **die**?
when accompanying verbs meaning *to happen*	*Wie **ist** das **passiert**?* How **did** that **happen**? *Etwas Schlimmes **ist geschehen**.* Something bad **has happened**.
when the verbs *bleiben* and *sein* are used	*Wie lange **bist** du bei ihnen **geblieben**?* How long **did** you **stay** at their place? *Wo **ist** sie gestern **gewesen**?* Where **was** she yesterday?

Ausnahme

Some verbs that normally take *sein,* such as *fahren* (to go by vehicle) and *fliegen* (to fly), take *haben* when they have a direct object or if the sentence describes an activity rather than motion from one place to another.

*Wir **sind** nach Berlin **geflogen**.*
We **flew** to Berlin.

*Der Copilot **hat** das Flugzeug nach Berlin **geflogen**.*
The copilot **flew** the plane to Berlin.

*Sie **ist** zur Insel **geschwommen**.*
She **swam** over to the island.

*Gestern **hat** sie stundenlang **geschwommen**.*
Yesterday, she **went swimming** for hours.

Exercise 1

In the following exchanges (written in the present tense), indicate which verbs would take *sein* or *haben* in the present perfect.

1. Leonhard: Ich glaube, dass es schneit.

   Ralf: Nein, nein, das Wetter wird besser.

   Sein: _____ Haben: _____

2. Anette: Warum gehst du nicht ins Kino, wenn es dir langweilig ist?

   Melanie: Weil ich keine Lust habe, einen Film zu sehen.

   Sein: _____ Haben: _____

3. Heinrich: Fahren sie irgendwohin oder bleiben sie zu Hause?

   Peter: Sie machen gar nichts.

   Sein: _____ Haben: _____

Exercise 2

Haben or *sein*? Circle the correct helping verb to complete each sentence.

1. Du siehst schlecht aus. Was hat/ist dir passiert?

2. Ihr seid ganz fit, weil ihr im Winter jeden Tag gejoggt habt/seid.

3. Wieso haben/sind sie so spät gekommen? Haben/Sind sie eine Panne gehabt?

4. Nach dem Spiel haben/sind wir im Stadion geblieben und haben/sind ordentlich gefeiert.

5. In welchem Krankenhaus hast/bist du geboren und wer hat/ist deine Mutter ins Krankenhaus gefahren?

Exercise 3

Complete each sentence with the correct form of *sein* or *haben* and the past participle of the infinitive given in parentheses. Note: Both strong and weak verbs are included below.

1. Du _____ viel zu langsam

_____! (laufen)

2. Monika _____ sich eine neue Hose

_____. (kaufen)

3. Heute _____ ich in die Stadt

_____. (fahren)

4. Ich _____ zwei Stunden in der Stadt

_____. (bleiben)

5. Er _____ erst gegen 18.00 Uhr

_____. (kommen)

Exercise 4

Translate these sentences by determining when to use *haben* and when to use *sein* based on the context.

1. He sailed to Jamaica.

_____

_____

2. We sailed on Lake Constance.

_____

_____

3. We surfed in Hawaii.

_____

_____

4. She surfed to the island.

_____

_____

5. They drove all night.

_____

_____

6. He drove the car to the shore.

_____

_____

57

For past participles of verbs with separable prefixes, the prefix *ge-* is placed between the separable prefix and the verb stem. The suffix, *-t* for weak verbs and *-en* for strong verbs, is added to the end.

Infinitive	Past Participle
abkaufen (to buy something from)	abgekauft
aufstehen (to get up/stand up)	aufgestanden
loslassen (let go of)	losgelassen
mitteilen (to inform someone of)	mitgeteilt
wegwerfen (to throw away)	weggeworfen

Sie **hat** das Papier **weggeworfen.**
She **threw** the paper **away.**

The past participle of a verb with an inseparable prefix (*be-, emp-, ent-, er-, ge-, mis-, ver-,* or *zer-*) is formed without the prefix *ge-*.

Infinitive	Past Participle
beschließen (to decide; to conclude)	beschlossen
besuchen (to visit)	besucht
empfehlen (to recommend)	empfohlen
entscheiden (to decide)	entschieden
erzählen (to tell)	erzählt
gewinnen (to win)	gewonnen
misslingen (to fail)	misslungen
verkaufen (to sell)	verkauft
verstehen (to understand)	verstanden
zerstören (to destroy)	zerstört

Er hat sie **besucht.**
He **visited** her.

Sylvia **hat** das Spiel **gewonnen.**
Sylvia **won** the game.

Achtung!
The prefixes *be-, emp-, ent-, er-, ge-, miss-, ver-,* and *zer-* are inseparable.

The prefixes *durch-, über-, unter-, um-, wieder-,* and *wider-* can be both separable and inseparable. They are always inseparable when unstressed.

Infinitive	Past Participle
durchbrechen (to break through)	durchbrochen (inseparable)
durchdringen (to penetrate)	durchgedrungen (separable)
unterstreichen (to underline; to emphasize)	unterstrichen (inseparable)
untergehen (to sink; to go under/down)	untergegangen (separable)
umarmen (to hug)	umarmt (inseparable)
umziehen (to move, as in a residence/to change clothes, when reflexive)	umgezogen (separable)

Wann **seid** ihr **umgezogen**?
When **did** you (plural) **move**?

Achtung!
Verbs with both separable and inseparable prefixes can be either weak or strong depending on their stem.

Exercise 1
Indicate whether the following verbs have separable prefixes (S) or inseparable prefixes (I). Then circle the correct past participle.

1. anziehen — S I — geanzogen — angezogen
2. gefallen — S I — gegefallen — gefallen
3. zurückrufen — S I — zurückruft — zurückgerufen
4. missverstehen — S I — missverstanden — gemissversteht
5. verursachen — S I — geverursacht — verursacht

Exercise 2
Provide the correct past participle for the each weak separable-prefix verb below.

1. aufhören _____

2. zumachen _____

3. einkaufen _____

4. zurückholen _____

5. ausrutschen _____

6. abstürzen _____

7. loskriegen _____

8. mitmachen _____

9. wegfegen _____

10. ausrichten _____

Exercise 3

The paragraph below describes a typical morning routine. Change each verb from the present tense to the present perfect tense. Determine whether *sein* or *haben* is the appropriate auxiliary, and include the correct past participle form.

Ich stehe um 6.00 Uhr auf. Zuerst dusche ich mich. Dann rasiere ich mir die Beine. Danach ziehe ich mich an, putze mir die Zähne und wasche mir nochmal die Hände. Dann kämme ich mir das Haar und schminke mich. Ich bemühe mich und obwohl ich mich beeile, ärgere ich mich, weil ich keine Zeit zum Frühstücken habe.

_____

_____

_____

_____

_____

_____

_____

Exercise 4

Provide logical answers to the following questions using the suggested prompt for each response and the present perfect tense of the verb in parentheses.

Beispiel:　Hast du gestern die Farbe gekauft?
　　　　　Ja, und heute (bemalen) <u>habe ich die Wände</u>
　　　　　<u>bemalt.</u>

1. Hast du gehört, dass er gestern seine ganzen Möbel verkauft hat?

Ja, und heute (wegwerfen) _____

_____.

2. Hat er dir gestern erzählt, ob du für nächste Saison einen Vertrag bekommst?

Nein, und heute (mitteilen) _____

_____.

3. Haben Sie am Samstag wirklich ein neues Haus gekauft?

Ja, und heute (entscheiden) _____

_____.

4. Ist gestern wegen des Hochwassers die Straße gesperrt gewesen?

Ja, und heute (zerstören) _____

_____.

5. Haben wir dir nicht gestern gesagt, dass man auf dem Viktualienmarkt alles am billigsten bekommt?

Doch, aber heute (empfehlen) _____

_____.

58

Past participles are used for several verb tenses, voices, and moods. Past participles can also be used as adjectives.

The past participle can be combined with an auxiliary verb in the present tense to form the present perfect tense to describe events that have already happened.

> *Wir **haben** nichts **gesehen.***
> We **did**n't **see** anything.

The past participle can be combined with an auxiliary verb in the past tense to form the past perfect (pluperfect) tense to describe past events that occurred prior to another past event.

> *Sie **hatten** ihn schon **gefunden.***
> They **had** already **found** him.

The past participle can be combined with a form of the verb *werden* (to become) to form the passive voice in a variety of tenses.

> *Die Fenster **wurden zerbrochen.*** (past subjunctive)
> The windows **were broken.**

A past participle can follow the verb *sein* to serve as a predicate adjective describing the result of a process.

> *Das Haus **ist abgebrannt.***
> The house **is burnt down.**

A past participle can act as an adjective when preceding a noun that it modifies. In these cases, the past participle takes the appropriate adjective ending to agree with the noun.

> *Das **abgebrannte** Haus wird neu gebaut.*
> The **burnt-down** house is being rebuilt.

Just as other adjectives can become nouns if they describe a person (masculine or feminine depending on the person) or things (neuter), so can past participles acting as adjectives. As with other adjectival nouns, the proper adjective ending and capitalization are required.

> ***Das Gefundene** liegt auf dem Tisch.*
> **The thing that was found** is on the table.

> ***Der Gesuchte** wurde gefunden.*
> **The boy who was being sought** was found.

Exercise 1

Rewrite the sentences below changing from present tense to present perfect tense using the past participle.

1. Kerstin spielt gern Tennis.

_____

_____

_____

2. Mutti backt Kekse für uns.

_____

_____

_____

3. Herr Wagner ruft seinen Kollegen an.

_____

_____

_____

4. Der Sportler trainiert jeden Tag.

_____

_____

_____

5. Der Zug kommt am Abend an.

_____

_____

_____

Exercise 2

Change the following sentences from the active voice to the passive voice using the past participle and the verb *werden.*

1. Die Studentin schreibt die Prüfung.

_____

_____

_____

2. Hans wäscht das Auto.

_____

_____

_____

3. Karla erzieht die Kinder.

_____

_____

_____

4. Diese Lehrerin unterrichtet Deutsch.

_____

_____

_____

5. Marcel verkauft die Maschinen.

_____

_____

_____

Exercise 3

Fill in the blanks below with the past participle of the verb in parentheses used as an adjective or adjectival noun. Remember to use proper adjective endings.

1. Hast du das _____ gefunden? (suchen)

2. Das Haus ist schon _____. (verkaufen)

3. Die _____ Gläser sind noch auf der Theke. (zerbrechen)

4. Diese Sachen sind schon _____. (erledigen)

5. Das _____ wird nicht vergessen. (versprechen)

59

While the present perfect tense is the past tense form used primarily in conversation, the imperfect tense (simple past) is primarily found in written texts such as newspapers, novels, fairy tales, and reports.

Regular verbs form the imperfect by adding -te to the verb stem. They then add an ending that corresponds to the appropriate personal pronoun.

	Personal Pronoun	Ending	Imperfect Form
	ich	–	kaufte
	du	-st	kauftest
kaufen (to buy)	er/sie/es	–	kaufte
	wir	-n	kauften
	ihr	-t	kauftet
	sie/Sie	-n	kauften

Ich **kaufte** eine neue Jacke.
I **bought** a new jacket.

Eine Bombe **explodierte.**
A bomb **exploded.**

Achtung!

Regular verbs that end in either -*d* or -*t*, or -*m* or -*n* preceded by a consonant other than *l* or *r*, add -*ete* to the verb stem in the imperfect.

	Personal Pronoun	Ending	Imperfect Form
	ich	–	arbeit**ete**
	du	-st	arbeit**ete**st
arbeiten (to work)	er/sie/es	–	arbeit**ete**
	wir	-n	arbeit**ete**n
	ihr	-t	arbeit**ete**t
	sie/Sie	-n	arbeit**ete**n

Sie **redeten** miteinander.
They **talked** to each other.

Er **atmete** tief **ein.**
He **took a** deep **breath.**

Irregular verbs form the imperfect through a variety of verb stem changes, which need to be memorized. However, the endings that they add are straightforward.

	Personal Pronoun	Ending	Imperfect Form
	ich	–	**lief**
	du	-st	**lief**st
laufen (to run)	er/sie/es	–	**lief**
	wir	-en	**lief**en
	ihr	-t	**lief**t
	sie/Sie	-en	**lief**en
	ich	–	**kam**
	du	-st	**kam**st
kommen (to come)	er/sie/es	–	**kam**
	wir	-en	**kam**en
	ihr	-t	**kam**t
	sie/Sie	-en	**kam**en

Er **kam** nach Hause aber **lief** plötzlich wieder weg.
He **came** home but suddenly **ran** away again.

Mixed verbs also form the imperfect in a variety of ways, which need to be memorized. As with irregular verbs, mixed verb endings are fairly straightforward.

	Personal Pronoun	Ending	Imperfect Form
	ich	-te	**brach**te
	du	-test	**brach**test
bringen (to bring)	er/sie/es	-te	**brach**te
	wir	-ten	**brach**ten
	ihr	-tet	**brach**tet
	sie/Sie	-ten	**brach**ten

Personal Pronoun	Ending	Imperfect Form
ich	-te	**dach**te
du	-test	**dach**test
er/sie/es	-te	**dach**te
wir	-ten	**dach**ten
ihr	-tet	**dach**tet
sie/Sie	-ten	**dach**ten

denken
(to think)

Er **dachte,** dass er das Turnier gewinnt.
He **thought** that he was going to win the tournament.

Achtung!

The endings of regular and mixed verbs follow a pattern going from the infinitive to the imperfect to the past participle(-en → -te → -t). Knowing one form can help when learning the other.

Infinitive	Imperfect	Past participle
kauf**en**	kauf**te**	gekauf**t**
arbeit**en**	arbeit**ete**	gearbeit**et**
bring**en**	brach**te**	gebrach**t**

Exercise 1

For each verb below, provide the imperfect form corresponding to the given pronoun.

1. regnen: es _____

2. fragen: ich _____

3. machen: du _____

4. verkaufen: wir _____

5. schauen: Sie _____

Exercise 2

Fill in the blanks in the news headlines below. Use the proper imperfect form of the weak verb in parentheses.

1. 12-Jähriger _____ aus Fenster. (stürzen)

2. Hochwasser _____ vermutlich acht Tote. (fordern)

3. Passanten _____ Frau mit Kind das Leben. (retten)

4. Gasflasche _____ bei einem Grillfest. (explodieren)

5. GrazerInnen _____ beste Anti-Hundekot-Kampagne. (wählen)

Exercise 3

In the paragraph below, a husband is describing his wife's daily routine. Fill in the blanks below by conjugating the verbs in parentheses in the imperfect tense.

Meine Ehefrau (**1.**) _____ (kommen) um 19.00 Uhr

nach Hause. Sie (**2.**) _____ (gehen) sofort in

die Küche und (**3.**) _____ _____ (sich

holen) etwas zu essen. Dann (**4.**) _____ sie (**5.**)

_____ ihre Schuhe (**6.**) _____ (sich

ausziehen) und (**7.** _____ _____ auf

das Sofa (sich setzen). Nachdem sie das Essen (**8.**) _____

(essen), (**9.**) _____ sie den Fernseher

(**10.**) _____ (einschalten). Es war Freitag und sie

(**11.**) _____ _____ (sich freuen)

sehr auf das Wochenende.

60

61 Verbs *Conversational Uses of the Imperfect Tense*

Although the present perfect tense is typically used to discuss events in the past and is even referred to as the conversational past, there are a few verbs that tend to be used in the imperfect tense in conversation.

The auxiliary verbs *haben* and *sein* are used in the imperfect tense more often than in the present perfect. *Haben* is a mixed verb, and *sein* is an irregular verb.

haben (to have)		sein (to be)	
ich hatte	I had	*ich war*	I was
du hattest	you had	*du warst*	you were
er/sie/es hatte	he/she/it had	*er/sie/es war*	he/she/it was
wir hatten	we had	*wir waren*	we were
ihr hattet	you (pl.) had	*ihr wart*	you (pl.) were
sie/Sie hatten	they/you (formal) had	*sie/Sie waren*	they/you (formal) were

*Brigitte **hatte** gestern Gebutstag.*
Yesterday **was** Brigitte's birthday.

***Warst** du gestern auf der Arbeit?*
Were you at work yesterday?

The modal verbs are also used in the imperfect tense more often than in the present perfect. The modals are mixed verbs.

	dürfen (to be allowed to)	können (to be able to)	mögen (to like to)
ich	*durfte*	*konnte*	*mochte*
du	*durftest*	*konntest*	*mochtest*
er/sie/es	*durfte*	*konnte*	*mochte*
wir	*durften*	*konnten*	*mochten*
ihr	*durftet*	*konntet*	*mochtet*
sie/Sie	*durften*	*konnten*	*mochten*

	müssen (to have to)	sollen (to ought to)	wollen (to want to)
ich	*musste*	*sollte*	*wollte*
du	*musstest*	*solltest*	*wolltest*
er/sie/es	*musste*	*sollte*	*wollte*
wir	*mussten*	*sollten*	*wollten*
ihr	*musstet*	*solltet*	*wolltet*
sie/Sie	*mussten*	*sollten*	*wollten*

*Ludger **konnte** das Fleisch nicht essen.*
Ludger **couldn't** eat the meat.

*Birgit **musste** zurückkehren.*
Birgit **had** to turn around.

When the word *als* is used to mean *when,* the imperfect tense usually accompanies it.

***Als** Sigrid jung **war,** ging sie mit ihrer Schwester in die Schule.*
When Sigrid **was** young, she walked to school with her sister.

***Als** Klaus und Wiebke nach Hause **mussten, war** es schon sehr spät.*
When Klaus and Wiebke **had** to leave, it **was** already very late.

Exercise 1

Use the correct imperfect form of *haben* or *sein* to complete the following sentences.

1. Margrit _____ immer müde.

2. Pius und Georg _____ neue Anzüge.

3. Wo _____ du die ganze Zeit?

4. Was _____ ihr in eurem Koffer?

5. _____ Sie damals Angst?

Exercise 2

Use the correct imperfect form of the modal verb in parentheses to complete the following sentences.

1. Was _____ Elisabeth machen? (wollen)

2. Und dann _____ wir das Buch lesen. (sollen)

3. Elke _____ danach mit ihrem Hund spazierengehen. (müssen)

4. Lena und Kerstin _____ sich
Motorräder kaufen.(dürfen)

5. _____ du deinen Rücksack nicht
finden? (können)

6. Wann _____ ihr abfahren? (wollen)

7. Ich _____ ihm eine E-Mail schicken.
(müssen)

8. Das Lied _____ wir nicht vom Internet
runterladen. (dürfen)

9. Ute _____ sich die Sendung nicht
anschauen, weil ihr Fernseher kaputt war. (können)

10. Klaus und Martin _____ unbedingt ins
Kino gehen. (wollen)

Exercise 3

**Use the imperfect tense to create a logical ending for
each sentence below.**

1. Als ich jung war, _____

_____

2. Als wir Urlaub machten, _____

_____

3. Als Karin Austauschstudentin war, _____

_____

4. Als du in der Küche warst, _____

_____

5. Als Heinz-Peter bei Siemens arbeitete, _____

_____

Exercise 4

**Norbert and Norma are coworkers discussing their
weekend. Create a brief exchange between the two using
the simple past in natural conversation.**

_____

_____

_____

_____

_____

_____

_____

_____

_____

_____

_____

_____

_____

_____

_____

_____

61

The pluperfect (past perfect) tense is used to establish the sequence in which two events occurred in the past.

The pluperfect tense is formed by combining the simple past tense form of the auxiliary verbs *haben* (to have) or *sein* (to be) + the past participle.

Present Perfect Tense	Past Perfect Tense
*Ich **habe** mir einen Rock **gekauft.***	*Ich **hatte** mir einen Rock **gekauft.***
I **have bought** myself a skirt./ I **bought** myself a skirt.	I **had bought** myself a skirt.
*Wir **sind** nach Frankfurt **geflogen.***	*Wir **waren** nach Frankfurt **geflogen.***
We **have flown** to Frankfurt./ We **flew** to Frankfurt.	We **have flown** to Frankfurt./ We **had flown** to Frankfurt.

The pluperfect tense is used to indicate an event that took place before another event in the past. The second event (chronologically) is presented in either the present perfect or the imperfect (simple past) tense. There is no difference in meaning between the present perfect tense and the simple past.

> *Bevor ich mir die Zähne **geputzt habe** (second event, present perfect), **hatte** ich **gefrühstückt.** (first event, past perfect)*
> Before I **had brushed** my teeth, I **had eaten** breakfast.

Regardless of their order in the sentence, the event that occurred first in the past (chronologically) will always be in the pluperfect (past perfect).

> *Ich **hatte** mich **geduscht,** bevor ich mich angezogen habe. (second event in present perfect)*
> *Ich **hatte** mich **geduscht,** bevor ich mich anzog. (second event in simple past)*
> I **had taken** a shower before I got dressed.

> *Ich habe mich angezogen, nachdem ich mich **geduscht hatte.** (second event in present perfect)*
> *Ich zog mich an, nachdem ich mich **geduscht hatte.** (second event in simple past)*
> I got dressed after I **had taken** a shower.

Exercise 1

Give the *ich* form in the pluperfect tense of the verbs below. Remember to include the proper form of the auxiliary verb.

1. tragen _____

2. lesen _____

3. Ski fahren _____

4. waschen _____

5. kosten _____

6. vermieten _____

7. schließen _____

8. steigen _____

9. heißen _____

10. bleiben _____

Exercise 2

You recently took a trip to Munich. Below are the events of your trip in the order that they occurred. Use the clues below to create five sentences about your trip. Use the pluperfect for those events that occurred first.

Event 1: im Internet surfen
Event 2: ein Hotel finden
Event 3: ein Zimmer buchen
Event 4: einen Flug buchen
Event 5: nach München fliegen

Beispiel: I did 5 after I did 1.
Ich bin nach München geflogen/flog nach München, nachdem ich im Internet gesurft hatte.

1. After I did 1, I did 2.

_____

_____

_____

2. I did 3 after I did 2.

_____

_____

_____

3. Before I did 4, I did 3.

_____

_____

_____

4. I did 4 before I did 5.

_____

_____

_____

Exercise 3

Write a brief paragraph using the pluperfect tense to describe the steps in your morning routine in relation to each other. Use the phrases below to prompt your writing.

sich anziehen
frühstücken
sich duschen
Zähne putzen
sich die Haare kämmen

_____

_____

_____

_____

_____

_____

_____

Exercise 4

Translate the following exchange between two friends into German using the pluperfect where appropriate.

Martina: Where were you yesterday?
Manfred: I had to go into the city because my boss (female) had called yesterday morning.
Martina: Why?
Manfred: She couldn't get into the office because she had forgotten her key.

_____

_____

_____

_____

_____

62

The future tense describes an event that is going to happen. The future tense usually is formed by combining the verb *werden* (to become) with an infinitive.

	Singular	Plural
werden (to become)	*ich werde* I will	*wir werden* we will
	du wirst you will	*ihr werdet* you (plural) will
	er/sie/es wird he/she/it will	*sie/Sie werden* they/you (formal) will

In the future tense, *werden* is conjugated to agree with the subject. In a simple sentence, the infinitive is placed at the end.

> *Wir **werden** Kaffee **trinken**.*
> We **will drink** coffee.

The future tense can be used in many situations. The future tense can express

a promise	*Ich **werde** dich **anrufen**.* I **will call** you.
a plan	***Werden** wir unterwegs irgendwo **anhalten**?* **Will** we **stop** somewhere on the way?
a certainty	*Sie **wird** jetzt **denken,** dass ich ein schlechter Fahrer bin.* Now she **must think** that I'm a lousy driver.
a strong suspicion	*Er **wird** wohl einen gebrochenen Finger **haben**.* His finger **must be broken**.
a prediction or prognosis	*Morgen **werden** wir das Spiel **gewinnen**.* We **are going to win** the game tomorrow.
an emphatic sdemand	*Du **wirst** jetzt die Teller **abwaschen**!* You **are going to do** the dishes now!

Alltagssprache

In English, the future tense is used to express any action that is certain to happen. In German, when an expression of time is used to indicate that an action will obviously be happening in the future, the present tense is usually used.

*Ich rufe dich am **Samstag** an.*
I will call you on **Saturday.**

***Morgen** gewinnen wir das Spiel.*
We are going to win the game **tomorrow.**

Exercise 1

Fill in the blanks below with the correct form of the verb *werden*.

1. Ich _____ das Problem sicherlich lösen.

2. Glaubst du, dass Ralf den Schlüssel wieder finden

_____?

3. _____ du irgenwann auch so viel Erfolg

haben wie ich?

4. Ich hoffe, dass ihr zur Party kommen _____.

5. Morgen _____ es wieder schneien.

Exercise 2

You share a house with four friends: Karin, Martin, Sabina, and Thomas. The five of you are dividing up the work. Use the table below to compose four sentences describing who will do what.

Name	Aufgabe
du	Geschirr spülen
Karin	staubsaugen
Martin und Sabina	Wäsche waschen
Thomas	WC putzen

1. _____

_____

2. _____

_____

3. _____

_____

4. _____

_____

Exercise 3

Although the following sentences are in the present tense, they indicate an action to take place in the future. Remove the time expressions from each sentence, and change the verb from the present tense to the future tense. Be sure to watch word order.

Beispiel: Heute Abend gehen wir kegeln.
                  <u>Wir werden kegeln gehen.</u>

1. Morgen hole ich mein Auto von der Reparatur ab.

_____

_____

2. Nächste Woche fliegt er nach Düsseldorf.

_____

_____

3. Übernächste Woche klettern sie in den Alpen.

_____

_____

Exercise 4

Make the demands below more emphatic by changing them from the imperative to the future tense. Remember to identify the subject in the new sentence.

Beispiel: Zeigt mir, wo ihr das Geld versteckt habt!
                  <u>Ihr werdet mir zeigen, wo ihr das Geld versteckt habt!</u>

1. Sag mir jetzt die Wahrheit.

_____

_____

2. Sagen Sie mir, mit dem Sie telefoniert haben.

_____

_____

3. Wirf jetzt den ganzen Müll weg.

_____

_____

Exercise 5

Use the prompts below and the reflexive verbs to describe what you are going to do when you wake up tomorrow morning.

1. Zuerst _____

_____

2. Dann _____

_____

3. Danach _____

_____

4. Nachdem ich das mache, _____

_____

5. Zum Schluss _____

_____

63

In the active voice, the subject of the sentence is the person or thing performing the action. In the passive voice, the subject of the sentence is the person or thing on which the action is performed. In passive voice, the agent (the person or thing performing the action) is often omitted.

Passive constructions in German are formed by using the verb *werden* (to become) + the past participle.

Active	Passive
*Der Bäcker **backt einen** Kuchen.* The baker **is baking** a cake.	*Ein Kuchen **wird gebacken.*** A cake **is being baked.**
*Sie **beobachtet** euch.* She **is observing** you all.	*Ihr **werdet beobachtet.*** You all **are being observed.**
*Ich **werfe** die Bälle.* I **am throwing** the balls.	*Die Bälle **werden geworfen.*** The balls **are being thrown** by me.

Achtung!

The direct object (in the accusative case) in active voice becomes the subject (in the nominative case) in passive voice. An indirect object in active voice remains an indirect object in passive voice.

Active	Passive
Wir** sagen **dir** immer **die Wahrheit. **We** always tell **you the truth.**	**You** are always told **the truth.**
***Ich** gebe **ihm das Geld**.* I am giving **him the money.**	**The money** is being given to **him.**

The passive voice can take various tenses. These tenses are constructed by changing the tense of *werden* accordingly.

imperfect (simple past) tense	*Ich **wurde** gesehen.* I **was** seen.
present perfect tense	*Ich **bin** verhaftet **worden.*** I **have been** arrested.
past perfect tense	*Ich **war** gelobt **worden.*** I **had been** praised.

Achtung!

The past participle of *werden* in the passive voice is *worden*, not *geworden*.

Exercise 1

Use the passive voice in present perfect tense to describe what is taking place in the five pictures below. Use the verbs and nouns in the word pool below in constructing your sentences.

ein Baby	zwei Verbrecher	zwei Schauspieler
ein Ehepaar	ein Fisch	verhaftet
geschminkt	getauft	fotografiert
gefangen		

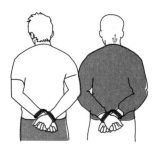

1. _____

2. _____

3. _____

_____

4. _____

_____

5. _____

_____

Exercise 2

Change each sentence below from the active voice to the passive voice.

1. Der Bauer melkt die Kühe.

_____

_____

2. Seine Frau mistet den Stall aus.

_____

_____

3. Der Junge sammelt die Eier ein.

_____

_____

4. Das Mädchen füttert das Pferd.

_____

_____

5. Die Nachbarin streichelt die Katze.

_____

_____

Exercise 3

You've just bought a new electric razor. Use the prompts below to describe in passive voice in the past perfect tense the six steps you went through after you brought it home.

Beispiel: Rasierapparat kaufen
Zuerst war der Rasierapparat gekauft worden.

1. zuerst alles auspacken

_____

_____

2. dann die Gebrauchsanweisung lesen

_____

_____

3. dann kontrollieren, ob etwas fehlt

_____

_____

4. danach die Batterien richtig einlegen

_____

_____

5. danach elektrischen Rasierapparat einschalten

_____

_____

64

In the passive voice, the person or thing performing the action is usually omitted. When the agent is not omitted, either the preposition *von* (+ dative) or *durch* (+ accusative) is used.

The preposition *von* is used when the action is being performed by a person or specific institution.

*Ein Kuchen wird **vom** Bäcker gebacken.*
A cake is being baked **by** the baker.

*Das Fest wird **vom** Verein organisiert.*
The festival is being organized **by** the club.

The preposition *durch* is used when the action is being performed by an inanimate object or an anonymous or generic institution.

*Das Haus wird **durchs** Feuer zerstört.*
The house is being destroyed **by** the fire.

*Das Projekt wird **durch** eine Stiftung finanziert.*
The project is being financed **by** charity.

Achtung!

When used with the definite article, the prepositions *von* and *durch* can be contracted.

von + dem = vom (from the, by the)
durch + das = durchs (through the, by the)

The German passive voice can be used to form the impersonal passive construction, which does not have a direct English translation. In the impersonal passive construction, the passive voice subject is not identified since there may not have been a direct object in the active voice sentence. In such cases, the article *es* (it) is often used as the subject.

Active	Passive
Wir werden heute noch viel arbeiten.	***Es** wird heute noch viel noch gearbeitet.*
We're going to work a lot more today.	A lot more work is going to be done today.
Sie diskutierten lange.	***Es** wurde lange diskutiert.*
They discussed (things) for a long time.	The discussion lasted a long time.

Ausnahme

If another part of speech is the first element of the sentence, *es* is left out of the impersonal passive construction. This construction is often seen on posted signs or as a warning.

***Hier** wird Deutsch gesprochen.*
German is spoken **here.**

***Nächstes Jahr** werden neue Häuser gebaut.*
New homes will be built **next year.**

***Hier** wird nicht geparkt.*
You are not allowed to park **here.**

***Im Restaurant** wird nicht geraucht.*
You are not allowed to smoke in **the restaurant.**

Exercise 1

Change the sentences below from the passive voice to the active voice, using the agent as the subject.

1. Das Buch wird vom Autor geschrieben.

_____

_____

2. Der Wagen wird vom Mechaniker repariert.

_____

_____

3. Das Schiff wurde vom Kapitän gesteuert.

_____

_____

4. Die Sendung ist zum ersten Mal von einer Frau moderiert worden.

_____

_____

5. Die Wäsche war vom Babysitter gewaschen worden.

_____

_____

Exercise 2

Answer the questions using the information in parentheses. Answer first in the active voice, then rewrite your answer in a passive construction.

Beispiel:
Was hat den Schaden verursacht? (das Wasser)
Das Wasser hat den Schaden verursacht.
Der Schaden ist durch das Wasser verursacht worden.

1. Was hat das Haus zerstört? (das Feuer)

_____

_____

_____

2. Was hat die Brücke beschädigt? (das Hochwasser)

_____

_____

_____

3. Was hat die Ernte ruiniert? (ein Sandsturm)

_____

_____

_____

Exercise 3

Rewrite the following sentences in impersonal passive using _es_ as the new subject.

1. Sie arbeiteten bis Mitternacht.

_____

_____

2. Wir flirteten im Chatroom.

_____

_____

3. Die Reporter berichteten über die Entführung.

_____

_____

4. Die Wissenschaftler betrieben drei Jahre lang Forschung.

_____

_____

5. Um 10.00 Uhr servierten die Flugbegleiterinnen die Getränke.

_____

_____

Exercise 4

Use the passive voice and the verbs provided to describe what goes on in each place listed below.

grillen   essen   tanzen
spielen   lernen

1. Halle: _____

_____

2. Party: _____

_____

3. Bibliothek: _____

_____

4. Restaurant: _____

_____

5. Garten: _____

_____

65

Imperatives are present tense forms used to make commands, give requests, or offer suggestions. There are three imperative forms in German, related to the three forms of the pronoun *you:* the *du* form, *ihr* form, and *Sie* form.

To form the *Sie* imperative, use the *Sie* conjugation of the verb and invert the word order so that the verb is in first position, followed by the pronoun.

Present Tense	Sie-form Imperative
Sie **kommen** herein.	**Kommen** Sie herein!
You **are coming** in.	**Come** in!

The *ihr* imperative is formed using the *ihr* conjugation of the verb without the *ihr* pronoun.

Present Tense	ihr-form Imperative
Ihr **gebt** mir zwei Euro.	**Gebt** mir zwei Euro!
You (plural) **are giving** me two Euros.	**Give** me two euros, you (plural)!

The *du* imperative is generally formed using the *du* conjugation of a verb without the *-st* ending. The pronoun is not generally included.

Present Tense	du-form Imperative
Du **gehst** nach Hause.	**Geh** nach Hause!
You **are going** home.	**Go** home!
Du **antwortest** mir.	**Antworte** mir!
You **are answering** me.	**Answer** me!

Alltagssprache

Although the pronoun is generally left out of the *du* imperative, the *du* pronoun is used for emphasis when showing a contrast.

*Geh **du** diesmal! Ich gehe nicht mehr hin.*
You go this time! I'm not going there anymore.

The present tense of verb stems ending in a sibilant (hissing consonant sound) -s, -z, or -ß add only -t. Therefore, in the *du* imperative form, only the *-t* is dropped from the *du* conjugation.

Present Tense	du-form Imperative
Du **isst** nicht so viel Eis!	**Iss** nicht so viel Eis!
You don't **eat** so much ice cream.	Don't **eat** so much ice cream!
Du **liest** diesen Artikel.	**Lies** diesen Artikel!
You are **reading** this article.	**Read** this article!

Irregular verbs that take an umlaut in the *du* form drop the umlaut in the *du* imperative form.

Present Tense	du-form Imperative
Du **läufst** schneller.	**Lauf** schneller!
You **run** faster.	**Run** faster!

Verbs that end in *-eln* and *-ern* have irregular *du* imperative forms.

Present Tense	du-form Imperative
Du **klingelst** noch mal.	**Klingle** noch einmal!
You **ring** the bell again.	**Ring** the bell again!
Du **wanderst** nie allein.	**Wandere** nie allein!
You never **hike** alone.	Don't ever **go hiking** alone!

Ausnahme

The verbs *haben*, *sein,* and *werden* have irregular imperative forms. *Sein* is irregular in all three imperative forms. *Haben* and *werden* are irregular only in the *du* form.

Sie imperative:
Seien Sie vorsichtig!	**Be** careful!

ihr imperative:
Seid nicht so dumm!	Don't **be** so stupid!

du imperative:
Sei nicht immer so schüchtern!	Don't **be** so shy all the time!
Hab Geduld! Ich bin fast fertig.	**Be** patient! I'm almost done.
Sei froh!	**Be** happy!

Achtung!

In all three imperative forms, verbs with separable prefixes remain separated.

Hören Sie **auf** zu meckern!
Stop complaining!

Räum dein Zimmer **auf**!
Clean up your room!

Exercise 1

Provide the three imperative forms for each verb below.

1. kaufen:

_____

2. machen:

_____

3. finden:

_____

4. schlafen:

_____

5. sammeln:

_____

6. sein:

_____

Exercise 2

Change the following commands from the *ihr* imperative form to the *du* imperative form.

1. Ruft die Polizei an!

_____

2. Macht ein Foto von mir!

_____

3. Gebt ihm zehn Euro!

_____

4. Schickt mir eine SMS!

_____

5. Esst mehr Gemüse!

_____

Exercise 3

Create sentences using the *ihr*-imperative form with the elements provided below.

1. mit / ihr / helfen / mal / Hausaufgaben / ihren

_____

_____

2. andere / Hosen / anziehen / euch

_____

_____

3. Buch / Woche / lesen / mindestens / die / ein

_____

_____

Exercise 4

Form verb and noun pairs from the pool below. Use each pair to create strong suggestions in the *Sie* imperative form.

Verbs:

schreiben	wegwerfen	treiben
sparen	haben	

Nouns:

Sport	E-Mail	Angst
Müll	Geld	

Beispiel: trinken, Saft
Trinken Sie mehr Saft. Saft ist ganz gesund.

1. _____

2. _____

3. _____

4. _____

5. _____

66

Just as verbs have tenses based on the time of the action they refer to, verbs also have *moods.* Most verbs are used in the indicative mood, which is used when discussing events or situations that are real or certain. When verbs are used to talk about things that are not (yet) real or certain, the subjunctive mood is used.

The general subjunctive (called subjunctive II in German) has two present tense forms: a one-word form and a two-word form. Verbs in the one-word form look similar to their imperfect (simple past) tense form.

*Ich **kaufte** eine Bluse.*
I **would buy** a blouse.

*Es **wäre** nett.*
It **would be** nice.

Alltagssprache

The names *subjunctive II* and *subjunctive I* for the general and special subjunctive, respectively, come from the fact that subjunctive II is derived from the second principle part (the simple past or imperfect tense) and subjunctive I is derived from the first principle part (the infinitive).

Weak verbs in the one-word form of the present tense subjunctive are identical to their simple past forms.

*Ich **kaufte** mir einen Rucksack, wenn ich das Geld dazu hätte.*
I **would buy** myself a backpack if I had the money for it.

Mixed verbs whose stem includes the vowels *a, o,* or *u* add an umlaut in the one-word present tense subjunctive.

*Er **dächte** das auch!*
He **would think** so too!

Ausnahme

In the subjunctive II present tense, mixed verbs that end in *-nnen,* such as *nennen* (to name), take an *e* rather than an *ä,* as would be expected in the subjunctive.

*Wenn sie ein Mädchen hätte, **nenne** sie es Liesel.*
If she had a girl, she **would name** her Liesel.

Strong verbs add the endings below to their simple past stem. They also add an umlaut if their stem vowel is *a, o,* or *u.*

	Singular	Plural
sein (to be)	*ich wär**e*** I would be	*wir wär**en*** we would be
	*du wär**est*** you would be	*ihr wär**et*** you (plural) would be
	*er/sie/es wär**e*** he/she/it would be	*sie/Sie wär**en*** they/you (formal) would be

The two-word form of the subjunctive is formed by combining the subjunctive of *werden* (to become) + the infinitive.

	Singular	Plural
sein (to be)	*ich würde gehen* I would go	*wir würden gehen* we would go
	du würdest gehen you would go	*ihr würdet gehen* you (plural) would go
	er/sie/es würde gehen he/she/it would go	*sie/Sie würden gehen* they/you (formal) would go

*Ich **würde** eine Bluse **kaufen.***
I **would buy** a blouse.

*Es **würde** nett **sein.***
It **would be** nice.

Alltagssprache

Although there is no difference in meaning between the one-word and the two-word forms of the present subjunctive, the two-word form is used most often in conversation except with the verbs *sein, haben,* and *wissen* and the modal verbs.

*Anja: Was **würdest** du **machen**, wenn du hier **wärest**?*
*Albert: Ich **hätte** keine Zeit, etwas Schönes zu machen, denn ich **müsste** viel **arbeiten.***

Anja: What **would** you **do** if you **were** here?
Albert: I **would**n't **have** any time to do anything nice because I **would have to work** a lot.

The subjunctive mood can be used to make polite requests and wishes. The subjunctive is also used to set conditions or discuss things that are contrary to reality.

mögen (to like)
***Möchtest** du einen Kaffee trinken?*
Would you **like** to drink a (cup of) coffee?

sein (to be)
*Ich wünschte, ich **wäre** reich.*
I wish I **were** rich.

haben (to have); *reisen* (to travel)
*Wenn ich mehr Zeit **hätte, würde** ich viel **reisen.***
If I **had** more time, I **would travel** a lot.

wissen (to know)
*Wenn ich das nur **wüsste**!*
If only I **knew**!

Exercise 1

Give the *ich* form of the following verbs in both the one-word form and the two-word form of the present tense subjunctive.

Beispiel:
kaufen: kaufte _____   würde kaufen _____

	One-word Form	Two-word Form
1. sein:	_____	_____
2. haben:	_____	_____
3. trinken:	_____	_____
4. fahren:	_____	_____
5. spielen:	_____	_____
6. tanzen:	_____	_____

Exercise 2

Fill in the blanks below with the two-word form of the present tense subjunctive using the infinitive in parentheses.

1. _____ du bitte das neue Programm

_____? (laden)

2. _____ Sie gerne _____?
(mitkommen)

3. Was _____ du _____?
(machen)

4. Bettina _____ lieber Sport

_____. (treiben)

5. Beate _____ die Nachrichten lieber

online _____. (lesen)

Exercise 3

Fill in the blanks with the one-word form of the present tense subjunctive of the infinitive in parentheses.

1. Wenn er nach Hause _____,

_____ wir anfangen. (kommen, können)

2. Das _____ nett. (sein)

3. Wenn sie rechtzeitig zur Arbeit _____,

_____ es kein Problem. (gehen, geben)

4. _____ Sie was zu essen? (mögen)

5. _____ du Lust, mit uns nach Mallorca zu

fliegen? (haben)

Exercise 4

Translate the following sentences into German using the present tense subjunctive.

1. I wish I could buy him this jacket.

_____

_____

2. Would you (formal) like to fly home today?

_____

_____

3. If he knew that, he would be able to answer the question.

_____

_____

67

The past tense of the general subjunctive (subjunctive II) is used to express events that did not happen in the past, but could have, should have, or would have.

The past tense subjunctive is formed by combining the present perfect tense + the subjunctive form of the auxiliary verbs *sein* or *haben*.

	Singular	Plural
sein (to be)	*ich wäre gegangen* I would have gone	*wir wären gegangen* we would have gone
	du wärest gegangen you would have gone	*ihr wäret gegangen* you all would have gone
	er/sie/es wäre gegangen he/she/it would have gone	*sie/Sie wären gegangen* they/you (formal) would have gone
haben (to have)	*ich hätte gekauft* I would have bought	*wir hätten gekauft* we would have bought
	du hättest gekauft you would have bought	*ihr hättet gekauft* you all would have bought
	er/sie/es hätte gekauft he/she/it would have bought	*sie/Sie hätten gekauft* they/you (formal) would have bought

*Ich wünschte, wir **wären Ski laufen gegangen.*** I wish we **would have gone skiing.**

As with the present perfect tense, modal verbs in the past subjunctive take a double infinitive construction rather than a past participle.

*Wir **hätten mitkommen können,** wenn wir das gewusst hätten.* We **would have been able to come along** if we had known that.

Exercise 1

Complete the sentences below by matching the words in column A with the appropriate clauses in the past tense subjunctive in column B.

A	B
____ 1. Wenn wir uns wärmer angezogen hätten,	a. wäre es ihm leichter gewesen, den Text zu verstehen.
____ 2. Wenn er den Wortschatz gelernt hätte,	b. hätten wir Licht haben können.
____ 3. Wenn ich das Auto hätte reparieren lassen,	c. wäre es uns nicht so kalt gewesen.
____ 4. Wenn du die Steckdose gefunden hättest,	d. hätten wir auf der Reise kein Problem gehabt.

Exercise 2

Rewrite the sentences below, changing them from the present subjunctive to the past subjunctive.

1. Ich würde eine Suchmaschine gebrauchen.

2. Wir würden uns die großen Kakteen anschauen.

3. Du würdest dich warm anziehen.

4. Sie würden einen Film runterladen.

5. Ich würde bei ihr bleiben.

_____

_____

6. Sie würde den Schnee selber schaufeln.

_____

_____

7. Ihr würdet einen Baum einpflanzen.

_____

_____

8. Er würde dir mit der Arbeit helfen.

_____

_____

9. Wir würden nach Hause fliegen.

_____

_____

10. Würdest du umziehen?

_____

_____

Exercise 3

Complete the following sentences by adding a meaningful past tense subjunctive clause.

1. Wenn Richard die E-Mail verschickt hätte,

_____

_____

2. Wenn Lena etwas anders studiert hätte,

_____

_____

3. Wenn Karl sein Handy bei sich gehabt hätte,

_____

_____

4. Wenn Monika früher zum Arzt gegangen wäre,

_____

_____

Exercise 4

Write a brief paragraph in response to the question below. Use the past subjunctive in composing your response.

Was hätten Sie letztes Jahr gemacht, wenn Sie das Geld und die Zeit dazu gehabt hätten?

_____

_____

_____

_____

_____

_____

_____

_____

_____

_____

_____

_____

_____

68

69 Verbs Modals in Subjunctive II

The general subjunctive (subjunctive II) of a modal verb is formed from the stem of the simple past (imperfect tense). An umlaut is added to those modals that have an umlaut in the infinitive form.

Infinitive	Simple Past	Subjunctive
dürfen to be allowed to	ich durfte I was allowed to	ich dürfte I would be allowed to; I might
können to be able to	ich konnte I was able to	ich könnte I would be able to; I could
mögen to like to	ich mochte I liked to	ich möchte I would like to
müssen to have to	ich musste I had to	ich müsste I would have to
sollen to ought to	ich sollte I was supposed to	ich sollte I should
wollen to want to	ich wollte I wanted to	ich wollte I would want to

Achtung!

The general subjunctive forms of *sollen* and *wollen* forms are identical to their simple past forms.

The subjunctive forms of *können* and *mögen* are often used to form polite requests. They are the most common of the subjunctive modal verbs.

Könnten Sie das Fenster bitte zu machen?
Could you please close the window?

Möchten Sie sonst noch etwas?
Would you like anything else?

The past tense subjunctive of the modals is formed with the subjunctive form of the auxiliary verb *haben* + a double infinitive construction using the modal.

Dann hätte ich mir ein Bluse kaufen können.
Then I **could have bought** myself a blouse.

Achtung!

The auxiliary verb precedes the double infinitive construction when verb-last word order is called for in the past tense subjunctive, as in a subordinate clause.

Wenn er das nur hätte wissen dürfen!
If only he **had been permitted to know** that!

Exercise 1

Fill in the blanks below with the subjunctive form of the modal in parentheses.

1. _____ Markus mit uns zusammen im Garten arbeiten? (mögen)

2. Wir würden mitkommen, wenn wir _____. (dürfen)

3. Peter und Nina _____ ihre Pässe mitnehmen, wenn sie ins Ausland fliegen würden. (müssen)

4. _____ du die frischen Tomaten pflücken? (können)

5. Wiebke und Jürgen _____ deinen Artikel lesen, wenn du schon damit fertig wärest. (wollen)

Exercise 2

Create a polite response to the following polite requests in the subjunctive.

1. Möchten Sie noch ein paar Minuten warten?

_____

_____

2. Möchten Sie mit jemandem anders sprechen?

_____

_____

3. Könnten Sie bitte Ihren Mantel zur Garderobe bringen?

_____

_____

4. Könnten Sie mir bitte helfen?

_____

_____

5. Möchten Sie noch eine Tasse Kaffee?

_____

_____

Exercise 3

The following sentences contain modals in the present tense subjunctive. Rewrite each sentence using the modal in the past tense subjunctive.

1. Beate und Ludger könnten den Rasen mähen.

_____

_____

2. Ich dürfte den Kuchen essen!

_____

_____

3. Wir sollten das wissen.

_____

_____

4. Du müsstest selber zur Bank gehen.

_____

_____

5. Wenn er den Wein nur trinken wollte!

_____

_____

Exercise 4

Translate the following sentences into German using the subjunctive tense with the modal verbs.

1. She would have to eat vegetarian.

_____

_____

2. The child would be allowed to play outside.

_____

_____

3. You (familiar, plural) should have been able to download that.

_____

_____

4. If only I could have eaten more ice cream!

_____

_____

5. The students should have done their homework.

_____

_____

69

The special subjunctive (subjunctive I) implies objectivity (neither certainty nor doubt). The subjunctive I is often used when reporting news or events and in making certain wishes and commands.

The subjunctive I is formed by adding the subjunctive endings to the infinitive stem.

	Singular	Plural
haben (to have)	ich hab**e** I would have	wir hab**en** we would have
	du hab**est** you would have	ihr hab**et** you (plural) would have
	er/sie/es hab**e** he/she/it would have	sie/Sie hab**en** they/you (formal) would have

Der Angeklagte **werde** *freigesprochen.*
The accused **will be** released.

Achtung!

In most cases, the *ich, wir,* and *sie/Sie* forms of the subjunctive verb are identical to those of the present tense indicative mood. To make the use of the subjunctive clear in these instances, the general subjunctive (subjunctive II) is used to replace these forms.

Present indicative:
Ich **habe** *das schon.*   I already **have** that.

Subjunctive I:
Ich **habe** *das schon.*   I already **would have** that.

Subjunctive II:
Ich **hätte** *das schon.*   I already **would have** that.

Ausnahme

The verb *sein* is irregular in the subjunctive.

Singular	Plural
ich sei I would be/was	wir seien we would be/were
du seist you would be/were	ihr seit you (plural) would be/were
er/sie/es sei he/she/it would be/was	sie/Sie seien they/you (formal) would be/were

Der andere **sei** *um 12.00 Uhr gekommen.*
The other one **was here** at 12:00.

The special subjunctive is used to make objective reports.

Die Autofahrer **seien** *nicht verletzt.*
The drivers **were** not injured.

The special subjunctive is used in several expressions that express wishes and commands. Some common expressions include:

Gott **sei** *Dank!*
Thank God!

Sei *froh!*
Be happy!

Exercise 1

Give the _ich_ form of the special subjunctive for each infinitive below.

1. kommen _____

2. sein _____

3. haben _____

4. werden _____

5. wollen _____

6. können _____

7. wissen _____

8. sollen _____

9. mögen _____

10. lassen _____

Exercise 2

Translate the following sentences into German using the speical subjunctive.

1. He was buying a book.

_____

_____

2. She was jogging in the park.

_____

_____

3. The children took along their books.

_____

_____

4. They were tidying up their room.

_____

_____

5. He decided for it.

_____

_____

Exercise 3

Fill in the blanks below with the special subjunctive form of the verb in parentheses.

1. Der Verkäufer _____ nicht mit den Kunden. (sprechen)

2. Der Markt _____ stabil. (sein)

3. Die Preise _____ noch höher. (steigen)

4. Die Nachfrage _____ groß. (werden)

5. Die Kunden _____ der Reklame nicht. (glauben)

70

Indirect speech is used to express what someone said without quoting verbatim.

The special subjunctive (subjunctive I) is most often used when expressing an indirect quote.

*Der Präsident sagte, er **sei** damit einverstanden.*
The president said that he **was** in agreement.

Ausnahme

In most cases, the *ich, wir,* and *sie/Sie* forms of the subjunctive verb are identical to those of the present tense indicative mood. To make the use of the subjunctive clear in these instances, the general subjunctive (subjunctive II) is used to replace these forms.

Present indicative:
*„Wir **haben** das schon."*
"We already **have** that."

Subjunctive I:
*Er sagte, wir **haben** das schon.*
He said we already **had** that.

Subjunctive II:
*Er sagte, wir **hätten** das schon.*
He said we already **had** that.

When there is a clear distinction between subjunctive I and the present indicative, subjunctive II may still be used for indirect speech. In these instances, subjunctive II implies doubt.

Present indicative:
*„Er **ist** krank."*   "He **is** sick."

Subjunctive I (objective):
*Sie sagte, er **sei** krank.*   She said he **was** sick.

Subjunctive II (doubt):
*Sie sagte, er **wäre** krank.*   She said he **was** sick.

The subject of a verb often changes when moving from direct to indirect speech.

Direct speech:
*„Wir **gehen** morgen in die Stadt", sagte Rolf."*
"**We're going** to the city tomorrow," said Rolf.

Indirect speech:
*Rolf sagte, **sie gingen** morgen in die Stadt.*
Rolf said **they were going** to the city tomorrow.

The past perfect subjunctive is used in indirect speech to indicate that an activity occurred before the original speaker remarked on it.

Direct speech:
*„**Wir sind** gestern in die Stadt **gegangen**", sagte Rolf.*
"**We went** to the city yesterday," said Rolf.

Indirect speech:
*Rolf sagte, **sie seien** gestern in die Stadt **gegangen**.*
Rolf said **they went** to the city yesterday.

When a command (imperative) is indirectly quoted, the verb *sollen* (to ought to; should) is used to introduce the action.

Direct speech:
*„**Nehmen** Sie den roten Wein", sagte der Verkäufer.*
"**Take** the red wine," said the salesman.

Indirect speech:
*Der Verkäufer sagte, wir **sollten** den roten Wein **nehmen**.*
The salesman said we **should take** the red wine.

The conjunction *ob* (whether; if) is used to introduce a *yes/no* question in indirect speech.

Direct speech:
***Hast** du Geld bei dir?" fragte er.*
"Do you **have** money on you?" he asked.

Indirect speech:
*Er fragte, **ob** ich Geld bei mir hätte.*
He asked **if** I had money on me.

The same interrogative word used to ask an informational question in direct speech is used to introduce that question in indirect speech.

Direct speech:
*„**Wer** ist der Richter?" fragte er.*
"**Who** is the judge?" he asked.

Indirect speech:
*Er fragte, **wer** der Richter sei.*
He asked **who** the judge was.

The two-word form of the subjunctive II is most often used in indirect speech except with the verbs *sein, haben,* and *wissen* and the modals.

*Sie sagte, sie **würde** die Rechnung **bezahlen**.*
She said she **would pay** the bill.

Exercise 1

Rewrite the direct quotes below using indirect speech.

1. „Wir sind sehr glücklich", sagte Monika.

_____

_____

2. „Der Kellner hat es empfohlen", sagte Christian.

_____

_____

3. „Die Putzfrau wird das aufräumen", sagte die Dame.

_____

_____

4. „Verdienst du viel?" fragte der Student

_____

_____

Exercise 2

You just returned from a doctor's appointment and are reporting what the doctor told you to a friend. Use *sollen* in the special subjunctive (subjunctive I) to express the following commands.

1. „Nehmen Sie ab!"

_____

_____

2. „Essen Sie mehr Gemüse!"

_____

_____

3. „Nehmen Sie zwei Aspirin!"

_____

_____

4. „Machen Sie diese Übungen!"

_____

_____

Exercise 3

You are interviewing a friend about his or her life and are asking the following questions. Use indirect speech to create a paragraph reporting his or her answer.

Wo bist du geboren?
Wie alt bist du?
Wie viele Geschwister hast du?
Wohnst du noch bei deinen Eltern?
Arbeitest du oder studierst du?

_____

_____

_____

_____

_____

_____

_____

_____

_____

The stem changes that irregular verbs undergo must be memorized. Most common irregular verbs can be grouped by similar vowel changes in the stem.

The following common vowel changes occur in the present tense second- and third-person singular (*du, er, sie, es*). All other present tense forms are regular.

	Singular	Plural
a → ä	*ich fahre* I go	*wir fahren* we go
	*du **fährst*** you go	*ihr fahrt* you (plural) go
	*er/sie/es **fährt*** he/she/it goes	*sie/Sie fahren* they/you (formal) go
e → ie	*ich sehe* I see	*wir sehen* we see
	*du **siehst*** you see	*ihr seht* you (plural) see
	er/sie/es darf he/she/it sees	*ssie/Sie sehen* they/you (formal) see
e → i	*ich gebe* I give	*wir geben* we give
	*du **gibst*** you give	*ihr gebt* you (plural) give
	*er/sie/es **gibt*** he/she/it gives	*ssie/Sie geben* they/you (formal) give

Some common irregular verbs grouped by these vowel changes include:

a → ä
- *fahren* (to go, by vehicle)
- *fallen* (to fall)
- *gefallen* (to please + dative)
- *hin.fallen* (to fall down)
- *fangen* (to catch)
- *an.fangen* (to begin, to start)
- *empfangen* (to receive a guest)
- *halten* (to hold)
- *an.halten* (to stop)
- *behalten* (to keep)
- *erhalten* (to receive)
- *laden* (to load)
- *auf.laden* (to upload)
- *ein.laden* (to invite)
- *herunter.laden* (to download)
- *lassen* (to leave, to allow, to let, to have done)
- *laufen* (to walk, to run)
- *schlafen* (to sleep)
- *aus.schlafen* (to sleep in)
- *ein.schlafen* (to fall asleep)

- *tragen* (to carry, to wear)
- *wachsen* (to grow)
- *waschen* (to wash)

e → ie
- *geschehen* (to happen)
- *lesen* (to read)
- *sehen* (to see)
- *stehlen* (to steal)

e → i
- *brechen* (to break)
- *essen* (to eat, as a person)
- *fressen* (to eat as an animal)
- *geben* (to give)
- *sprechen* (to speak)
- *sterben* (to die)
- *treffen* (to meet)
- *vergessen* (to forget)
- *werden* (to become)
- *werfen* (to throw)

Achtung!

A verb retains the stem change even after taking a prefix (separable or inseparable).

schlafen (to sleep)	*Er **schläft** lange.* He **sleeps** a long time.
aus.schlafen (to sleep in)	*Er **schläft** am Wochende **aus**.* He **sleeps** in on the weekend.
ein.schlafen (to fall asleep)	*Er **schläft** jetzt **ein**.* He's **falling asleep** now.

Achtung!

The irregular verb *nehmen* (to take) has both a vowel and a consonant change in the second- and third-person singular (*du, er, sie, es*).

	Singular	Plural
nehmen (to take)	*ich nehme* I take	*wir nehmen* we take
	*du n**imm**st* you take	*ihr nehmt* you (plural) take
	*er/sie/es n**im**mt* he/she/it takes	*sie/Sie nehmen* they/you (formal) take

Verb stems ending in a sibilant (-s, -z, -ß) add only a -t to their stem in the *du* form.

	Singular	Plural
	ich esse I eat	*wir essen* we eat
essem (to eat)	*du isst* you eat	*ihr esst* you (pl.) eat
	er/sie/es isst he/she/it eats	*sie/Sie essen* they/you (formal) eat

4. Sie lädt Monika ein. (ich)

_____

_____

5. Ich vergesse, wie sie heißt. (er)

_____

_____

Exercise 1

Fill in each blank below by conjugating the infinitive form of the irregular verb in parentheses.

1. Kristina und ich _____ heute Abend im griechischen Restaurant. (essen)

2. Der Student _____ die Zeitung jeden Tag. (lesen)

3. Wann _____ du normalerweise _____? (einschlafen)

4. _____ er jede Woche eine Karte von ihr? (erhalten)

5. _____ Sie Ihren neuen Anzug zum Bewerbungsgespräch? (tragen)

Exercise 2

Rewrite each of the sentences below by conjugating the verb according to the new subject in parentheses.

1. Du wirst gesund. (wir)

_____

_____

2. Sie waschen die Wäsche. (sie, singular)

_____

_____

3. Wir geben ihm einen neuen Computer. (du)

_____

_____

Exercise 3

Use the present tense form of the verbs below to describe what is happening in each picture.

einsteigen, fahren, halten, hinfallen, laufen, sehen

1. _____

2. _____

_____

3. _____

_____

4. _____

_____

72

There are a variety of ways to express the verb *to like* in German.

The adverb *gern* (gladly) is used to describe an activity that one enjoys doing. The use of this adverb literally expresses that one does something *gladly*.

*Sie fährt **gern** Ski.*
She **likes** to ski./She skis **gladly**.

*Das mache ich **gern**.*
I **like** to do that./I do that **gladly**.

To make polite requests expressing what someone *would like* to do or *would like* to have, the modal verb *mögen* (to like) is used in the subjunctive mood.

***Möchtest** du mitfahren?*
Would you **like** to ride along?

***Möchten** Sie eine Tasse Tee?*
Would you **like** a cup of tea?

To express that one *likes* an object, use either the verb *gefallen* (which requires the dative case) or *mögen* in the indicative mood. Both verbs are irregular, though *gefallen* is generally used only in the third person.

	Singular	Plural
gefallen (to please, to be pleasing)	*er/sie/es gefällt* he/she/it is pleasing	*sie gefallen* they are pleasing
mögen (to like)	*ich mag* I like	*wir mögen* we like
	du magst you like	*ihr mögt* you all like
	er/sie/es mag he/she/it likes	*sie/Sie mögen* they/you (formal) like

*Das neue Bild **gefällt** mir sehr.*
I **like** the new picture a lot./The new picture is very pleasing to me.

*Ich **mag** das neue Bild.*
I **like** the new picture.

The modal verb *mögen* in the indicative mood can be used to express liking for a person.

*Ich **mag** dich sehr.*
I **like** you a lot.

The construction *gern . . . haben* can also be used to express liking for a person. This construction is equivalent to the use of *mögen* in the indicative mood.

*Ich **habe** dich **gern**.*
I **like** you.

Achtung!

Lieben or *lieb haben* translates as *to love*. This verb expresses a strong emotion with regard to another person and is not appropriate for expressing fondness with regard to things.

*Ich **liebe** dich, Gustav./Ich **hab'** dich **lieb**, Gustav.*
I **love** you, Gustav.

*Der Teddybär **gefällt** mir **sehr**!*
I **love** the teddy bear!

Exercise 1

Fill in each blank below by conjugating the infinitive form of the verb in parentheses.

1. Was _____ er essen?
(mögen, subjunctive mood)

2. _____ Ihnen die neue Farbe?
(gefallen)

3. _____ ihr euren neuen Lehrer?
(mögen, indicative mood)

4. Ich _____ ihn sehr gern. (haben)

5. _____ dir die neuesten Autos?
(gefallen)

6. Wir _____ am Sonntag abfliegen.
(mögen, subjunctive mood)

7. _____ ihr die neue Nachbarin
wirklich gern? (haben)

8. Dich _____ ich schon lange!
(mögen, indicative mood)

Exercise 2

Complete each sentence by choosing the most appropriate expression from the options below and conjugating the verb accordingly. Use each expression only once.

gefallen
mögen (indicative)
mögen (subjunctive)
gern haben
gern

1. _____ Ihnen die neue Mode?

2. Spielt ihr _____ Tennis?

3. _____ du mich _____?

4. Die Gruppe _____ schon heute abfahren.

5. Er _____ dich sehr.

Exercise 3

Translate the following sentences into German.

1. She likes to play the piano.

_____

_____

_____

2. They would like to pay with a credit card.

_____

_____

_____

3. The children like to play outside.

_____

_____

_____

4. Do you like her a lot?

_____

_____

_____

5. I like your new dress.

_____

_____

_____

73

74 Word Order Verb Second

In a simple statement the conjugated verb is always placed in second position, meaning it is the second grammatical element but not necessarily the second word.

In most German sentences, the subject takes first position in front of the verb, as in English.

> *Der schwarze Hund liegt* unter dem Baum.
>   1   2
>
> **The black dog is lying** under the tree.
>   1   2

On some occasions, an element other than the subject will take first position. This is done for emphasis but does not change the meaning of the sentence. In these cases, the subject follows directly after the conjugated verb.

> *Heute Abend* (time expression) *gehen* wir ins
>   1   2
> Konzert.
> We **are going** to the concert **this evening.**
>   2   1

> *Den Roman* (direct object) *habe* ich schon vor langer
>   1   2
> Zeit gelesen.
> I **have** already read **that novel** a long time ago.
>   2   1

> *Der Frau* (indirect object) *habe* ich nichts zu sagen.
>   1   2
> I don't **have** anything to say to **that woman.**
>   2   1

> *Als wir jung waren* (dependent clause), *gingen* wir
>   1   2
> gerne reiten.
> **When we were young**, we **used to** like **to go**
>   1   2
> (horseback) riding.

Achtung!

As in English, a comma is included when a dependent clause takes the first position in a German sentence.

> *Wenn er mich besucht, bringt* er immer Blumen *mit.*
> Whenever he visits me, he always brings flowers along.

Ausnahme

Coordinating conjunctions, such as *und* (and) and *oder* (or), and words such as *ja* (yes) and *nein* (no) do not have an effect on word order.

> *Ja, ich möchte* ein Glas Wasser.
> 0   1   2
> **Yes, I would like** a glass of water.
> 0   1   2

> *Ich fahre* in die Stadt, *und er bleibt* zu Hause.
> 1   2   0   1   2
> **I am going** into the city, **and he is staying** at home.
>   1   2   0   1   2

Exercise 1

Reorder the sentences below so that an element other than the subject is in first position. Insert commas where necessary.

1. Er zieht nächstes Jahr nach Düsseldorf um.

_____

_____

2. Sie nimmt ihren Bruder nicht mit.

_____

_____

3. Sie haben mir nichts erzählt.

_____

_____

4. Ich weiß nicht, wann Heinrich ankommt.

_____

_____

5. Wir werden nach Deutschland fliegen, wenn wir genug Geld dazu haben.

_____

_____

Exercise 2

Organize the following elements into logical sentences with the verb in second position. Conjugate the verb to agree with the subject.

1. Tobias / Fußball / heute Nachmittag / spielen.

_____

_____

2. die Trainer / mit den Spielern / arbeiten / stundenlang.

_____

_____

3. haben / gestern Abend / wir / gesungen.

_____

_____

4. ich / es / mögen / er / lächeln / , / wenn.

_____

_____

5. Maria / kochen / , / er / wenn / arbeiten.

_____

_____

Exercise 3

Answer the following in complete German sentences. Be sure to use proper word order in your responses.

1. Lesen Sie oft?

_____

_____

_____

2. Was ist Ihr Lieblingsroman?

_____

_____

_____

3. Wo kaufen Sie Ihre Bücher ein?

_____

_____

4. Gehen Sie oft in die Stadtbibliothek?

_____

_____

5. Können Sie auf Deutsch lesen?

_____

_____

74

75 Word Order *Verb First*

On some occasions, the conjugated verb takes first position in German. The subject follows directly behind it.

Verbs take first position when asking a *yes/no* question.

> ***Liegt der Hund*** *unter dem Baum?*
>   1   2
> **Is the dog lying** under the tree?
> 1a   2   1b

Ausnahme

Yes/no questions can also be formed by adding certain expressions, such as *oder* (or), *nicht wahr* (not true), or *gell* (valid) to the end of a sentence. In these constructions, the verb takes second position.

Der Hund liegt unter dem Baum, ***nicht wahr****?*
The dog is lying under the tree, **isn't it**?

Verbs take first position when creating the imperative in the *Sie* form or *wir* form.

> ***Gehen Sie*** *jetzt nach Hause!*
>   1   2
> **Go** home now!
> 1

> ***Bleiben wir*** *bis morgen!*
>   1   2
> **Let us stay** until tomorrow!
> 1a   2   1b

Ausnahme

The *du* and *ihr* forms of the imperative also take the verb in first position. However, typically no subject is used unless for emphasis/contrast.

Geh/Geht nach Hause!
Go home!

Geh ***du*** *nach Hause!/Geht* ***ihr*** *nach Hause!*
(No,) **you** go home!

Exercise 1

Reorder the sentences below so that they ask *yes/no* questions.

1. Stefanie trinkt immer Rotwein.

_____

_____

2. Maximilian isst gern italienisch.

_____

_____

3. Birgit und Heike wollen nicht ins Restaurant gehen.

_____

_____

4. Du möchtest lieber hier bleiben.

_____

_____

5. Wir fahren heute Abend in die Stadt.

_____

_____

Exercise 2

Make the following sentences into *yes/no* questions by adding an appropriate phrase to the end and maintaining verb-second word order. Then reorder them into *yes/no* questions by placing the conjugated verb in first position.

1. Hans-Peter studiert Geologie.

_____

_____

2. Monika schreibt heute eine Eintrittsklausur.

_____

_____

3. Viele Studenten haben mehr als zehn Semester studiert.

_____

_____

4. Du hast einen Studienplatz bekommen.

_____

_____

5. Wir werden im Studentenwohnheim wohnen.

_____

_____

Exercise 3

You've got some housework to do, but you'd like some help. Take the following verb phrases and create both the *Sie-* and *wir*-form imperatives. Then give the English equivalent.

1. im Garten arbeiten

_____

_____

_____

2. die Blumen gießen

_____

_____

_____

3. Gemüse pflanzen

_____

_____

_____

4. den Rasen mähen

_____

_____

_____

75

76 Word Order *Verb Last*

In some sentences, the conjugated verb goes to the end of a clause or sentence.

Verbs are placed last in a dependent clause that is introduced by a subordinating conjunction.

*Ich lese die Zeitung, **weil** ich endlich mal Zeit **habe.***
I'm reading the newspaper, **because** I finally **have** time.

Verbs are placed last in a dependent clause that is introduced by a question word.

*Er weiß nicht, **wann** er wieder mal vorbeikommen **kann.***
He doesn't know **when** he **can** come back by again.

Verbs are placed last in a relative clause that is introduced by a relative pronoun.

*Sind das die Schuhe, **die** du gestern angehabt **hast**?*
Are these the shoes **that** you **had on** yesterday?

Ausnahme

There are occasions when the conjugated verb is not the last part of a verb-last clause. If a double infinitive construction is part of the clause or sentence, it comes after the conjugated verb.

*Hast du gewusst, dass sie das **hätte machen können**?*
Did you know that she **could have done** that?

Exercise 1

Reorder the words below to form logical sentences. Double lines indicate the start of a new clause. Be sure to use a comma.

1. ich / nicht / weiß // er / ob / kommen / wird / morgen.

_____

_____

2. er / für / Deutsch / sich / interessiert // weil / nach / er / will / Deutschland.

_____

_____

3. Sie / geschrieben / hat // nicht / Chicago / nach / will / dass / sie.

_____

_____

4. weißt / du // liegt / Ingolstadt / wo?

_____

_____

5. der / gesagt / Schaffner / hat // der / soll / Zug / wann / ankommen.

_____

_____

6. das / der / Mann / ist // dem / mit / haben / wir / geredet.

_____

_____

7. sind / das / Studenten / die // Eltern / deren / kennst / du?

_____

_____

Exercise 2

Fill in the blanks below with the correct form of the verbs in parentheses. Watch the verb order in your answer.

1. Weißt du, wann er Geburtstag _____?
(wird /haben)

2. Ist das die Frau, die er _____

_____? (kennen lernen/wollte)

3. Das ist nicht, wie er das _____?
(machen/wollte)

4. Kennst du die Mädchen, die er _____

_____? (mitbringen/sollen/ hätte)

5. Weißt du, ob er _____?
(mitkommen/wird)

6. Stimmt es, dass sie das selber _____?
(hat/gekocht)

3. My sister knows who is in my class.

_____

_____

_____

4. Do you know if she will dance with me?

_____

_____

_____

5. That was the woman whose husband I met yesterday.

_____

_____

_____

Exercise 3

Translate the following sentences using the correct word order.

1. Do you know where the bookstore is?

_____

_____

_____

2. They are going to Europe, because they have friends there.

_____

_____

_____

76

Elements of time, manner, and place follow specific rules of word placement.

Following a conjugated verb, the elements of time, manner, and place are always in that order.

> *Wir fahren **morgen mit dem Schiff nach Hamburg.***
>   T   M   P
> We're going **tomorrow by ship to Hamburg.**

Achtung!

To remember word order, students of German use the word *tempo* (speed). The consonants stand for the first letter of the three elements in their respective order: **t**ime, **m**anner, and **p**lace.

Achtung!

Any of the three elements may appear as the first element of a sentence for emphasis. The remaining elements following the conjugated verb still fall in their proper order. In each case, the conjugated verb remains in second position, with the subject following.

> ***Morgen** fahren wir **mit dem Schiff nach Hamburg.***
>   T   M   P
> **Tomorrow,** we're going **by ship to Hamburg.**

> ***Mit dem Schiff** fahren wir **morgen nach Hamburg.***
>   M   T   P
> **We're going **by ship tomorrow to Hamburg.**

> ***Nach Hamburg** fahren wir **morgen mit dem Schiff.***
>   P   T   M
> **We're going **to Hamburg tomorrow by ship.**

Verb forms that are typically placed at the end of a sentence, such as past participles or infinitives, follow expressions of time, manner, and place.

> *Wir sind gestern mit dem Schiff nach Hamburg **gefahren.***
> We **went** yesterday by ship to Hamburg.

> *Wir wollten gestern mit dem Schiff nach Hamburg **fahren.***
> We wanted ***to go*** yesterday by ship to Hamburg.

Most expressions of manner are adverbs and prepositional phrases.

> *Wir gehen **zusammen** ins Kino.*
> We're going **together** to the movies.

> *Wir gehen **mit unseren Freunden** ins Kino.*
> We're going **with our friends** to the movies.

Exercise 1

Reorder the following elements to form logical sentences. Begin each sentence with the subject and use proper word order following the conjugated verb.

1. wir / heute Abend / ins Kino / gehen / zusammen.

_____

_____

2. Sylvia und Karl / mit Maria / essen / im Restaurant / um 18.00 Uhr.

_____

_____

3. alleine / im Wald / wandere / ich / am Tag.

_____

_____

4. dieses Wochenende / schnell / meine Eltern / zu Oma / fahren.

_____

_____

5. Gregor / ständig / arbeitet / am Computer / jeden Tag.

_____

_____

_____

Exercise 2

The following sentence answers all three questions below. Rewrite the answer according to the emphasis indicated in each question.

Jürgen arbeitet morgen Abend mit seiner Lerngruppe im Gemeinschaftsraum.
Jürgen is studying tomorrow evening with his study group in the common room.

1. Wann arbeitet Jürgen mit seiner Lerngruppe im Gemeinschaftsraum?

_____

_____

_____

2. Mit wem arbeitet Jürgen morgen Abend im Gemeinschaftsraum?

_____

_____

_____

3. Wo arbeitet Jürgen morgen Abend mit seiner Lerngruppe?

_____

_____

_____

Exercise 3

You recently took a brief vacation. Write a paragraph describing when you left, with whom you went, and to where you traveled. Then describe what you did each day, how you went about doing it, and where you did these things.

_____

_____

_____

_____

_____

_____

_____

_____

_____

_____

_____

_____

_____

77

When a verb has both a direct and an indirect object, a strict word order is followed depending on whether the objects are nouns or pronouns.

If both the direct and indirect object are noun phrases, the dative (indirect object) comes before the accusative (direct object).

*Peter und Nina geben **dem Hund sein Futter**.*
Peter and Nina are giving **the dog his food.**

If one of the two objects is a pronoun, the pronoun comes first in the sentence.

*Peter und Nina geben **ihm sein Futter**.*
Peter and Nina are giving **him his food.**

*Peter und Nina geben **es dem Hund**.*
Peter and Nina are giving **it to the dog.**

If both of the objects are pronouns, the accusative (direct object) comes before the dative (indirect object).

*Peter und Nina geben **es ihm**.*
Peter and Nina are giving **it to him.**

Achtung!

The most typical verbs that take both a direct and an indirect object are often referred to as *give, show, tell* verbs since one generally gives something (direct object) to someone (indirect object), shows something to someone, or tells something to someone.

*Hast du ihr die Nachrichten **erklärt**?*
Did you **explain** the news to her?

Exercise 1

Rewrite each sentence below, replacing the boldface object with a pronoun and altering the word order if necessary. Be sure the new pronoun agrees in number, case, and gender with the object that it is replacing.

1. Margrit kocht **ihren Kindern** eine Suppe.

_____

_____

2. Uwe singt seiner Freundin **ein Lied.**

_____

_____

3. Nina und Bettina backen ihren Eltern **Kekse.**

_____

_____

4. Wiebke und Dominik schreiben **ihrem Großvater** einen Brief.

_____

_____

5. Wir bringen unseren Nachbarn **eine Flasche Wein.**

_____

_____

6. Die Kinder schenken **ihrer Mutter** frische Blumen.

_____

_____

7. Der Vater baut **den Kindern** einen Schneemann.

_____

_____

8. Thomas erzählt dem Publikum **einen Witz.**

_____

_____

Exercise 2

Rewrite the following sentences three times based on the model below. First, replace only the direct object with a pronoun. Second, replace only the indirect object. Third, replace both objects. Be sure to watch word order with each change.

Beispiel:
Marcel und Tanja schenken ihrer Großmutter eine Vase.
Marcel und Tanja schenken sie ihrer Großmutter.
Marcel und Tanja schenken ihr eine Vase.
Marcel und Tanja schenken sie ihr.

1. Julia strickt ihrem Freund einen Pullover.

_____

_____

_____

2. Ich zeige dem Beamten meinen Ausweis.

_____

_____

_____

_____

3. Karl erzählt den Touristen einen Witz.

_____

_____

_____

_____

4. Gibst du der Kellnerin das Trinkgeld?

_____

_____

5. Der Professor erklärt den Studenten die Aufgabe.

_____

_____

_____

Exercise 3

You're preparing a party! Write a paragraph describing what you do to prepare. Describe what you say, cook, purchase, make, bring, etc., and to/for whom.

_____

_____

_____

_____

_____

_____

_____

_____

_____

78

Cardinal numbers are those numbers used to count items in a set.

Cardinal numbers in German are written out as one word, without a hyphen.

0	*null*
1	*eins*
2	*zwei/zwo*
3	*drei*
4	*vier*
5	*fünf*
6	*sechs*
7	*sieben*
8	*acht*
9	*neun*
10	*zehn*
11	*elf*
20	*zwanzig*
21	*ein**und**zwanzig*
121	*einhunderteinundzwanzig*

A decimal or a space is used to mark the thousands place.

1.213: eintausendzweihundertdreizehn
one thousand two hundred thirteen

2 000: zweitausend
two thousand

A comma is used to mark a decimal space.

4,5: vier komma fünf
4.5: four point five (four and a half)

6,07: sechs komma null sieben
6.07: six and seven one-hundredths

Years are stated by the hundreds or thousands. The expression *im Jahre* (in the year), which is not considered formal in German, may or may not accompany the year. *Im Jahre* is not formal in German. Stating the year by itself still implies *in*.

***im Jahre** 1965:* ***im Jahre** neunzehnhundertfünfundsechzig*
in the year 1965 (nineteen sixty-five)

2007: zweitausendsieben
in two thousand seven

Cardinal numbers can be used in combination with the suffixes *-mal* and *-fach* to indicate the number of repetitions or duplications.

*ein**mal**, zwei**mal**, drei**mal** . . .*
once, twice, thrice . . .

*ein**fach**, zwei**fach**, drei**fach** . . .*
single, twofold, threefold . . .

The cardinal numbers are used to perform simple math functions.

+	*plus*
–	*minus*
×	*mal*
/	*durch*
=	*gleich/ist/macht*

2 + 3 = 5:   *zwei plus drei gleich fünf*
two plus three equals five

The cardinal numbers are also used along with the following expressions when telling time.

nach (after)   *Viertel* (quarter)   *um* (at)
vor (till)   *halb* (half, toward the next hour)

12:30:   *Es ist halb eins.*
It is half-past twelve.

12:30:   *Es ist zwölf Uhr einunddreißig.*
It's twelve thirty-one.

Exercise 1

Write out the numbers indicated below.

1. 1.105

_____

2. 321

_____

3. 74

_____

4. 6,5

_____

5. 682

_____

6. 2.610

_____

Exercise 2

What comes next in the sequence mathematically? Give the number as a word.

1. null, zwei, vier, sechs, . . .

_____

2. eins, drei, neun, siebenundzwanzig, . . .

_____

3. zehn, zwanzig, dreißig, . . .

_____

4. achtzig, fünfundsiebzig, siebzig, . . .

_____

5. zwei, vier, acht, sechzehn, . . .

_____

Exercise 3

Write out the years given below.

1. im Jahre 1987

_____

2. im Jahre 1996

_____

3. im Jahre 2010

_____

Exercise 4

Complete the mathematical equations below, giving the answer as a word.

1. null mal sechs ist

_____

2. achtundzwanzig durch vier ist

_____

3. einundvierzig minus zwei ist

_____

4. vierzehn plus zweiundsechzig ist

_____

5. neun mal acht ist

_____

Exercise 5

Write out the times indicated below.

1. 12:05 P.M.

_____

2. 11:00 A.M.

_____

3. 8:30 P.M.

_____

4. 4:45 A.M.

_____

79

Ordinals are numbers used to indicate a sequence (first, second, third, and so on).

The stems of ordinal numbers are formed by adding -t- to numbers from two through 19 and -st- to numbers 20 and higher.

zwei**t**- (second)
einundzwanzig**st**- (twenty-first)

Ausnahme

There are some exceptions to the normal ordinal-stem pattern. They must be memorized.

erst- (first)
dritt- (third)
siebt- (seventh)
acht- (eighth)

When used in context, ordinals act as adjectives and take the appropriate adjective ending to agree with the noun they modify.

Das ist unser **zweiter** Hund.
This is our **second** dog.

Nach der **zwanzigsten** Probe hat es geklappt.
After the **twentieth** try, it worked.

The ordinals are often used for both the days and months when indicating a date. A period (.) is used after a number to indicate that it should be read as an ordinal. All dates are masculine. The day is given before the month.

der 3. Oktober
der dritte Oktober } the third of October
der 3.10.
der dritte zehnte

Der 3.10. war ein schöner Tag.
The 3rd of October was a nice day.

den 3. Oktober
den dritten Oktober } the third of October
den 3.10.
den dritten Oktober

Heute haben wir den 3.10.
Today is the 3rd of October.

am 3. Oktober
am dritten Oktober } on the third of October
am 3.10.
am dritten zehnten

Am 3.10. haben wir gefeiert.
We celebrated on the 3rd of October.

Fractions are formed by adding an -l to an ordinal number. When fractions are used in combination with whole numbers, no joining word (such as and) is used.

Ich brauche $\frac{3}{4}$ Liter Wein für das Rezept.
Ich brauch drei **Viertel** Liter Wein für das Rezept.
I need three-**fourths** ($\frac{3}{4}$) of a liter of wine for the recipe.

Ausnahme

The fraction $\frac{1}{2}$ (one-half) is not based on an ordinal. One-half is read as a noun (ein Halb).

Ich brauche **ein halbes** Kilo Brot.
I need **a half** a kilogram of bread.

Wir hatten **zweieinhalb** Zentimeter Regen gestern.
We had **two-and-a-half** ($2\frac{1}{2}$) centimeters of rain yesterday.

Alltagssprache

The expression $1\frac{1}{2}$ (one and a half) can be read eineinhalb. However, in colloquial German speech one often hears anderthalb.

Exercise 1

Write out the fractions below as they would be said in German.

1. $\frac{1}{10}$

_____

2. $2\frac{1}{4}$

_____

3. $\frac{5}{8}$

_____

4. $\frac{3}{4}$

_____

5. $1\frac{1}{2}$

Exercise 2

Write out your answers to the following questions using only words. Use ordinals for both the day and month when giving dates.

1. Wann haben Sie Geburtstag?

_____

_____

_____

2. Wann fängt der Sommer an?

_____

_____

_____

3. Wann ist der Tag der Arbeit?

_____

_____

_____

4. Wann feiert man den schweizerischen Nationalfeiertag?

_____

_____

_____

5. Wann ist Silvester?

_____

_____

_____

Exercise 3

Translate the following sentences into German using the proper words for the ordinal numbers.

1. We met each other on the 5th of September.

_____

_____

_____

2. Hans is in the fifth grade.

_____

_____

_____

3. Four-fifths of the class understands him.

_____

_____

_____

4. She is the first in her class.

_____

_____

_____

5. They will leave on the 30th of May.

_____

_____

_____

80

German-speaking countries use the metric system.

Weights are given in terms of grams and kilograms (1 kg = approx. 2.2 lbs)

ein Gramm (one gram)
ein Kilo(gram) (one kilogram)
ein Pfund (= *ein halbes Kilo*) (one pound)

*Ich bräuchte ein halbes **Kilo** Brot, bitte.*
I need a half **a kilogram** of bread, please.

Measures are given in terms of centimeters, meters, and kilometers (1 km = approx. 0.6 mile).

ein Zentimeter (one centimeter)
ein Meter (one meter)
ein Kilometer (one kilometer)

*Wir müssen nur noch einen **Kilometer** laufen.*
We only have to walk one more **kilometer.**

Achtung!

As in English, when reading off distances that are fractions (with decimals), one reads the whole number first.

*Wir laufen nur **30,40** m zum Wald.*
*Wir laufen nur **dreißig** Meter **vierzig** zum Wald.*
We only walk **30.4** meters to the woods.

Achtung!

To give measures for areas or volumes, meters are squared (*Quadratmeter*) or cubed (*Kubikmeter*).

Das Schlafzimmer ist nur 6 m².
Das Schlafzimmer ist nur sechs Quadratmeter.
The bedroom is only six meters squared.

Monetary units for Austria and Germany are given in terms of *cents* and *Euros*. Monetary units in Switzerland are given in terms of *Rappen* and *Schweizer Franken* (SF). When reading off prices that are fractions (with decimals), one reads the higher unit (*Euros* or *Franken*), then the smaller units (*Cents* or *Rappen*).

*Das Kleid kostet **EUR 60,40**.*
*Das Kleid kostet **sechzig Euro vierzig**.*
The dress costs **60 euros and 40 cents.**

Exercise 1

Write out the following amounts as one would say them.

1. 1 Kg

_____

2. 2,30 m

_____

3. 0,50 SF

_____

4. 4 m³

_____

5. $1\frac{1}{2}$ Kg

_____

Exercise 2

Answer each question with the most appropriate quantity from the options below.

50 Quadratmeter
3,50 SF
100 Kilometer
30,- Euro
3,1 Kilo

1. Wieviel kostet das Brot?

_____

_____

2. Wie teuer ist das Hemd?

_____

_____

3. Wir groß ist die Wohnung?

_____

_____

_____

4. Wie weit ist es nach Hamburg?

_____

_____

_____

5. Wie viel wiegt das Baby?

_____

_____

_____

3. We live 40 kilometers from Frankfurt.

_____

_____

_____

4. I need a meter of material.

_____

_____

_____

5. How many cubic meters do they need?

_____

_____

_____

Exercise 3

Translate the following sentences into German using the appropriate terms for quantity.

1. Two kilograms of apples costs three euros.

_____

_____

_____

2. He is nearly two meters tall.

_____

_____

_____

81

Conjunctions are used to link words, phrases, clauses, and parts of sentences. Coordinating conjunction link two elements of equal weight equal weight with respect to importance. Coordinating conjunctions have no effect on word order within the clause.

The coordinating conjunctions in German are typically preceded by a comma.

*Ich lerne Deutsch, **aber** meine Nichte lernt Italienisch.*
I am learning German, **but** my niece is learning Italian.

Achtung!

If two clauses connected by *aber* (but), *sondern* (but, with negatives), or *und* (and) have the same subject, the subject does not need to be repeated in the second clause.

*Ich finde das Buch interessant, **aber ich finde** den Film langweilig.*
*Ich finde das Buch interessant, **aber** den Film langweilig.*
I think the book is interesting, **but (I think)** the movie is boring.

Some common coordinating conjunctions include:

aber (but)	*Meine Mutter will mir eine Hose kaufen, **aber** ich möchte lieber einen Schal.* My mom wants to buy me a pair of pants, **but** I would prefer a scarf.
denn (for, since, because)	*Mein Vater hat eine Mahnung bekommen, **denn** er hat die Telefonrechnung nicht bezahlt.* My dad got an overdue notice, **because** he didn't pay the phone bill.
oder (or)	*Kannst du mich zum Flughafen bringen, **oder** sollte ich mit der Bahn fahren?* Can you give me a ride to the airport **or** should I take the train?
sondern (but, but rather)	*Das Päckchen ist nicht für mich, **sondern** (es ist) für meinen Bruder.* The package isn't for me, **but rather** (it is) for my brother.
und (and)	*Der Arzt schaut sich gerade die Röntgenbilder an **und** ich bin sehr nervös.* The doctor is taking a look at the x-rays **and** I'm very nervous.

Exercise 1

Match each sentence in column A with the coordinating conjunction and clause that best completes it from column B below.

A	B
_____ **1.** Ich bin allergisch gegen Pilze	a. oder lieber draußen auf dem Balkon?
_____ **2.** Hast du Lust in der Küche zu essen	b. aber ihre Schwester hat drei.
_____ **3.** Der Erich kommt nicht mit ins Kino,	c. sondern ich gehe bloss zu meiner Freundin..
_____ **4.** Die Andrea hat keine Kinder,	d. denn er hat morgen eine wichtige Prüfung.
_____ **4.** Heute Abend fahre ich doch nicht nach Stuttgart,	e. und ich esse Tomaten nur ungern.

Exercise 2

Compose a logical beginning for each sentence.

1. _____

_____

und ich weiß wo du wohnst.

2. _____

_____

sondern ich werde zu Hause bleiben.

3. _____

_____

denn ein Brief braucht zu lang.

4. _____

_____

oder trinkst du lieber einen Kaffee?

5. _____

_____

aber heute geht es mir viel besser.

Exercise 3

The paragraph below discusses the writer's mother and her animals. Complete the paragraph by filling in the appropriate coordinating conjunctions.

Meine Mutter hat zwei Katzen, drei Hunde **(1.)** _____

____ auch ein Pferd. Das Pferd bleibt gerne in seinem Stall

(2.) _____ es grast am liebsten draußen auf der

Wiese. Ich hoffe, dass meine Mutter das Pferd nie verkauft,

(3.) _____ es ist ein tolles Pferd

(4.) _____ ich liebe es. Ich merke langsam wie

viel Spaß ich mit Tieren habe. Deswegen werde ich nicht wie

geplant Architektur studiern, **(5.)** _____ ich werde

Tierärztin werden. Ich freue mich sehr darauf

(6.) _____ ich werde schon im kommenden

Sommer in einem Zoo arbeiten. Wenn du mich fragst, ob ich

lieber im Londoner Zoo arbeiten will **(7.)** _____ ob

ich lieber im Berliner Zoo arbeite, das weiß ich leider nicht.

Exercise 4

Use the coordinating conjunctions to write five sentences about what you did last week. Perhaps you wanted to do x and y. Maybe you didn't want to do x but rather y.

1. _____

_____

_____

2. _____

_____

_____

3. _____

_____

_____

4. _____

_____

_____

5. _____

_____

_____

82

Subordinating conjunctions link independent (main) and dependent (subordinate) clauses in a sentence.

Unlike coordinating conjunctions, subordinating conjunctions do affect word order. When a subordinating conjunction is used, the conjugated verb is placed at the end of the dependent clause. The main clause and subordinate clause are separated by a comma.

> *Ich möchte Deutsch lernen, **weil** ich Familie in Deutschland **habe.***
> I would like to learn German, **because** I **have** family in Germany.

Some common subordinating conjunctions include:

bevor (before)	*Ich hatte schon gefrühstückt, **bevor** ich mir die Zähne geputzt habe.* I had already eaten breakfast before I brushed my teeth.
da (because)	*Sie ist sehr hilfreich, **da** sie das alles gut verstehen kann.* She is very helpful, **because** she can understand all of this well.
dass (that)	*Es war mir nicht bewusst, **dass** ich die Akte hätte aufbewahren sollen.* I was not aware **that** I was supposed to keep the file.
nachdem (after)	*Er hat sie abgeholt, **nachdem** er getankt hatte.* He picked her up **after** he stopped for gasoline.
ob (whether, if)	*Sie weiß nicht, **ob** sie heiratet.* She does not know **if** she is going to get married.
obwohl (although)	*Wir mussten zweimal halten, **obwohl** die Fahrt gar nicht so lang war.* We had to stop twice, **although** the drive wasn't long at all.
solange (as long as)	*Ich werde nach Italien, **solange** du mitreist.* I will go to Italy, **as long as** you come along.
während (while)	*Er hat das Lied geschrieben, **während** sie geschlafen hat.* He wrote the song **while** she was sleeping.
weil (because)	*Ich bringe einen Regenschirm mit, **weil** es bestimmt regnen wird.* I am bringing an umbrella along, **because** it's definitely going to rain.
wenn (if, when)	*Sie würde sich freuen, **wenn** du sie anrufen würdest.* She would be happy **if** you would call her.

Participles or infinitives are placed directly ahead of the conjugated verb in the subordinate clause.

> *Er ware gern mitgefahren, wenn er das **gewusst** hätte.*
> He would have gone along if he had **known** that.

> *Wir werden es versuchen, obwohl er uns nicht gut **verstehen** kann.*
> We'll try it, although he can't **understand** us well.

Ausnahme

When double infinitives appear in a subordinate clause, the conjugated verb goes directly in front of the double-infinitive construction. The double infinitive is placed at the end of the clause.

> *Sie hat sich geärgert, weil sie das nicht hätte **wissen können.***
> She was angry because she **could** not have **known** that.

The subordinate clause can precede the main clause. In these cases, a comma is placed before the main clause and the main clause begins with the conjugated verb.

> ***Weil ich Durst habe,** werde ich viel Wasser trinken.*
> ***Because I am thirsty,** I will drink a lot of water.*

> ***Dass er Bürgermeister war,** habe ich nicht gewusst.*
> I did not know **that he was mayor.**

Exercise 1

Circle the correct subordinating conjunction to complete each sentence.

1. Ich kaufe mir ein Handy, weil/dass ich immer erreichbar sein will.

2. Kannst du mir bitte sagen, weil/ob der ICE nach Berlin auch sonntags verkehrt?

3. Wusstet ihr, ob/dass „Malcolm mittendrin" täglich in ORF gezeigt wird?

4. Julia hat noch nicht gesagt, ob/weil sie mit ins David Hasselhof Konzert geht.

Exercise 2

Fill-in the correct subordinating conjunction in the blanks below

1. Ich werde ihn fragen, _____ er mal auf Mallorca war.

2. Weiß sie überhaupt, _____ ich heute Geburtstag habe?

3. Ich werde nicht dran gehen, _____ du mich anrufst.

4. Wir haben den Bus verpasst, _____ wir uns nicht beeilt haben.

5. Leider habe ich vergessen, _____ ich hätte aufräumen sollen.

Exercise 3

Unscramble the elements below to form logical sentences.

1. neuen / sparen / weil / Computer / Ernst / er / muss / Geld / kaufen / einen / will

_____

_____

2. gibt / nicht / ob / Ich / noch / Eintrittskarten / es / weiß

_____

_____

3. Die Frau / adoptiert / gesagt / dass / sie / hat / aus China / hat / ein Baby

_____

_____

4. gehen / Wir / weil / einen Kaffee / wollen / ins Café / trinken / wir

_____

_____

5. wenn / den Weg / mehr / Er / wird / vorsichtig / ist / nicht / finden / er / ist / nicht

_____

_____

Exercise 4

Use the appropriate conjunction to combine the sentences below.

1. Stimmt es? Du wohnst in Zürich?

_____

_____

2. Peter isst eine große Portion Eis. Er hat immer noch Hunger.

_____

_____

3. Wir haben keine Ahnung. Haben wir morgen eine weitere Sitzung?

_____

_____

4. Ist es wahr? Sie haben die Eishockey-Meisterschaft gewonnen?

_____

_____

5. Brigitte ist traurig. Ihr Freund hat mit ihr Schluß gemacht.

_____

_____

Nicht and *kein* are two German words commonly used to negate sentences.

Nicht is the equivalent of saying *not*. Nicht is always used in combination with a definite article. For general negation, *nicht* follows the subject, the conjugated verb, and all objects (direct and indirect).

> *Er gibt dem Kind **den** Ball **nicht**.*
> He is **not** giving **the** ball to the child.

Ausnahme

Nicht may precede a specific object for emphasis. In these instances, an alternative object is often provided, introduced by *sondern*, for comparison.

> *Er gibt dem Kind **nicht den Ball, sondern den Zug**.*
> He is **not** giving the child **the ball, but rather the train**.

> *Er gibt **nicht dem Kind** den Ball, **sondern dem Mann**.*
> He is **not** giving the ball to **the child, but rather to the man**.

Kein replaces *nicht* + the indefinite article *ein* to mean *not a* or *not any*. Kein takes the same endings as *ein* and precedes the noun being negated.

	M.	F.	Neuter	Pl.
Nom.	kein	keine	kein	keine
Acc.	keinen	keine	kein	keine
Dat.	keinem	keiner	keinem	keinen
Gen.	keines	keiner	keines	keiner

> *Ich habe **einen** Garten.*   I have **a** garden.
> *Ich habe **keinen** Garten.*   I do **not** have **a** garden.

> *Ein Apfel ist **eine** Frucht.*   An apple is **a** fruit.
> *Brokkoli ist **keine** Frucht.*   Broccoli is **not a** fruit.

Kein can also mean *no*.

> *Ich habe **kein** Auto.*
> I have **no** car. (I don't have a car.)

> *Ich trinke **kein** Bier.*
> I drink **no** beer. (I don't drink beer.)

Achtung!

As in English, singular nouns in German often become plural in the negative, especially when making a generalization. *Kein* becomes plural in these instances.

> *Magst du **eine Tomate**?*
> Would you care for **a tomato**?

> *Nein, danke, ich esse **keine Tomaten**.*
> No, thanks, I do **not** eat **tomatoes**.

Exercise 1

Answer the following questions in the negative. Use complete sentences beginning with *Nein, . . .* (*No, . . .*) and either *nicht* or *kein* in your response.

1. Ist das ein Stuhl?

   _____

   _____

2. Ist das eine Tafel?

   _____

   _____

3. Ist das deine Mutter?

   _____

   _____

4. Ist das ein Fenster?

   _____

   _____

5. Stimmt es, dass ihre Lieblingsstadt Hamburg ist?

   _____

   _____

6. Fährt Luise nach Rostock?

   _____

   _____

7. Haben Sie einen Wecker?

_____

_____

8. Schwimmt Julia jeden Tag?

_____

_____

9. Kennen Sie eine berühmte Schauspielerin?

_____

_____

Exercise 2

For each affirmative statement below, use _nicht_ to negate the action in relation to the direct object in parentheses. Use _nicht_ in your negation. Then write a second sentence using _kein_ to make a general negative statement about the object.

Beispiel:
Das werde ich trinken. (Der Saft)
Den Saft werde ich nicht trinken.
Ich trinke keinen Saft.

1. Das wird er kaufen. (Die Schuhe)

_____

_____

2. Das werden wir schreiben. (Die Geschichte)

_____

_____

3. Das werden Sie essen. (Die Banane)

_____

_____

4. Das wirst du verkaufen. (Der Stuhl)

_____

_____

5. Das werde ich spenden. (Das Geld)

_____

_____

Exercise 3

Use the information in the table below to construct a question and negative answer statement about what people do and don't do.

Beispiel: Ist DJ Ötzi Formel-1-Pilot? Nein, er ist kein Formel 1 Pilot, sondern Sänger, also fährt er keinen Ferrari.

Beruf	Aktion	Ja	Nein
Formel-1-Pilot (M)	fährt einen Ferrari	Michael Schumacher	DJ Ötzi
Sänger (M)	schreibt Lieder	DJ Ötzi	Claudia Schiffer
Model (neuter)	hat einen Fototermin	Claudia Schiffer	Angela Merkel
Politikerin (F)	hält eine Rede	Angela Merkel	Michael Schumacher

_____

_____

_____

_____

_____

_____

_____

_____

84

85 Negation *Negative Expressions*

There are several expressions that can be used to negate a sentence in German.

Nichts can be used to mean *nothing* or *not . . . anything.*

> *Ich sehe **nichts.***
> I do **not** see **anything.**/I see **nothing.**

Nie can be used to mean *never.*

> *Er spielt **nie** fair.*
> He **never** plays fairly.

Niemand can be used to mean *no one* or *not anyone.*

> ***Niemand** kennt uns.*
> **No one** knows us.

Achtung!

Niemand takes the masculine strong endings in the accusative and dative cases (*-en* and *-em*, respectively).

> *Hier kennen wir **niemanden.***
> We don't know **anyone** here.

> *Sie sprechen mit **niemandem.***
> They don't talk to **anyone.**

Nirgend- is used in combination with the question words *wo* (*-hin/-her*) (where to/from), *wann* (when), and *wie* (how) to express the negative. This use is similar to how the prefix *no* is used in English to indicate *nowhere, never* (at no time), and *no way,* respectively.

> *Ich kann meine Schlüssel **nirgendwo** finden.*
> I can**not** find my keys **anywhere.**

> *Das kann er **nirgendwie** schaffen.*
> There's **no way** he can manage that.

Alltagssprache

Although not considered polite, the *nirgend-* forms of negation can stand alone in response to questions.

Wohin gehst du?	Where are you going?
Nirgendwohin.	**Nowhere.**

Exercise 1

Fill in each blank below with the most appropriate negative expression.

1. Ich habe _____ dagegen.

2. _____ wird es wissen.

3. Das hast du _____ gesagt.

4. Das habe ich echt _____ gesehen.

5. Der Arzt meinte, er konnte _____ dafür.

Exercise 2

You are tired of being asked to report to your older sibling about everything you do. With one word, reply negatively to his or her questions below.

1. Wohin gehst du?

_____

2. Was isst du?

_____

3. Wann machst du deine Hausaufgaben?

_____

4. Wem schickst du diese E-Mail?

_____

5. Wann räumst du endlich dein Zimmer auf?

_____

Exercise 3

Answer the following questions in the negative. Use complete sentences and the negative expression indicated in parentheses.

1. Was machst du am Wochenende? (nichts)

_____

_____

2. Wann wirst du alleine singen? (nie)

_____

_____

3. Mit wem redet ihr? (niemand)

_____

_____

_____

4. Wen hat sie angesprochen? (niemand)

_____

_____

_____

85

To ask a *yes/no* question in German, simply place the conjugated verb in first position.

*Das **ist** seine Mutter.*	***Ist** das seine Mutter?*
This **is** his mother.	**Is** this his mother?

Alltagssprache

As in English, the voice rises at the end of a spoken question.

Informational questions begin with a question word followed by the conjugated verb.

wer?	who? (nom., in reference to the subject)	***Wer** ist das?* **Who** is that?
wen?	whom? (acc., in reference to the direct object)	***Wen** fragst du?* **Whom** are you asking?
wem?	to/for whom? (dat., in reference to the indirect object)	***Wem** gibt er die Blumen?* **To whom** is he giving the flowers?
was?	what?	***Was** ist das?* **What** is that?
wo?	where?	***Wo** sind die Messer?* **Where** are the knives?
wohin?	where to? (toward)	***Wohin** fährt er?* **Where** is he driving **to**?
woher?	where from? (away from)	***Woher** kommen Sie?* **Where** are you **from**?
wessen?	whose?	***Wessen** Brille ist das?* **Whose** (eye)glasses are those?
wann?	when?	***Wann** kommt ihr?* **When** are you guys coming?
warum?/ wieso?/ weshalb?	why?	***Warum/Wieso/Weshalb** hast du es eilig?* **Why** are you in a hurry?
wieso?	why?	***Wieso** rennst du?* **Why** are you running?
weshalb?	why?	***Weshalb** weint er?* **Why** is he crying?
wie?	how?	***Wie** kommst du in die Stadt?* **How** are you getting downtown?
wie viel?	how much?	***Wie viel** kostet das?* **How much** does that cost?
wie viele?	how many?	***Wie viele** Kinder hat sie?* **How many** children does she have?
welcher?	which?	***Welcher** Tisch ist billiger?* **Which** table is cheaper?
was für? (+ *ein*)	what kind (of)?	***Was für ein** Wagen ist das?* **What kind of** car is that?

Achtung!

Welcher (which?) is the nominative masculine form of *welch-*, one of the *der*-words. *Welch-* takes the same ending as *der* to agree with the subject. The nominative feminine form is *welche*, and the nominative neuter form is *welches*.

***Welche** Sendung ist das?*
 Which show is this?

*Mit **welcher** Hand schreibt er?*
 What hand does he write with?

The noun *für* (kind) generally requires the accusative case for any noun associated with it. However, in the expression *was für* (what kind?), the associated noun remains in the same case it would normally be in given the context of the sentence.

*Was für **ein Wagen** (nom.) ist das? Das ist ein deutscher Wagen.*
 What kind of **car** (subject) is that? This is a German car.

*Was für **einen Wagen** (acc.) willst du? Ich will einen deutschen Wagen.*
 What kind **of car** (direct object) do you want? I want a German car.

*In was für **einem Wagen** (dat.) sitzt sie? Sie sitzt in einem deutschen Wagen.*
 What kind of **car** (indirect object) is she sitting in? She is sitting in a German car.

In a question, a second verb, such as a past participle or an infinitive, takes the same position it would in a declarative sentence.

*Was hast du **gesagt**?*
 What did you **say**?

*Wo wirst du **wohnen**?*
 Where will you **live**?

Exercise 1

From the options below, choose the response that best answers each question below.

Dreieinhalb Stunden.   Am kommenden Wochenende.
Thomas Mann.   Mit der U-Bahn.   Er telefoniert.

1. Was macht Martin gerade?

_____

_____

2. Wie lange dauert die Fahrt nach Basel?

_____

_____

3. Wie kommst du nach Hause?

_____

_____

4. Wann ist die Stadtfest?

_____

_____

5. Wer hat die Geschichte geschrieben?

_____

_____

Exercise 2

You are checking out a new website and are asked to complete a personal profile. Respond to each of the profile questions below.

1. Wie heißt du?

_____

_____

2. Wo wohnst du?

_____

_____

3. Wie alt bist du?

_____

_____

Exercise 3

Michael Schaumgartner, a friend of a friend, has written a brief description of himself as a personal introduction on his website. Based on the information in his paragraph below, compose three questions that you could ask about Michael.

Ich heiße Michael Schaumgartner. Ich komme aus Innsbruck und bin 27 Jahre alt. Ich habe einen Bruder und eine Schwester. Mein Bruder heißt Mathias und ist Bauingeneur. Meine Schwester heißt Sabine und ist Krankenschwester. Ich wohne mit meiner Freundin in einer kleinen Wohnung. An den Wochenenden gehen wir gerne im Park spazieren. Mein Lieblingssport ist Handball, und mein Lieblingsessen ist Fisch.

1. _____

_____

2. _____

_____

3. _____

_____

86

Wo-compounds are used to ask informational questions about things (as opposed to people) when a preposition is present.

The *wo*-compound is a question word used to ask for specific information about things. A *wo*-compound is formed by adding *wo-* to the beginning of the preposition.

> **Wodurch** seid ihr gefahren?
> Wir fuhren **durch** den Park.
> **What** did you drive **through**?
> We drove **through** the park.

> **Womit** hat er das geschrieben?
> Er hat das **mit** einem Bleistift geschrieben.
> **What** did he write this **with**?
> He wrote that **with** a pencil.

> **Wovor** hat sie geparkt?
> Sie hat **vor** der Garage geparkt.
> **What** did she park **in front of**?
> She parked **in front of** the garage.

If the preposition begins with a vowel, *wor-* is added to the beginning.

> **Worum** seid ihr gefahren?
> **What** did you drive **around**?

> Wir fahren **um** das Haus.
> We're driving **around** the house.

Wo-compounds are formed with nearly all of the accusative and dative prepositions and the two-way prepositions.

> **Woran** wolltest du den Spiegel hängen?
> **What** did you want to hang the mirror **on**?

> **Worüber** hat der neue Autor geschrieben?
> **What** did the new author write **about**?

> **Wovon** wirst du ihm erzählen?
> **What** will you tell him **about**?

Ausnahme

Wo-compounds are not used in questions that refer to a person. For these questions, the preposition is followed by *wer*, *wen*, or *wem*, depending on the case.

> **Für wen** machst du das?
> Das mache **ich für** meinen Bruder.

> **For whom** are you making that?
> I'm making this **for** my brother.

Although *wo*-compounds typically translate into English as the preposition + *what*, some *wo*-compounds are used in specific expressions that do not translate directly.

> *woraus* (out of what is something made)
> **Woraus** ist die neue Tischdecke?
> **What** is the new tablecloth **made of**?

> *wobei* (whereas)
> Sie meint, sie kennt ihn sehr gut, **wobei** er sie gar nicht kennt.
> She thinks she knows him very well, **whereas** he doesn't know her at all.

> *wozu* (what for? why?)
> **Wozu** brauchst du das?
> **Why** do you need that?

Exercise 1

Fill in the blanks below with either the appropriate *wo*-compound or a preposition followed by *wer*, *wen*, or *wem*.

1. Weißt du, _____ er sich interessiert?

2. Weißt du, _____ er oft ausgeht?

3. Weißt du, _____ er gestern Abend erzählt hat?

4. Weißt du, _____ er glaubt?

5. Weißt du, _____ er gern spricht?

Exercise 2

Compose a question that would elicit each response below. Use the information in bold to determine which question word would be most appropriate.

Beispiel: Wir wissen viel **über die aktuelle Politik.**
<u>Worüber wisst ihr/wissen Sie viel?</u>

1. Hier riecht es **nach Rauch.**

_____

_____

2. Susanna wird **an dem Wettbewerb** teilnehmen.

_____

_____

3. Lorenz und Jürgen warten **auf Claudia.**

_____

_____

4. Du sollst **über deine Lebenserfahrungen** schreiben.

_____

_____

5. Jeanette hat Angst **vor Hunden.**

_____

_____

6. Barbara schreibt **mit einem Bleistift.**

_____

_____

7. Ich schreibe einen Brief **an Onkel Franz.**

_____

_____

8. Wir erinnern uns **an die Sommerferien.**

_____

_____

Exercise 3

Translate the following dialog between Anja and Andreas into German using the proper *wo*-compounds.

Anja: What do you think of the new word-processing program at work?
Andreas: Well, at first I feared it, because I'm not very interested in technology, and such things simply frighten me. But over time it's okay.
Anja: Christina was really worried about it. But I don't know myself what she wanted to warn us about. I find the new program simply great!
Andreas: What are you waiting for, then? Back to work!

_____

_____

_____

_____

_____

_____

_____

_____

_____

_____

_____

_____

_____

87

Question words and *wo*-compounds can be used to introduce subordinate (dependent) clauses in both statements and questions.

A question word can be used to introduce a subordinate clause within a question. A comma is used to separate the main clause and the subordinate clause. The conjugated verb is placed at the end of the clause.

*Weißt du, **wo** sie **wohnt**?*
Do you know **where** she **lives**?

Achtung!

When asking for details about a prepositional phrase, a *wo*-compound is used when referring to an object as opposed to a person. A preposition + *wer/wen/wem* (who) is used when referring to a person.

*Wissen Sie, **woran** er Interesse hat?*
Do you know **what** he is interested **in**?

*Wissen Sie, **für wen** er arbeitet?*
Do you know **for whom** he works?

*Wissen Sie, **mit wem** er arbeitet?*
Do you know **with whom** he works?

Question words can also introduce a subordinate clause within a statement. Some common examples of main clauses that lead to subordinate clauses include:

Ich weiß (nicht), . . .	I (don't) know . . .
Ich weiß Bescheid/genau . . .	I know for sure/ exactly . . .
Ich frage mich . . .	I wonder . . .
Ich habe keine Ahnung . . .	I have no idea . . .

*Er fragt sich, **wie** sie das gemacht hat.*
He wonders **how** she did that.

*Sie hat keine Ahnung, **wofür** er sich interessiert.*
She has no idea **what** he is interested **in.**

*Ich weiß Bescheid, **mit wem** sie telefoniert.*
I know exactly **whom** she is calling.

Exercise 1

Use the clues below to determine which question word would complete each sentence.

1. Weißt du, _____ sie wohnt? (where)

2. Wisst ihr, _____ er übernachtet? (at whose house)

3. Ich habe keine Ahnung, _____ man das macht. (how)

4. Wir wollen nicht wissen, _____ sie nach Hause gekommen ist. (when)

5. Sie fragt sich, _____ so was hätte machen können. (who)

6. Er hat keine Ahnung, _____ das so ist. (why)

7. Ich weiß, _____ sie sich freut. (what)

8. Wissen Sie, _____ das ist? (what)

9. Er weiß genau, _____ sie ausgeht. (with whom)

10. Wisst ihr, _____ er geholfen hat? (whom)

Exercise 2

Die Polizei ruft an! Use the table to compose six sentences explaining what you do and don't know about Robert.

Wo hat er übernachtet?	Ja/bei Jeanette
Wo ist er jetzt?	Nein
Wer hat zuletzt mit ihm gesprochen?	Ja/Monika
Wann hat er gestern das Haus verlassen?	Ja/um 00 abends
Warum will er weg?	Nein

Wie fährt er normalerweise nach Berlin?	Ja/mit dem Zug

Beispiel: Ja, ich weiß, wo Robert übernachtet hat. Er war bei Jeanette.

1. _____

_____

_____

2. _____

_____

_____

3. _____

_____

_____

4. _____

_____

_____

5. _____

_____

_____

6. _____

_____

_____

Exercise 3

Translate the following sentences into German using the correct question words.

1. We know where we're going.

_____

_____

2. She has no idea where she's going to live.

_____

_____

3. He knows exactly what he wants.

_____

_____

4. I have no idea what he's interested in.

_____

_____

5. Do you know what they're waiting for?

_____

_____

88

In German, there are three ways to translate *when*.

Als is used to mean *when* in reference to circumstances in the past. *Als* is generally used with the imperfect (simple past) tense.

> **Als** ich jung war, gingen wir im Dorf zur Schule.
> **When** I was young, we went to school in the village.

Achtung!

Als can also translate *as* or *than*.

> **Als** Kind wollte ich immer ein Pferd.
> **As** a child I always wanted a horse.

> Er ist dünner **als** sein Bruder.
> He is thinner **than** his brother.

Wenn is used to mean *when, whenever,* or *if* to introduction a conditional statement.

> **Wenn** er nach Hause kommt, können wir essen gehen.
> **When** he comes home, we can go out to eat.

> **Wenn** es viel schneit, müssen wir nicht in die Schule.
> **If** it snows a lot, we don't have to go to school.

Achtung!

Ob can also mean *if*, but it is used in the sense of *whether or not*.

> Ich weiß nicht, **ob** wir morgen in die Schule müssen.
> I don't know **if** we have to go to school tomorrow.

Wann is a question word used to ask *when* in reference to time, as in *at what time*.

> **Wann** fährt der nächste Zug ab?
> **When/ At what time** does the next train leave?

Exercise 1

Fill in the blank with the appropriate expression of *when*.

1. Ich weiß nicht, _____ die Party anfängt.

2. _____ er in München wohnte, studierte er dort an der Technischen Universität.

3. _____ du es willst, können wir zusammen fahren.

4. _____ wolltest du die Ausstellung besuchen?

5. Sie hebt immer sofort ab, _____ er sie anruft.

Exercise 2

Compose a logical end for each sentence below.

1. Weißt du, wann _____

_____

_____

2. Als wir anfingen, _____

_____

_____

3. Ich werde mitfahren, wenn _____

_____

_____

4. Wenn ich das wüsste, _____

_____

_____

5. Weiß Sabina, wann _____

_____

_____

Exercise 3

Translate the following exchange between Georg and Gerturd into German.

Georg: When is the plumber coming?
Gertrud: I don't know if he's coming today.
Georg: If he's not coming until tomorrow, he could at least call.
Gertrud: When I spoke with him, he wasn't able to say for sure.

_____

_____

_____

_____

_____

_____

_____

_____

89

90 Other *Wenn and Falls*

Both *wenn* and *falls* can translate as *if*. They each have specific functions, though *falls* is more limited in use.

Wenn is used to mean *if* when expressing a condition for which the conclusion is definite (indicative mood) or a condition that is not likely to be met (subjunctive mood). Wenn can translate as *if only* or *if it were the case that . . . but it's not.*

> **Wenn** *es regnet, werden wir nicht gehen.* (indicative)
> **If** it rains, we're not going.

> **Wenn** *ich Geld hätte, würde ich einkaufen gehen.* (subjunctive)
> **If only** I had money, I would go shopping.

Conditions using *wenn* can be set in the present or in the past.

> **Wenn** *er das weiß, wird er es uns sagen.*
> **If** he knows, he will tell us.

> **Wenn** *er das gewusst hätte, hätte er es uns schon gesagt.*
> **If** he had known, he would have told us already.

Alltagssprache

If *wenn* is left out of a sentence in the indicative mood, then the verb typically introduces the conditional (*wenn*) clause. *Dann* (then) or *so* (in that case) introduces the main clause in these cases. There is no change in meaning between the three options.

> **Wenn** *es regnet, bleiben wir hier.*
> *Regnet es,* **dann** *bleiben wir hier.*
> *Regnet es,* **so** *bleiben wir hier.*
> **If** it rains, we're staying here.

Achtung!

In the present time subjunctive, the one-word form of the subjunctive is generally used in the *wenn* clause, and the two-word form of the subjunctive (*würde* + the infinitive) is used in the main clause.

> *Wenn ich* **wüsste, würde** *ich es dir* **sagen.**
> If I **knew, I would tell** you.

Similar to *wenn*, *falls* is used in the indicative mood to express a condition for which the conclusion is certain. Falls can translate as *if* in the sense of *in the event that . . .*

> **Falls** *es regnet, bleiben wir hier.*
> **In the event that** it rains, we're staying here.

Achtung!

Wenn and *falls* have similar meanings when expressing a condition when the conclusion is definite. However, *wenn* indicates an event that is certain to occur (or certain to not occur) but the timing of which is uncertain or not known (whenever). *Falls* can only be used when there is uncertainty regarding whether the event itself will occur.

> **Wenn** *die Sonne untergeht, muss ich nach Hause.*
> **Whenever** the sun goes down, I have to go home.

> **Falls** *es morgen regnet, komme ich nicht vorbei.*
> **If (in the event that)** it rains tomorrow, I will not come over.

Exercise 1

Use the context of each sentence to determine whether *wenn* or *falls* should be used.

1. Ich bin doch hier, _____ er nicht kommt.

2. _____ du willst, kann er dir helfen.

3. _____ du möchtest, würde er dabei sein.

4. Wir würden dich öfters anrufen, _____ du ein Handy hättest.

5. _____ sie hier wären, würden wir zusammen tanzen gehen.

Exercise 2

Rewrite each sentence below by removing *wenn* or *falls*.

1. Wenn die Sonne scheint, machen wir ein Picknick.

_____

_____

2. Wenn/falls das Haus verkauft wird, ziehen wir um.

_____

_____

3. Wenn das Semester anfängt, haben wir weniger Freizeit.

_____

_____

4. Wenn/falls sie nach Hause kommen, bleiben sie bei uns.

_____

_____

Exercise 3

Change the following sentences from the subjunctive with _wenn_ to the indicative with _falls_.

1. Wenn wir Geld bräuchten, würden wir die Wohnung vermieten.

_____

_____

2. Wenn er mehr Zeit hätte, würde er einiges in der Stadt erledigen.

_____

_____

3. Wenn sie ihr Handy dabei hätte, würde sie ihn anrufen.

_____

_____

4. Wenn Nina das Geld hätte, würde sie ihren Sohn in Belgien besuchen.

_____

_____

5. Wenn Markus hier wäre, würde er uns besuchen.

_____

_____

Exercise 4

Translate the following sentences into German using the correct word for _if._

1. If I were going to the university, I would take the subway.

_____

_____

2. In the event that I don't go, can you please bring me something?

_____

_____

3. If you go to the store, will you pick me up a loaf of bread?

_____

_____

4. If she had the time, she would read more.

_____

_____

5. In the event that he gets sick, I will take his place.

_____

_____

Pronouns are used after a preposition when referring to a person. When referring to things, a so-called *da*-compound is used.

Da-compounds are formed by adding *da* to the beginning of the preposition.

*Wir fuhren **durch** den Park.*	*Wir fuhren **dadurch**.*
We drove **through** the park.	We drove **through it**.
*Er läuft **vor** das Haus.*	*Er läuft **davor**.*
He is walking **in front of** the house.	He is walking **in front of it**.

If the preposition begins with a vowel, *dar-* is added.

*Wir fahren **um** das Haus.*	*Wir fahren **darum**.*
We're driving **around** the house.	We're driving **around it**.
*Die Weinflasche ist **in** der Kiste.*	*Die Weinflasche ist **drin**.*
The wine bottle is **in** the carton.	The wine bottle is **in it**.

Da-compounds can be formed with nearly all of the accusative and dative prepositions, as well as the two-way prepositions.

*Er hängt das Bild **an** die Wand.*	*Er hängt das Bild **daran**.*
He is hanging the picture **on** the wall.	He is hanging the picture **on it**.
*Sie schreibt **mit** dem Kugelschreiber.*	*Sie schreibt **damit**.*
She is writing **with** the pen.	She is writing **with it**.
*Der Hund liegt **unter** dem Tisch.*	*Der Hund liegt **darunter**.*
The dog is lying **under** the table.	The dog is lying **under it**.

Ausnahme

Da-compounds are not used when the pronoun following a preposition refers to a person.

*Das mache ich **für** meinen Bruder.*
I'm making this **for** my brother.

*Das mache ich **für** ihn.*
I'm making this **for** him.

Although the *da*-compounds typically translate into English as the preposition + a pronoun, some form specific expressions in German.

dabei (on one's person)
*Hast du Geld **dabei**?*
Do you have money **on you**?

damit (so that)
*Ich fahre mit, **damit** ich erklären kann, wie man dahin kommt.*
I'm riding along **so that** I can explain how to get there.

darum (for that reason)
***Darum** will ich nicht mitkommen.*
For that reason, I don't want to come along.

dazu (in addition, else)
*Möchten Sie noch was **dazu**?*
Would you like anything **else**?

Exercise 1

Respond to the following questions in the affirmative (,,Ja, ich . . . "). Use either a *da*-compound or a preposition + pronoun if the statement refers to a person.

1. Bist du für den neuen Kandidaten?

   _____

   _____

2. Bist du gegen Atomkraftwerke?

   _____

   _____

3. Sitzt du neben dem großen Regal?

   _____

   _____

4. Hast du das von deinem Freund bekommen?

   _____

   _____

5. Wohnst du hinter der Post?

_____

_____

Exercise 2

Match each prepositional phrase to the question it most likely answers. Then replace that prepositional phrase with the appropriate *da*-compound to complete the crossword puzzle below.

a. auf dem Tisch   d. unter dem Tisch
b. am Tisch   e. vor dem Fernseher
c. uber dem Tisch   f. im Regal

Across	Down
1. Wo ist das neue Buch? ____	**1.** Wo ist der Teppich? ____
2. Wo sind die Stühle? ____	**3.** Wo ist das Licht? ____
3. Wo ist der Sessel? ____	
4. Wo ist die Vase? ____	

Exercise 3

Translate the following sentences into German using the appropriate *da*-compounds.

1. He told us about it.

_____

_____

2. Lay the book on top of it.

_____

_____

3. Are you going between them? (them = two objects, e.g., cars)

_____

_____

4. She's interested in it.

_____

_____

5. I don't have any money on me.

_____

_____

91

Other *Du, Ihr, and Sie*

In German, there are three ways to translate *you* and *your.*

The personal pronoun *du* is used to address a person with whom the speaker is familiar. The personal pronoun *ihr* is used to address more than one person with whom the speaker is familiar. Both pronouns are used with family members (young and old), with friends, and with fellow students (to show companionship).

Nom.	Acc.	Da.	Possessive Adjective
du (you)	dich (you)	dir (to/for you)	dein (your)
ihr (you, pl.)	euch (you, pl.)	euch (to/for you, pl.)	euer (your)

*Mama, wo bist **du**?*
Mom, where are **you**?

*Oma und Opa, seid **ihr** heute zu Hause?*
Grandma and Grandpa, are **you** at home today?

*Alex, wir warten auf **dich**.*
Alex, we're waiting for **you**.

*Alex und Monika, wir warten auf **euch**.*
Alex and Monika, we're waiting for **you**.

Ausnahme

Children, regardless of familiarity, are addressed using the familiar form of *you.*

*Wo ist **dein** Bruder, Maria?*	Where is **your** brother, Maria?
*Wo ist **eure** Mutter, Kinder?*	Where is **your** mother, children?

The pronoun *Sie* can be singular or plural and is used to address a person on formal terms. *Sie* is used with strangers; non-related elders; coworkers; persons of authority, such as teachers and coaches; and any situation that calls for a show of respect.

Nom.	Acc.	Dat.	Possessive Adjective
Sie (you)	Sie (you)	Ihnen (to/for you)	Ihr (your)

*Könnten **Sie** das bitte wiederholen, Herr Braun?*
Could **you** please repeat that, Mr. Brown?

*Kann ich **Ihnen** behilflich sein, Frau Schmidt?*
Can I help **you**, Ms. Schmidt?

Achtung!

In general, the pronoun *Sie* is used in situations where the speaker is not on a first-name basis, including exchanges with neighbors.

Alltagssprache

Historically, at most German offices and work places, the formal *Sie,* together with the formal titles *Herr* (Mr.) and *Frau* (Ms.), is used even with coworkers who have worked together for years. Recently, a *mixed form* of address is being used that combines the first name with *Sie,* to show respect.

***Inge,** können **Sie** diesem Kunden helfen?*
Inge, can **you** help this customer?

Alltagssprache

Generally speaking, students at German universities are addressed by their professors with the formal *Sie* and the titles *Herr* (Mr.) and *Frau* (Ms.) as an acknowledgment of adulthood. As a sign of respect, professors are addressed by students with *Sie* unless the professor permits the informal address. Traditionally, this moment of acknowledged camraderie is celebrated with a *Bruderschaftstrunk* (drink to brotherhood) at a local bar.

Alltagssprache

Until the spelling reform at the turn of this century, the various forms of the pronouns *du* and *ihr* were capitalized in personal letters as a sign of respect. Today, only the formal pronoun *Sie* is capitalized in all instances.

Exercise 1

Determine if the situation described below requires the formal (F) *you* or the informal (I) *you* by German standards.

_____ **1.** You are meeting your friend's parents for the first time.

_____ **2.** You are speaking on the phone with a travel agent.

_____ **3.** You are writing an email to a prospective employer.

_____ **4.** You are asking your neighbor, Markus, to mow your lawn.

_____ **5.** You need to ask a child you do not know to move his bike from behind your car.

Exercise 2

Fill in the blanks below with the appropriate form of *du, ihr,* or *Sie.*

1. Arbeiten _____ schon lange hier?

2. Seit wann studierst _____ in Freiburg?

3. Ich sehe _____ so selten, Gregor.

4. Bei _____ fühle ich mich immer wie zu Hause, Peter und Nina.

5. Herr Wagner, rufen _____ mich bitte morgen zurück.

6. Habt _____ schon gegessen?

7. Mit wem redest _____ denn so lange?

8. _____ Referat war wirklich gut, Stefan und Markus!

9. Maria, gibst _____ mir _____ Handynummer?

10. Frau Baumgarten, sind _____ noch da?

Exercise 3

Translate the following sentences into German using the correct form of *you.*

1. Uwe, what would you like to drink?

_____

_____

2. Lutz and Karin, have you been waiting long?

_____

_____

3. Mr. and Mrs. Holzer, did you receive my letter?

_____

_____

4. Dad, I can't hear you.

_____

_____

5. Viktor and Maria, we will need both of you and your car.

_____

_____

92

The verb *haben* (to have) can be combined with a noun to form several common German expressions. These expressions do not translate word for word into English.

Durst haben (to be thirsty)
> **Hast** du **Durst**?
> **Are** you **thirsty**?

Hunger haben (to be hungry)
> Ich **habe Hunger.**
> I'm **hungry.**

Lust haben (to have the desire to/to want to/to feel like doing something)
> **Hast** du **Lust,** mit uns nach Italien zu fliegen?
> Do you **want to** fly to Italy with us?

Angst haben (to be afraid)
> Er will sich keinen Horrorfilm anschauen, denn er **hat** immer **Angst.**
> He doesn't want to watch a horror movie, because **he's** always **afraid.**

Glück haben (to be lucky/to have good luck)
> Sie **hat** immer **Glück** beim Lottospiel.
> She **is** always **lucky** when she plays the lottery.

Pech haben (to be unlucky/to have bad luck)
> **Pech gehabt**!
> (You/I) **had bad luck**! (Too bad!)

Spaß haben (to have fun)
> Wir **haben** immer **Spaß,** wenn wir uns sehen.
> We always **have fun** when we see each other.

Interesse haben (an) (to be interested [in])
> Er **hat Interesse** daran.
> He **is interested in** that.

Exercise 1

Use the table to create a response to each question below. Include the correct *haben* expression in your answers.

Robert	will essen
Wilhelm	ist unglücklich
Konstanza	will etwas trinken
Diana	will etwas tun
Margrit	ist erschrocken

1. Wer hat Durst?

_____

_____

2. Wer hat Angst?

_____

_____

3. Wer hat Hunger?

_____

_____

4. Wer hat Pech?

_____

_____

5. Wer hat Lust, etwas zu machen?

_____

_____

Exercise 2

Respond to each question below in the negative by stating, *Nein, ich habe kein(e)(n) . . .*

1. Hast du Interesse daran?

_____

_____

2. Hast du Glück gehabt?

_____

_____

3. Hast du Angst beim Achterbahnfahren?

_____

_____

4. Hast du Hunger?

_____

_____

5. Hast du Lust, ihren nächsten Roman zu lesen?

_____

_____

Exercise 3

Translate the following sentences into German.

1. You (familiar, singular) were really lucky.

_____

_____

2. We had a lot of fun.

_____

_____

3. Why is he afraid?

_____

_____

4. Is she thirsty?

_____

_____

5. Are you (formal) interested in that?

_____

_____

93

Several common expressions in German use specific nouns with *machen* (to make/to do) and *tun* (to do). These expressions do not translate word for word into English.

einen Ausflug machen (to take a brief trip)
   Am Sonntag **machen** *wir* **einen Ausflug** *aufs Land.*
   On Sunday we're **taking a trip** to the country.

ein Foto machen (to take a picture)
   Kannst du bitte **ein Foto** *von uns beiden* **machen**?
   Can you please **take a picture** of both of us?

eine Freude machen (to make someone happy)
   Bring ihr ein paar Blumen mit, wenn du ihr **eine Freude machen** *willst.*
   Bring her a few flowers if you want **to make** her **happy.**

Gymnastik machen (to do exercises)
   Er **macht** *jeden morgen* **Gymnastik,** *um fit zu bleiben.*
   He **does exercises** every day in order to stay fit.

Hausarbeit machen (to do housework)
   Wir haben noch viel **Hausarbeit** *zu* **machen,** *bevor die Party anfängt.*
   We still have **to do** a lot of **housework** before the party starts.

Hausaufgaben machen (to do homework)
   Helga **macht** *ihre* **Hausaufgaben** *immer vor dem Abendessen.*
   Helga always **does** her **homework** before supper.

eine Pause machen (to take a break)
   Mach *doch* **eine Pause**, *wenn du müde bist.*
   Why don't you **take a break** if you're tired.

eine Reise machen (to take a trip)
   Wir **machen eine Reise** *nach London.*
   We're **taking a trip** to London.

ein Schläfchen machen (to take a nap)
   Das Kind **macht** *gerade* **ein Schläfchen.**
   The child **is taking a nap** just now.

Spaß machen (to be fun)
   Es **macht** *ihm immer* **Spaß,** *auf Deutsch zu reden.*
   He always **has fun** speaking German.

einen Gefallen tun (to do a favor)
   Kannst du mir bitte **einen Gefallen tun**?
   Can you please **do** me **a favor**?

Leid tun (to be sorry)
   Es **tut** *mir* **Leid,** *dass ich nicht dabei sein konnte.*
   I **am sorry** I couldn't be there.

weh tun (to hurt)
   Es **tut** *ihm immer* **weh,** *wenn er schnell laufen muss.*
   It always **hurts** him when he has to run quickly.

Exercise 1

Fill in the blanks below with the appropriate form of *tun* or *machen*.

1. Sollen wir schon jetzt eine Pause _____?

2. Du _____ deiner Großmutter immer eine Freude, wenn du sie besuchst.

3. Hat die Spritze dir weh _____?

4. Es _____ ihm wirklich Leid, dass du nicht gewonnen hast.

5. Ich wollte ihnen nur einen Gefallen _____.

Exercise 2

Complete each expression below with the appropriate noun.

1. Heute machen wir einen kleinen _____ und besuchen eine Fabrik in der Nähe.

2. Er macht immer so viele schöne _____, aber man muss sie auf seiner Webseite besichtigen.

3. Tut das dir der Hals _____, wenn du hustest?

4. Das macht immer _____, wenn wir den Vergnügungspark besuchen.

5. Hast du deine _____ für die Schule morgen fertig gemacht?

Exercise 3

Translate the following sentences into German using expressions with *machen* or *tun*.

1. He is supposed to do exercises every day.

   _____

   _____

2. She doesn't like to do the housework.

   _____

   _____

3. They were sorry that they could not come to the reception.

   _____

   _____

4. Katja never takes a break.

   _____

   _____

5. Paul is taking a nap.

   _____

   _____

94

Together with the verb *sein* (to be), the past participle can describe a condition or state of being that is the result of an action. In this construction, the past participle is used as a predicate adjective and is often confused with the passive voice, which also uses the past participle.

The passive voice is formed with *werden* + the past participle and describes a process that may or may not be complete.

*Das neue Programm **wird getestet.***
The new program **is being tested.**

*Das neue Programm **wurde getestet.***
The new program **was tested.**

***Sein* + the past participle is used to describe a state of being.**

*Diese Sachen **sind verkauft.***
These items **are sold.**

At times, the two constructions can look nearly identical. Context is used to determine which tense is being used.

*Das Haus **wird verkauft.***
The house **is being sold.** (in the process)

*Das Haus **ist verkauft.***
The house **is sold.** (state of being)

*Sein Bein **wird verletzt.***
His leg **is being injured.** (in the process)

*Sein Bein **ist verletzt.***
His leg **is injured.** (state of being)

Exercise 1

Im Büro: **You are at the office. Determine what has already been completed (*erledigt*) and what still remains to be (*unerledigt*) by determining whether the past participle is being used in the passive voice or in a *sein* construction.**

1. Das Formular ist ausgefüllt. erledigt unerledigt

2. Die Akten sind organisiert. erledigt unerledigt

3. Der Computer wird repariert. erledigt unerledigt

4. Der Kunde wurde angerufen. erledigt unerledigt

5. Die Dokumente müssen
   getippt werden. erledigt unerledigt

6. Der Direktor kann
   eingeladen werden. erledigt unerledigt

Exercise 2

Determine which of the following statements express a process (P) and which express a state of being (S).

1. Das Haus wurde verkauft.   P   S

2. Das Programm wird installiert.   P   S

3. Unser Gebäude ist vermietet.   P   S

4. Die Karten sind unterschrieben.   P   S

5. Der Flug war gebucht.   P   S

Exercise 3

Der Umzug: **You are moving. Write a paragraph in which you discuss what has already been done (*wurde gemacht*), what is completed (*ist gemacht*), and what still has yet to be done (*muss noch gemacht werden*). Use the expressions below and the correct past participle construction.**

den Nachbarn das übrige Essen schenken
die Zeitung abstellen
das Telefon umleiten lassen
die Rechnungen bezahlen
die Sachen einpacken
die Kisten aufladen
die Möbel transportieren lassen

95

There are several alternatives to the passive voice construction (*werden* + past participle).

The impersonal pronoun *man* (one) can be used with a verb in active voice to create a passive voice equivalent.

Passive:
Hier wird Deutsch gesprochen.
German is spoken here.

Hier wird nicht geparkt.
There's no parking here.

Active:
*Hier spricht **man** Deutsch.*
One speaks German here.

*Hier parkt **man** nicht.*
One doesn't park here.

The construction *sein + zu + infinitive* can be used to create a passive voice equivalent when combined with an adverb that describes the likelihood or manner with which an activity is performed. This construction can also be used when describing the necessity of an activity being done.

Passive:
*Kekse werden **leicht** gebacken.*
Cookies are **easily** baked.

*Geschirr **muss noch** gespült werden.*
The dishes are **still to (be)** wash(ed).

Active:
*Es **ist leicht**, Kekse **zu backen**.*
It **is easy to bake** cookies.

*Das Geschirr **ist noch zu spülen**.*
The dishes **still have to be washed**.

The construction *sich lassen + infinitive* can be used to create a passive voice equivalent when the passive voice construction contains the modal verb *können* (to be able to).

Passive:
*Das **kann** geklärt werden.*
That **can** be explained.

*Diese Bluse **kann** in der Waschmaschine gewaschen werden.*
This blouse **can** be washed in the washing machine.

Active:
*Das **lässt sich klären**.*
That **allows itself to (be) explain(ed)**.

*Diese Bluse **lässt sich** in der Waschmaschine **waschen**.*
This blouse **allows itself to (be) wash(ed)** in the washing machine.

Exercise 1

Rewrite the passive voice sentences below using *man* and the active voice.

1. In Paris wird Französisch gesprochen.

   _____

   _____

2. Im alten Kino werden klassische Filme gezeigt.

   _____

   _____

3. Mit dem neuen Computer wird die Arbeit viel schneller gemacht.

   _____

   _____

4. Im Winter wird der Schnee geschaufelt.

   _____

   _____

5. Die Zeitung wird früh geliefert.

   _____

   _____

Exercise 2

Complete the sentence below using the *sein + zu + infinitive* construction.

1. Es ist schwer,

_____

_____

2. Es ist unmöglich,

_____

_____

3. Es ist einfach,

_____

_____

4. Es ist unkompliziert,

_____

_____

Exercise 3

Use an appropriate passive voice alternative to rewrite each sentence below.

1. Das Auto muss noch gewaschen werden.

_____

_____

2. Dieses Haus kann leicht verkauft werden.

_____

_____

3. Diese Möbel werden leicht transportiert.

_____

_____

4. Die Kisten müssen noch gepackt werden.

_____

_____

5. Das kann elektronisch verschickt werden.

_____

_____

Exercise 4

Translate the following sentences into German using a passive voice alternative.

1. That isn't done.

_____

_____

2. The tickets still have to be sold.

_____

_____

3. This photo can be enlarged.

_____

_____

4. The electronic bills are easily paid.

_____

_____

5. Flowers aren't delivered on Saturday.

_____

_____

96

Interjections are short exclamations of emotion that can stand on their own. Similar to animal sounds, though they are intended to mimic what is natural, they tend to vary from language to language.

Some common German interjections include:

Ach (expresses surprise, as in *Oh!*)
Ach! Was haben wir hier?
Oh! What have we here?

Au!/Aue! (expresses pain, as in *Ouch!*)
Au! Das tut doch weh!
Ouch! That hurts, you know!

Haha! (expresses laughter, as in *Ha! Ha!*)
Haha! Das ist ja lustig!
Ha! Ha! That's really funny!

Quatsch! (expresses disagreement or disgust, as in *Well!*)
Quatsch! Das glaub' ich dir nicht!
Well! I don't believe you!

Some common animals, along with the verbs associated with them, include:

Animal	Verb	Sound
der Hahn (rooster)	*krähen* (to crow)	*kikeriki* (cockadoodledoo)
das Hühnchen (chick)	*piepsen* (to peep)	*piep piep* (peep peep)
der Hund (dog)	*bellen* (to bark)	*wau wau* (bowwow) *wuf wuf* (woof woof)
die Katze (cat)	*miauen* (to meow)	*miau* (meow)
die Kuh (cow)	*blöken* (to bleat)	*muh* (moo)
das Schwein (pig)	*grunzen* (to grunt)	*grunz grunz* (oink oink)
der Vogel (bird)	*zwitschern* (to tweet) *singen* (to sing)	*zwitscher zwitscher* (tweet tweet)

Exercise 1

Match to each situation described in column A to the appropriate interjection in column B.

	A	B
_____ **1.**	Der Mechaniker versteht endlich das Problem mit dem Auto.	a. Au!
_____ **2.**	Der Freund ist mit dir nicht einverstanden.	b. Quatsch!
_____ **3.**	Die Skifahrerin verletzt sich das Bein.	c. Ach!
_____ **4.**	Der Junge amüsiert sich beim Fernsehen.	d. Haha!

Exercise 2

Match each animal in column A to the appropriate verb in column B, then, in column C, provide the sound each animal makes.

A	B	C
_____ **1.** der Hund	a. blöken	_____
_____ **2.** die Katze	b. bellen	_____
_____ **3.** das Hühnchen	c. grunzen	_____
_____ **4.** der Hahn	d. miauen	_____
_____ **5.** die Kuh	e. piepsen	_____
_____ **6.** das Schwein	f. krähen	_____

Exercise 3

Translate the following sentences into German.

1. Ow! My finger hurts!

_____

_____

2. Why is the dog barking?

_____

_____

3. Ah! What do we have here?

_____

_____

4. The birds are singing in the trees.

_____

_____

5. Do you hear the cat meowing?

_____

_____

97

Particles are small words that can have a variety of meanings depending on their context. They add emphasis to a sentence or change its tone. In many cases, there is not a direct English equivalent, as their use tends to be idiomatic and may even be conveyed with a shrug or voice inflection.

Generally speaking, particles follow the subject, the conjugated verbs, and most objects of the verb, particularly pronouns.

> *Geben Sie ihr **doch** das Buch.*
> Why don't you give her the book, **after all.**

The particle *aber* can add emphasis to an exclamation.

> *Das hast du **aber** schön gemacht!*
> **My,** but you did that nicely!

> *Das hat **aber** viel gekostet!*
> That **really** cost a lot!

The particle *denn* can add emphasis to a question.

> *Was weißt du **denn**?*
> **So** what do you know?

> *Was ist **denn** los?*
> What **on earth** is the matter?

The particle *doch* is used to soften a command, making it into a suggestion. Using *doch* may be similar to adding *after all* to a sentence in English.

> *Fliegen Sie **doch** nach Mallorca.*
> Why don't you fly to Mallorca, **after all**?

> *Wir haben uns **doch** schon lange gekannt.*
> We've known each other for a long time **after all.**

> *Es liegt **doch** hier auf dem Tisch.*
> It's lying **right** here on the table.

The particle *erst* adds a conditional quality to a statement, similar to *not until* in an English time expression.

> *Wir fahren **erst** um 7.00 Uhr ab.*
> We are**n't** leaving **until** 7:00.

> ***Erst** morgen fangen unsere neuen Stunden an.*
> Our new hours do**n't** start **until** tomorrow.

The particle *ja* can add emphasis to a statement.

> *Das ist **ja** schön.*
> This is **really** nice.

> *Das kann ich **ja** machen.*
> That I can **really** do.

The particle *mal* can be used to turn an imperative into a more polite form of suggestion.

> *Schau **mal**!*
> Look **(at that)**!

> ***Mal** sehen!*
> **Well,** we'll see . . .

The particle *wohl* communicates probability when a situation or state of being is discussed.

> *Er ist **wohl** nicht zu Hause.*
> He is **probably** not at home.

> *Das ist sie **wohl**!*
> That's **probably** her (at the door)!

Exercise 1

Fill in each blank below with the appropriate particle from the options below. Use each particle only once.

aber	denn	mal
wohl	erst	

1. Bei uns fängt das neue Semester _____ im Oktober an.

2. Was tust du _____ da?

3. Nach der Wettervorhersage wird es _____ schneien.

4. Guck _____! Die sind schön!

5. Die ist _____ hübsch! Die will ich mir kaufen!

Exercise 2

Rewrite each sentence below using an appropriate particle.

1. Fahren wir bis zur nächsten Tankstelle.

_____

_____

2. Warum schaust du mich so an?

_____

_____

3. Er will morgen damit anfangen.

_____

_____

4. Tu das nicht!

_____

_____

5. Sie wird die Nächste sein.

_____

_____

Exercise 3

Translate the following sentences into German using the appropriate particle to modify the tone or meaning.

1. What on earth happened here?

_____

_____

2. That is really cheap!

_____

_____

3. It is probably too late.

_____

_____

4. I don't want to see the movie until next week.

_____

_____

5. Why don't you start tomorrow?

_____

_____

98

Other Basics of the German Spelling Reform

The German Spelling Reform was introduced in 1998 and was followed by a *transitional period* that was to last until 2005. During this period, new spellings and grammar were taught in all German schools, but both old and new were accepted as correct. Since the German Spelling Reform, texts can be found written in both systems, and several of the rules themselves have been adjusted as reforms are made to the reforms. Below is a partial list of new spellings and rules.

The German letter *ß* remains in use, but its use has changed and its occurrence is less frequent. The letter *ß* is now used only after long vowels and diphthongs. In instances where *ß* appeared as the final letter of a word or preceding a consonant after a short vowel, it is now replaced by *ss*.

Old spelling:	New spelling:	
daß	*dass*	(that)
du mußt	*du musst*	(you must)
groß	*groß* (no change)	(big)
heißen	*heißen* (no change)	(to be named)

Under the old rules, compound verbs composed of two verbs or of a noun + verb combination are written as one word. Under the new rules, they are written separately, as are their various forms (including the past participles). The nouns in these cases are capitalized.

Old spelling:	New spelling:	
kennenlernen	*kennen lernen*	(to get to know)
radfahren	*Rad fahren*	(to ride a bike)

Under the old rules, for compound nouns formed by a first-component noun ending in a double consonant and a second-component noun beginning with the same consonant, the consonants are reduced to two in a row. Under the new rules, all three of the identical consonants are retained in the newly formed compound.

Old spelling:	New spelling:	
Ballettänzerin	*Balletttänzerin*	(ballet dancer)

In letters written under the old rules, all forms of *you* are capitalized, including all forms of *du* and *ihr*. This is done as a means of showing respect. Under the new rules, only the forms of *Sie* remain capitalized in correspondence.

Old spelling:
Interessierst Du Dich auch dafür?

New spelling:
Interessierst du dich auch dafür?
(Are you also interested in that?)

Exercise 1

The words below follow the old spelling rules. Determine if there should be a change from *ß* to *ss*. Write out each word as it would appear under the *new* spelling rules.

1. daß

dass

2. wir mußten

wir mussten

3. du heißt

du heißt

4. weiß

weiß

5. ich wußte

ich wusste

6. groß

groß

7. er weiß

er weiß

8. die Straßenbahn

die Straßenbahn

9. der Großvater

der Großvater

10. sie ißt

sie isst

Exercise 2

Determine if there should be a change in spelling to any of the words below. Write out each word as it would appear under the *new* spelling rules.

1. die Telefonnummer

die Telefonnummer

2. der Geschirreiniger

der Geschirrreiniger

3. eislaufen

eis laufen

4. nacherzählen

nacherzählen

5. das Balletttheater

das Balletttheater

6. autofahren

Auto fahren

7. spazierengehen

spazieren gehen

8. die Mittagspause

die Mittagspause

9. die Buchhandlung

die Buchhandlung

10. loswerden

loswerden

Exercise 3

Transcribe the following letter from old rules to new rules.

Liebe Katja!

Weißt Du was?! Am 6.8. ziehe ich nach Koblenz um! Kannst Du das glauben? Das heißt, wir werden jetzt gleich in der Nähe sein! Wir können zusammen radfahren gehen, und im Winter können wir zusammen Richtung Süden fahren und dort skilaufen gehen!

Es ist kaum zu glauben, daß es schon fünf Jahre sind, seitdem wir uns zum ersten Mal kennengelernt haben! Wir waren zusammen auf der Schiffahrt auf der Donau. Erinnerst Du Dich daran?

Tja, langsam muß ich gehen . . .
Bis bald!

Dein,
Stefan

du
du
rad fahren
skilaufen
dass
schifffahrt
du dich

Liebe Katja,

99

Some German words similar in spelling to words in English have very different meanings from their English counterparts. These words are often referred to as *false friends*.

Some of the most common false friends in German, as well as some other confusing vocabulary, are given below.

aktuell	up-to-date, current (not *actual*) *Haben Sie einen **aktuellen** Stundenplan?* Do you have an **up-to-date** schedule?
die Toilette	a room with a toilet and a sink; bathroom
das Badezimmer	a room with a bathtub and sink, not a toilet; bathroom (In English, both may be translated as *bathroom*.) *Man wäscht sich im **Badezimmer**.* One washes oneself in **the bathroom.** *Das Kind muss dringend auf **die Toilette.*** The child has to go to **the bathroom** urgently.
die Bank	bench; bank *Wer sitzt auf **der Bank**?* Who is sitting on **the bench**?
bekommen	to get/receive
werden	to become; to turn; to get *Sie hat einen Brief **bekommen**.* She **received** a letter.
blau	the color blue or drunk (not *sad*) *Sein T-Shirt ist **blau**.* His T-shirt is **blue.** *Nach sechs Bier ist er bestimmt **blau**.* After six beers he is surely **drunk.**
brav	well behaved (not *brave*) *Er ist ein **braver** Hund.* He's a **well-behaved** dog.
die Brotmaschine	bread slicer (not bread machine/breadmaker) *Sie benutzt **die Brotmaschine**, wenn sie das Brot schneidet.* She uses **the bread slicer** when she cuts the bread.
der Chef/die Chefin	the boss (M/F)
der Koch/die Köchin	the chef/cook (M/F) *Unsere **Chefin** kennt alle.* Our **boss** knows everyone. *Der **Koch** hat das Essen vorbereitet.* **The cook** prepared the meal.
erster Stock	first floor (aboveground-level floor) *Sie wohnt im **ersten Stock**.* She lives on **the first floor.**

die Fabrik	factory
der Stoff	fabric; material *Herr Mejer arbeitet in **der Fabrik**.* Mr. Mejer works in **the factory.** *Aus welchem **Stoff** ist das Kleid?* What kind of **fabric** is the dress made of?
das Gift	poison
das Geschenk	present/gift *Der Mörder hat **Gift** in das Glas Wein getan.* The killer put **poison** into the glass of wine. *Er hat ihr ein schönes **Geschenk** gegeben.* He gave her a beautiful **gift.**
die Klasse	the class (group of people); the grade level
die Stunde	the course/class *Er ist in meiner **Klasse**.* He is in my **class/grade.** *Was habt ihr in der Deutsch**stunde** gemacht?* What did you all do in German **class**?
der Student/ die Studentin	student (M/F) (at university)
der Schüler/ die Schülerin	student (M/F) (in elementary or secondary school); pupil *Die **Studenten** haben demonstriert.* **The university students** demonstrated. *Die **Schüler** waren alle sehr brav.* **The pupils** were all very well behaved.
studieren	to attend a university; to major in a subject
lernen	to study (for a test or subject area)
arbeiten	to work; to study (alone or in a group) *Wo willst du **studieren**?* Where do you want **to attend university**? *Ich muss noch für Mathematik **lernen**.* I still have **to study** for math. *Wollen wir heute Abend zusammen **arbeiten**?* Do we want **to study** together tomorrow night?
wer	who
wo	where ***Wer** hat das gesagt?* **Who** said that? ***Wo** ist die Toilette?* **Where** is the bathroom?

winken to wave (not *to wink*)
Wir werden vom Bahnsteig **winken**.
We'll **wave** from the platform (at the train station).

9. Bernhard ___lernt___ für die Prüfung.

10. Der ___Student___ jobbt in der Mensa.

Exercise 1

Unscramble the letters below to form some of the false friends. Then unscramble the letters in circles to form another false friend.

1. D S U E E I T N R ___Studieren___

2. N N K I E W ___winken___

3. L U B A ___blau___

4. T F I G ___gift___

5. K M M N E B O ___bekommen___

Bonus: ___Student___

Exercise 2

Choose the appropriate word from the choices below to fill in each blank.

Schüler   lernt   wo
Gift   wer   Geschenk
Badezimmer   Toilette   studiert
Student

1. ___wo___ ist die Haltestelle?

2. Der Ring war ein sehr schönes ___Geschenk___.

3. Tanja ___studiert___ Kunstgeschichte.

4. Die Badewanne ist im ___badezimmer___.

5. ___wer___ sitzt an diesem Schreibtisch?

6. Die ___Schüler___ fahren mit dem Bus zur Schule.

7. Wir müssen ___Gift___ gegen die Ameisen kaufen.

8. Wo ist die ___toilette___?

Exercise 3

Complete the crossword puzzle below with the false friend described in each clue.

Across
3. wo etwas hergestellt wird
5. erhalten
8. hier kann man sich baden

Down
1. das ist man, wenn man sich benimmt
2. mit diesem Gerät schneidet man ein Laib
4. jemanden mit der Hand begrüssen
6. eine Gruppe von Schülern
7. betrunken

100

Irregular & Special Usage German Words

Note: phonetic pronunciation in parentheses

N-Nouns

der Affe (dair af.fe): *the ape*

der Architekt (dair ar.khi.tekt): *the architect*

der Bär (dair bair): *the bear*

der Bauer (dair bow.er): *the farmer*

der Elefant (dair e.le.fant): *the elephant*

der Gedanke (dair ge.dang.ke): *the thought*

der Glaube (dair glow.be): *the belief*

der Herr (dair hair): *the gentleman; sir*

der Journalist (dair zhur.na.list): *the journalist*

der Junge (dair yung.e): *the boy*

der Kollege (dair ko.lay.ge): *the colleague*

der Kunde (dair kun.de): *the customer*

der Löwe (dair ler.ve): *the lion*

der Mensch (dair mensh): *the person*

der Nachbar (dair nahkh.bahr): *the neighbor*

der Name (dair nah.me): *the name*

der Neffe (dair ne.fe): *the nephew*

der Patient (dair pa.tsee.ent): *the patient*

der Polizist (dair po.li.tsist): *the police officer*

der Präsident (dair pre.zi.dent): *the president*

der Prinz (dair prints): *the prince*

der Soldat (dair zol.dat): *the soldier*

der Student (dair shtu.dent): *the student (university level)*

der Tourist (dair tu.rist): *the tourist*

Strong Verbs & Their Principle Parts

Infinitive	Perfect Form	Past Participle
backen (bah.ken): *to bake*	backte	gebacken
beginnen (be.gin.en): *to begin*	begann	begonnen
bitten (bi.ten): *to request*	bat	gebeten
bleiben (blai.ben): *to stay*	blieb	geblieben
brechen (bre.khen): *to break*	brach	gebrochen
brennen (bren.nen): *to burn*	brannte	gebrannt
bringen (bring.en): *to bring*	brachte	gebracht
denken (deng.ken): *to think*	dachte	gedacht
entscheiden (ent.shai.den): *to decide*	entschied	entschieden
essen (e.sen): *to eat*	aß	gegessen
fahren (fah.ren): *to go (by vehicle)*	fuhr	gefahren
fallen (fal.len): *to fall*	fiel	gefallen
fangen (fang.en): *to catch*	fing	gefangen
finden (fin.den): *to find*	fand	gefunden
fliegen (flee.gen): *to fly*	flog	geflogen
geben (gay.ben): *to give*	gab	gegeben
gefallen (ge.fal.len): *to please*	gefiel	gefallen
gehen (gay.en): *to go (by foot)*	ging	gegangen
gelingen (ge.ling.en): *to succeed*	gelang	gelungen
geschehen (ge.shay.en): *to happen*	geschah	geschehen
gewinnen (ge.vi.nen): *to win*	gewann	gewonnen
haben (hah.ben): *to have*	hatte	gehabt
halten (hal.ten): *to stop; to hold*	hielt	gehalten
hängen (heng.en): *to hang*	hing	gehangen
heißen (hai.sen): *to be called*	hieß	geheißen
helfen (hel.fen): *to help*	half	geholfen

Infinitive	Perfect Form	Past Participle
kennen (ke.nen): to know	kannte	gekannt
kommen (ko.men): to come	kam	gekommen
laden (lah.den): to load	lud	geladen
lassen (lah.sen): to leave; to let	ließ	gelassen
laufen (low.fen): to run; to walk	lief	gelaufen
leiden (lai.den): to suffer	litt	gelitten
lesen (lay.zen): to read	las	gelesen
liegen (lee.gen): to lie	lag	gelegen
nehmen (nay.men): to take	nahm	genommen
nennen (ne.nen): to name	nannte	genannt
reiten (rai.ten): to ride	ritt	geritten
rennen (re.nen): to run	rannte	gerannt
riechen (rai.khen): to smell	roch	gerochen
rufen (roo.fen): to call; to cry out	rief	gerufen
scheinen (shai.nen): to shine	schien	geschienen
schlafen (shlah.fen): to sleep	schlief	geschlafen
schneiden (shnai.den): to cut	schnitt	geschnitten
schreiben (shrai.ben): to write	schrieb	geschrieben
schwimmen (shvi.men): to swim	schwamm	geschwommen
sehen (zay.en): to see	sah	gesehen
sein (zain): to be	war	gewesen
senden (zen.den): to send	sandte	gesandt
singen (zing.en): to sing	sang	gesungen
sinken (zin.ken): to sink	sank	gesunken
sitzen (zi.tsen): to sit	saß	gesessen
sprechen (shpre.khen): to speak	sprach	gesprochen

Infinitive	Perfect Form	Past Participle
stehen (shtay.en): to stand	stand	gestanden
steigen (shtai.gen): to climb	stieg	gestiegen
sterben (shter.ben): to die	starb	gestorben
tragen (trah.gen): to wear; to carry	trug	getragen
treffen (tre.fen): to meet	traf	getroffen
trinken (tring.ken): to drink	trank	getrunken
tun (toon): to do	tat	getan
vergessen (fer.ge.sen): to forget	vergaß	vergessen
verlieren (fer.lee.ren): to lose	verlor	verloren
waschen (va.shen): to wash	wusch	gewaschen
werden (ver.den): to become	wurde	geworden
wissen (vi.sen): to know	wusste	gewusst

Da-Compounds

daran (dah.rahn): *on it/them (vertically)*

darauf (dah.rowf): *on it/them (horizontally)*

daraus (dah.rows): *out of it/them*

dabei (dah.bai): *at it/them; on one's person*

dadurch (dah.durkh): *through it/them*

dafür (dah.für): *for it/them*

dagegen (dah.gay.gen): *against it/them*

dahinter (dah.hin.ter): *behind it/them*

damit (dah.mit): *with it/them; so that*

danach (dah.nakh): *after it/them*

daneben (dah.nay.ben): *next to it/them*

darin (dah.rin): *in it/them*

darüber (dah.rü.ber): *above it/them*

darum (dah.rum): *around it/them; for that reason*

darunter (dah.run.ter): *under it/them*

davon (dah.fon): *from it/them*

davor (dah.fawr): *in front of it/them*

dazu (dah.tsu): *to it/them; in addition; else*

dazwischen (dah.tsvi.shen): *between them*

Wo-Compounds

woran (vaw.rahn): *on what (vertically)*

worauf (vaw.rowf): *on what (horizontally)*

woraus (vaw.rows): *out of what (is something made)*

wobei (vaw.bai): *at what; whereas*

wodurch (vaw.durkh): *through what*

wofür (vaw.für): *for what*

womit (vaw.mit): *with what*

wonach (vaw.nakh): *after what*

worin (vaw.rin): *in what*

worüber (vaw.rü.ber): *above what; about what*

worum (vaw.rum): *around what*

worunter (vaw.run.ter): *under what*

wovon (vaw.fon): *from what; about what*

wovor (vaw.fawr): *in front of what*

wozu (vaw.tsu): *to what; what for; why*

Glossary of Grammar Terms

adjectival: A word or phrase that is related to or functions like an adjective and is used to describe a noun. For example: *The woman **who wrote the book** is my sister.* In this sentence, *who wrote the book* is an adjectival phrase that describes the noun *woman*.

adjective: A word that describes the quality or state of a noun. In the example *the **beautiful** dog, beautiful* is an adjective that describes the quality of *dog*.

adverb: A word that describes or enhances the meaning of a verb, adjective, another adverb, or sentence. An adverb answers *How? Where?* or *When?* In English, most adverbs end in *–ly*. For example: *slowly, hourly, softly.* Other common adverbs include: *there, now, yesterday.*

article: A word used in combination with a noun to indicate if that noun is definite (specific) or indefinite (generic). English has two articles: *the* (definite article) and *a/an* (indefinite article).

auxiliary: A verb that is used in combination with another verb when forming a specific tense or mood. In English, common auxiliary verbs include *to have* and *to be.* For example: *She **is** running, and he **has been** waiting.*

cardinal numbers: Numbers that are used when counting to describe how many of an item are present: *one, two, three...*

comparative: The form of a word, or the word construction, that is used to compare specific qualities between two things. In English, the comparative is generally formed by adding *–er* or *more/less* to an adjective or adverb. For example: *fast**er**, **more/less** intelligent.*

compound sentence: A sentence that has one main (independent) clause and one or more subordinate (dependent) clauses. *My father is generous* is an independent clause, and it can be part of a compound sentence when combined with a dependent clause: *My father is generous **when he gives me an allowance.***

conditional clause: A sentence or clause that describes a situation that is dependent on a condition explained by another clause or sentence. In English, conditional clauses generally begin with *if, unless,* or another conjunction with a similar meaning. For example: *I'll buy the cake **unless you don't want it.***

conditional mood: The form of a verb used when describing an imaginary situation that would happen in the future if a specific condition is met. In English, the conditional mood is formed with the auxiliaries *would* or *could* and a verb. For example: *I **would go** to the movies if you pay for my ticket. If you have enough time and money, we **could see** two movies.*

conjugation: The possible form a verb can take in a given tense to express person, number, and mood. In English, for example, the present tense conjugation of the verb *to be* is *am, are,* and *is.* The past tense conjugation for *to be* is *was* and *were.*

conjunction: A word that joins two or more words, phrases, or sentences. Conjunctions are either coordinating or subordinating, depending on how the two elements relate to each other. *And, but, because, unless*, and *if* are examples of common conjunctions in English.

coordinating conjunction: A conjunction that joins two elements that are on the same grammatical level, such as noun + noun, adjective + adjective, independent clause + independent clause. The coordinating conjunctions in English are *and, but, or, for, nor, yet,* and *so. The boy **and** the girl are swimming. The house is on fire, **and** the firemen are on the way.*

declarative sentence: A statement of fact or state of being, as opposed to a question, exclamation, or command. For example: *I would like to have pizza. The weather is nice. She has been working hard.*

declension: A group of nouns, pronouns, or adjectives that undergo the same kind of changes according to number, gender, and, in some languages, case.

demonstrative: A word that refers to a noun in terms of its proximity to the speaker. In English, demonstratives include *this, that, these,* and *those.*

dependent clause: See **subordinate clause**

direct object: The direct object in a sentence is usually a noun or pronoun that is directly affected by the action of the verb. The direct object will generally answer the question *what do you do (with the verb)?* In the sentence *I wrote **a letter,*** the noun *letter* is the direct object because it is directly affected by the verb (*wrote*).

disjunctive: A word used to establish a relationship of contrast or opposition between two or more things or events. For example, the preposition *but* is disjunctive: *I am stronger, **but** you are faster.*

future tense: A tense used to refer to events that have not yet occurred but will or are likely to happen. In English, the future tense can be formed in two ways: with the auxiliary *will* + a verb (*I **will read** that book tomorrow*) or with the present of *to be* + *going to* + a verb (*I **am going to read** that book tomorrow*).

future perfect tense: The future perfect refers to an event that is either currently in progress and will be finished in the future or that will begin and be finished in the future. In English, the

Glossary of Grammar Terms

future perfect is formed with the auxiliary *to have* in future tense (*will have*) + the past participle of a verb. For example: *I **will have finished** my project by the time you come back.*

gerund: A verb in a form ending in *-ing*. For example: *eating, writing, reading.* Gerunds can function as nouns in a sentence (***Smoking** is bad for you*). They are also the verb form used after a preposition (*Thanks **for** calling me back*).

imperative: The form of a verb used to give commands or orders. In the imperative form, the subject is often implied and is therefore omitted. The imperative can be either affirmative or negative. For example: *Go! Come! Don't speak! Don't eat!*

imperfect tense: A past tense form used to discuss repeated, habitual, or continued actions in the past. Though considered a separate tense in some languages, the imperfect tense is not considered a separate tense in English, and it is equivalent to the simple past and past progressive tenses. The imperfect is commonly formed using *used to* or *would*: *I **used to** visit my grandparents every Sunday. I **would** visit them every week.*

indefinite adjective: An adjective that refers to an undefined or inexact number or quantity. Common indefinite adjectives in English are *some, all, many, few, more, most,* and *several.*

independent clause: See **main clause**

indicative mood: The verb form used in declarative sentences or questions. The indicative is the most commonly used mood in most languages. For example: *She bought a cake. Are you OK?*

indirect object: The indirect object of a verb expresses who or what has been affected indirectly by the action of the verb. The indirect object is the receiver or beneficiary of the action and answers the question *To/for whom?* In the sentence *I wrote you a letter,* the pronoun *you* is the indirect object because it benefits from the action (the written letter).

infinitive: The base form of a verb. In English, the infinitive is expressed with the particle *to* + the verb. The infinitive is the form of the verb defined in a dictionary. For example: *to go, to eat, to come, to dance.*

interjections: A single word or phrase that conveys a strong emotion or an attitude, such as shock, surprise, delight, or disgust. Common interjections include *Ouch! Wow! Oh! Yuck!*

interrogative adjective: An adjective used in forming a question, asking for definition or clarification, and distinguishing among various choices. In English, interrogative adjectives include *what, which, who, whom,* and *whose.*

invariable: A word that never changes form, regardless of tense, number, or person. In English, prepositions are invariable. Verbs, however, are not because they change form depending on the tense and, occasionally, subject.

main (independent) clause: A sentence that expresses a complete thought on its own and does not depend on another clause to create meaning. For example: *I like cake. They have been traveling. Math is difficult.*

modal verb: In English, modal verbs are auxiliary verbs that express an attitude (doubt, desire, need) about the event expressed by another verb. Modal verbs are also used to make requests and ask permission. Modal verbs include *can, could, may, might, must, have to, should, shall, will,* and *would.* For example: *I **would** like to go to the movies. I **can** speak French.*

modify/qualify: To use a word or group of words to give further information about another noun or phrase, sometimes resulting in a change of meaning and/or form. Words are considered **modifiers** when they come before the word they alter. Words are considered **qualifiers** when they come after the word they alter. In the sentence *The **yellow** taxi **from New York,*** the adjective *yellow* modifies *taxi* and *from New York* qualifies it.

mood: All sentences are said to be in a specific mood, depending on the attitude and intentions of the speaker. The specific form of a past, present, or future tense verb in a given sentence indicates the mood.

nominal: A word or phrase that is related to or functions like a noun. For example: *I liked **what she gave me.*** In this sentence, *what she gave me* is a nominal phrase or clause because it functions like a noun describing *what I liked.* This nominal phrase is a direct object and can be replaced by a pronoun: *I liked **it.***

noun: A word referring to a person, an animal, a thing, a place, or an abstract idea. For example: *Steve, dog, teacher, book, California, love, freedom.*

object pronoun: Words used in place of the direct object in a sentence. The object pronouns in English are *me, you, him, her, it, us,* and *them.* In the sentence *I like cake,* the noun *cake* is the direct object and can be replaced by the direct object pronoun *it*: *I like **it.***

ordinal numbers: Numbers used when designating the place of items listed in a sequence: *first, second, third, fourth,* and so on.

participle (past and present): A verb form used as an adjective. The present participle is used in progressive tenses with the verb *to be* (*I am **reading***). The past participle is used in perfect tenses and in the passive voice with the verb *to be* (*the homework was **made***). In English, the present participle is formed by adding *-ing* to the verb (*I am **dancing**, they are **walking***), and the past participle is formed by adding either *-ed* to the verb (*danc**ed**, walk**ed***), or *-en* instead (*writt**en**, brok**en***). Some past participles are irregular (*sing/**sung**, eat/**ate***).

partitive adjective: A phrase used to express quantity when distinguishing a piece from the whole or when referring to an uncountable noun. For example: *a piece of cake, a slice of bread, a bunch of grapes, a pinch of salt.*

past tense: The verb tense used to describe events that occurred in the past. For example: *She **walked** to the store. He **ran** to the house.*

past perfect (pluperfect) tense: A past tense form that refers to an event completed in the past, prior to the beginning of another event that also occurred in the past. In English, the pluperfect tense is formed with the auxiliary *to have* in past tense (*had*) + the past participle. For example: *I **had read** the book before you told me the ending.*

possessive adjective: An adjective that indicates ownership or possession. In English, the possessive adjectives are *my, your, his, her, its, our, their.*

possessive pronoun: A pronoun that replaces a possessive adjective and its noun. In English, the possessive pronouns are *mine, yours, his, hers, its, ours, yours, theirs.* For example: *I bought my house. It is **mine.***

preposition: A word used to join nouns, adjectives, and pronouns with other words to indicate ownership, physical location, direction, or time. Prepositions are invariable, meaning they never change form. Some common English prepositions include *about, before, but, for, from, in, at, of,* and *on.* For example: *She sat **on** the bench. I left **before** you got there.*

present tense: The tense that describes an action taking place in present time or an action that is habitual. Present tense can also be used to describe facts or states of being in the present. For example: *She **reads** a book. I **go** to the movies every day. Madrid **is** the capital of Spain.*

present perfect tense: A past tense form that refers to an action that has been completed, occurred within a specific time period, or has results that continue up to a specific point in time. In English, the present perfect is formed with the auxiliary *to have* in present tense (*have, has*) + the past participle. For example: *I **have been** to New York twice.*

preterite tense: A past tense form used to discuss an action completed in the past, an action that happened only once, or an action that interrupted another in the past. For example: *I **saw** the movie yesterday. I **ran** into you while you were walking.* The preterite is also known as the simple past in English, though in some languages there is a distinction between the preterite and other past tenses.

progressive tenses: A progressive tense expresses an action that is in progress or is developing at a given time. Progressive tenses in English are formed with the auxiliary *to be* + the present participle (*-ing* form of a verb). A progressive action can be expressed in present tense (*I **am reading** a book now*), past (*She **was taking** notes during class*), and future (*We **will be eating** pizza next Saturday*).

pronoun: A word that replaces a noun or a noun phrase. English pronouns come in three forms: subject pronouns (for example, *I* and *we*), object pronouns (*me* and *us*), and possessive pronouns (*my/mine* and *our/ours*).

qualify: See *modify.*

reflexive verb: A verb used to imply that the subject is performing an action on itself. In English, reflexive verbs are expressed with the pronoun *–self* (*myself, herself, themselves,* etc.) or are implied by the verb alone. For example: *I **hurt myself.** I was **shaving.***

relative pronoun: Relative pronouns introduce a sentence or clause that gives additional information about a noun. The relative pronouns in English are *who, whom, whose, which,* and *that.* In the sentence *The man **who** called was my father,* the clause *who called* provides additional information about the noun *man.*

subject pronoun: Pronouns that replace the subject of a sentence. Subject pronouns have the same gender and number as the noun they replace. The subject pronouns in English are *I, you, he, she, it, we, you, they,* and *one.* In the sentence *My mother is nice,* the noun phrase *my mother* can be replaced by the subject pronoun *she: **She** is nice.*

subjunctive mood: The verb form used to express wishes, desires, emotions, uncertainty, and hypothetical or nonfactual situations. For example: *If I were you, I wouldn't go.*

subordinate (dependent) clause: A clause that does not express a complete idea on its own. A subordinate clause must be used with another clause or sentence (called a **main clause** or **independent clause**). In the sentence *They told me that she was not coming, that she was not coming* is the subordinate clause, since it does not form a complete idea on its own.

Glossary of Grammar Terms

subordinating conjunction: A conjunction that joins an independent clause with a dependent clause. Common subordinating conjunctions in English include *after, before, because, since, although, if, unless, until, while,* and *even if. I am going outside **even if** it is cold.*

superlative: The form of a word or the word construction used to show the most or the least in quantity, quality, or intensity. In English, the superlative is formed by adding *–est* or *most/least* to an adjective or adverb. For example: *tall**est,** **most** difficult.*

tense: Tense conveys when in time an event happened, how long it lasted, and whether the event has been completed. All tenses can be divided into one of three groups: present, past, and future. The specific form of a verb in a given sentence indicates the tense.

verb: A word that refers to an action or a state of being. For example: *to eat, to write, to read.*

voice: Voice indicates whether emphasis is placed on the person or thing causing the action or on the person or thing receiving the action. The voice of a sentence is either **active** or **passive.** In the **active voice,** the subject is the person or thing performing the action: ***She visited** the school.* In the **passive voice,** the subject is receiving the action of the verb: ***The school is visited** by her.* Two sentences can be written in different voices but still carry the same meaning. For example: *I ate the cake* (active voice). *The cake was eaten by me* (passive voice).

Answer Key

Exercise 1

Subject (circle)	Direct object (underline)
1. Sie	die Suppe
2. Er	den Ball
3. Mein Lehrer	eine E-Mail
4. Das weiße Haus	ein neues Dach an der Ecke
5. er	Seinen Vater

Exercise 2
1. Subject (nominative case)
2. Direct object (accusative)
3. Direct objects (accusative)
4. Subject (nominative)
5. Direct object (accusative)

Exercise 3
Possible answers:
1. Der Junge malt ein Bild.
2. Die Frau putzt das Haus.
3. Das Mädchen backt Kekse.
4. Die Kinder werfen den Ball.

Exercise 1
1. meinem Freund
2. ihren Eltern
3. dem Publikum
4. mir
5. deiner Tochter
6. uns
7. ihm
8. mir

Exercise 2

Subject (Nom.)	Direct object (Acc.)	Indirect object (Dat.)
1. Der Vater	ein schönes Abendessen	der Mutter
2. Ich	ein neues Fahrrad	meinem Bruder
3. wir	etwas	der alten Dame neben uns
4. Wir	eine Karte für das Konzert	dem alten Mann

Exercise 3
1. IO
2. OP
3. IO
4. OP
5. OP

Exercise 4
1. Sie kauft der Schwester eine CD.
2. Sie kauft der Tante einen Roman.
3. Sie kauft dem Onkel eine Pfeife.
4. Sie kauft dem Vetter ein Buch.

Exercise 1
1. d
2. e
3. a
4. c
5. b

Exercise 2

Subject (Nom.)	DO (Acc.)	IO (Dat.)	Possessive (Gen.)
1. du	den Bruder	–	dieses Mädchens
2. Er	Tennis	–	–
3. Die nette Dame	die Märchen	den Kindern	der Brüder Grimm
4. Unser Großvater	alte Fotos	uns	–
5. du	etwas	mir	–
6. Der Schwanz	–	–	der Katze
7. du	einen Tipp	mir	–
8. Meine Schwester	die Filme	–	des Regisseurs

Exercise 3
1. der Frau
2. des Mädchens
3. des Kunden (*n*-noun)
4. des Arbeiters
5. der Familie

Exercise 4
1. Das Auto/Der Wagen ihrer Mutter ist in der Garage.
2. Das Bein des Pferdes ist verletzt.
3. Der Einband des Buches ist neu.
4. Wo ist der Besitzer/die Besitzerin des roten Mercedes?
5. Hast du/haben Sie den neuen Teppich der Nachbarn gesehen?

Exercise 1
1. Siehst du die Bank? Die Bank steht in der Hauptstraße.
2. Siehst du das Restaurant? Das Restaurant steht in der Hauptstraße.
3. Siehst du die Bäckerei? Die Bäckerei steht in der Hauptstraße.

Answer Key

Exercise 2
1. den
2. Die
3. die
4. dem
5. Der

Exercise 3
Possible answers:
1. Ich schreibe der Oma die Karte.
2. Du schreibst dem Andreas die E-Mail.
3. Der Martin schreibt der Claudia ein Gedicht.
4. Sigrid schreibt dem Michael den Brief.
5. Elke und Jürgen schreiben den Kindern die Geschichte.

Exercise 4
1. Wo sind die Schlüssel?
2. Ist das das richtige Haus?
3. Sie wohnen im/in dem Libanon.

Workout 5 . . . . p. 10

Exercise 1
Possible answers:
1. Dieses Gebäude ist hoch.
2. Dieses Haus ist klein.
3. Dieser Fernseher ist alt.
4. Dieser Stuhl ist modern.

Exercise 2
1. Jede
2. Solche
3. Welches
4. diesen
5. Jedes
6. Welchen
7. Welchem
8. Manche
9. diesen
10. Jenem

Exercise 3
1. **Verkäuferin:** Welchen Tisch möchten Sie? Möchten Sie diesen Tisch?
   Kunde: Nein, danke, solche Tische mag ich nicht.
2. **Verkäuferin:** Welche Lampe möchten Sie? Möchten Sie diese Lampe?
   Kunde: Nein, danke, solche Lampen mag ich nicht.
3. **Verkäuferin:** Welche Vase möchten Sie? Möchten Sie diese Vase?
   Kunde: Nein, danke, solche Vasen mag ich nicht.
4. **Verkäuferin:** Welches Regal möchten Sie? Möchten Sie dieses Regal?
   Kunde: Nein, danke, solche Regale mag ich nicht.
5. **Verkäuferin:** Welches Sofa möchten Sie? Möchten Sie

dieses Sofa?
Kunde: Nein, danke, solche Sofas mag ich nicht.

Workout 6 . . . . p. 12

Exercise 1
1. eine
2. einen
3. einen
4. einem
5. ein

Exercise 2
1. Rolf will Schauspieler werden. = *Rolf wants to become an actor.*
2. Miriam will eine effiziente Managerin werden. = *Miriam wants to become an efficient manager.*
3. Stefan will ein effektiver Krankenpfleger werden. = *Stefan wants to become an effective nurse.*
4. Kirstin will Katholikerin werden. = *Kirstin wants to become a Catholic.*
5. Heinz will Deutscher werden. = *Heinz wants to become a German.*

Exercise 3
1. Eine Bank steht in der Hauptstraße. Wir brauchen eine Bank in der Nähe.
2. Ein Supermarkt steht in der Hauptstraße. Wir brauchen einen Supermarkt in der Nähe.
3. Ein Restaurant steht in der Hauptstraße. Wir brauchen ein Restaurant in der Nähe.

Workout 7 . . . . p. 14

Exercise 1
1. Nein, das ist nicht sein Computer. Das ist ihr Computer.
2. Nein, das ist nicht unsere/unsre/euere/eure/Ihre Haltestelle. Das ist ihre Haltestelle.
3. Nein, das ist nicht deine/Ihre Zeitung. Das ist meine Zeitung.
4. Nein, das ist nicht ihr Handy. Das ist sein Handy.
5. Nein, das ist nicht mein Wagen. Das ist ihr Wagen.

Exercise 2
1. Ihr (capitalized only because it is the first word)
2. deinem
3. ihren
4. meinem
5. unser

Exercise 3
Possible answers:
1. Ich gebe meinem Onkel meine E-Mailadresse.
2. Du gibst deiner Kollegin deine Handynummer.

3. Maria gibt/schenkt ihrer Schwester ihren Rock.

4. Christian gibt/schenkt seinem Freund sein Buch.

5. Peter und Nina geben/schenken ihrem Sohn ihren Wagen.

Workout 8 .... p. 16

Exercise 1
1. die Tochter
2. der Chef
3. die Maklerin
4. der Bruder
5. die Balletttänzerin
6. der Arbeiter
7. das Mädchen
8. der Wissenschaftler
9. das Fräulein
10. der Hund
11. die Kuh
12. die Katze
13. der Vater
14. der Lehrling
15. die Touristin
16. die Politikerin
17. der Neffe
18. der Journalist

Exercise 2
1. Unsere Tochter ist Wissenschaftlerin.
2. Ihr Sohn ist Politiker.
3. Das ist mein Hund.
4. Seine Vermieterin heißt Frau Braun.
5. Dieses Mädchen ist Balletttänzerin.

Exercise 3
1. die Flugbegleiterin
2. die Krankenpflegerin
3. die Verkäuferin
4. die Vermieterin
5. die Königin

Workout 9 .... p. 18

Exercise 1
1. das Aluminium	**6.** das Gold	**11.** das Silber
2. der Februar	**7.** das Rot	**12.** der Herbst
3. die Mayflower	**8.** das Schwimmen	**13.** die Boeing
4. der Montag	**9.** der Mercedes	**14.** das Hilton
5. die U.S. Constitution	**10.** der Frühling	**15.** das Radfahren

Exercise 2
1. das Büchlein	**6.** die Partei	**11.** die Tageszeitung
2. die Gesundheit	**7.** die Diskussion	**12.** die Demokratie
3. die Reportage	**8.** die Universität	**13.** die Miete

4. das Rennauto	**9.** der Sozialismus	**14.** die Butter
5. das Märchen	**10.** das Museum	**15.** das Stigma

Exercise 3
Masculine	Feminine	Neuter
Winter	Blockade	Studium
Anfänger	Universität	Indigo
Gegner	Tätigkeit	Lithium
Egoismus	Tendenz	Büro
November	Erholung	Einkommen
	Reaktion	Ritz

New words:
Wagen	Butter	Silber

Exercise 4
1. Das ist meine Straße.
2. Die Titanik war riesengroß.
3. Der Realismus ist viel interessanter.
4. Das Café Kranzler ist ein altes Café in Berlin.
5. Dieser Wissenschaftler/Diese Wissenschaftlerin interessiert sich für (das) Magnesium.

Workout 10 .... p. 20

Exercise 1
1. die Bleistifte
2. die Zeitungen
3. die Computer
4. die Handys
5. die Länder
6. die Hosen
7. die Prinzessinnen
8. die Tische
9. die Filme
10. die Tassen

Exercise 2
1. Die Bücher liegen da drüben.
2. Die Touristen fliegen nach Frankfurt.
3. Die Jungen kochen am Wochenende.
4. Die Studentinnen gehen in die Mensa.
5. Die Krankenpfleger bleiben im Zimmer.

Exercise 3
1. Der Schüler schreibt heute viel.
2. Der Autor wohnt hier.
3. Die Sekretärin tippt sehr schnell.
4. Der Profi kauft die Autos.
5. Die Lampe steht auf dem Tisch.

Workout 11 .... p. 22

Exercise 1
1. der Hausschlüssel

Answer Key

2. die Handynummer
3. der Teelöffel
4. die Handtasche
5. der Kaffeetisch
6. das Schreibwarengeschäft
7. das Telefonbuch
8. der Regenmantel
9. die Kaffeemaschine
10. der Schneemann

Exercise 2
1. die Telefonbücher
2. die Straßenlampen
3. die Studentenausweise
4. die Teeladen
5. die Krankenwagen

Exercise 3
Possible answers:
1. die Krankenschwester (nurse)
2. die Turnhalle (gymnasium)
3. das Federbett (feather bed)
4. der Wolkenkratzer (skyscraper)
5. das Altersheim (nursing home)

Exercise 4
1. the glove/mitten   (hand + shoe)
2. the hospital   (sick + house)
3. the desk   (write + table)
4. the dining room   (eat + room)
5. the strawberry   (soil + berry)
6. the thimble   (finger + hat)
7. the washcloth   (wash + cloth/rag)
8. the umbrella   (rain + shield)

Exercise 5
1. Wochenende
2. Winterfest
3. Schneemänner
4. Schlittschuhen
5. Handschuhe

Workout 12 .... p. 24

Exercise 1
✓	der Professor	✓	der Gedanke
	die Straße		die Frau
✓	der Affe		der Wissenschaftler
	das Mädchen		das Messer
	der Sessel	✓	der Name

den Professoren, dem Professoren, des Professoren
den Affen, dem Affen, des Affen
den Gedanken, dem Gedanken, des Gedankens
den Namen, dem Namen, des Namens

Exercise 2
1. der Prinz, den Prinzen, dem Prinzen, des Prinzen
2. der Glaube , den Glauben, dem Glauben, des Glaubens
3. der Herr, den Herrn, dem Herrn, des Herrn
4. der Löwe, den Löwen, dem Löwen, des Löwen
5. der Tourist, den Touristen, dem Touristen, des Touristen

Exercise 3
1. Die Frau schenkt dem Journalisten ein Foto.
2. Der Student kocht der Dame das Essen.
3. Der Mann zeigt dem Fotographen sein Werk.
4. Der Elefant gibt dem Touristen den Ball.
5. Das Mädchen erzählt dem Autoren eine Geschichte.

Workout 13 .... p. 26

Exercise 1
1. Es ist zu klein.
2. Er schläft im Wald.
3. Sie liegt neben der Lampe.
4. Sie stehen im Regal.
5. Es weint nicht oft.

Exercise 2
1. a. ich
2. a. Sie
3. c. Wir
4. c. ihr
5. b. du

Exercise 3
1. Sie
2. sie
3. sie
4. Sie

Exercise 4
1. you (plural, familiar)
2. it
3. you (formal, singular)
4. she
5. they

Workout 14 .... p. 28

Exercise 1
1. Der Lärm stört sie.
2. Der Räuber versteckt ihn.
3. Mutti will sie im Internet buchen.
4. Wir kennen es schon.
5. Wer hat ihn gesehen?

2. Wir singen **es.** Singst du **es** auch?

3. Meine Schwester spart **es.** Sparen wir **es** auch?

4. Du kennst **sie** seit langem. Kennt er **sie** auch seit langem?

5. Mein Vater probiert **ihn.** Probieren Sie **ihn** auch?

Exercise 3

1. Ich umarme sie.

2. Sie hat ihn gestern gesehen.

3. Habt ihr sie angerufen?

4. Wo hat er dich getroffen?

5. Kannst du mich mitnehmen?

Workout 15 .... p. 30

Exercise 1

1. Sagen Sie ihm, dass er morgen zurückrufen soll.

2. Gibst du ihm seinen Ball zurück?

3. Kannst du ihr deine Rollschuhe leihen?

4. Was schenkt er ihr zur Hochzeit?

5. Rainer hat ihm sein neues Handy gezeigt.

Exercise 2

1. Ich kaufe ihm das Wörterbuch. Ich kaufe es ihm.

2. Sie zeigt ihr ihre Übersetzung. Sie zeigt sie ihr.

3. Oliver schenkt ihnen einen Gutschein. Oliver schenkt ihn ihnen.

4. Will Maria ihnen ein Märchen erzählen? Will Maria es ihnen erzählen?

5. Weißt du schon, ob du ihm den Rasenmäher leihen kannst? Weißt du schon, ob du ihn ihm leihen kannst?

Exercise 3

1. Der Fussballspieler gibt seinem Fan ein Foto.

2. Sie schreibt ihr einen Brief.

3. Ich habe ihm ein kaltes Getränk gebracht.

4. Eva erzählt uns eine Geschichte.

5. Doris und Uwe haben es ihnen erklärt.

Workout 16 .... p. 32

Exercise 1

1. P

2. R

3. R

4. R

5. P

Exercise 2

1. D

2. A

3. A

4. D

5. D

Exercise 3

1. Die Kinder sind total dreckig. Ich hoffe, sie duschen sich bald.

2. Hast du vielleicht ein Taschentuch. Ich möchte mir die Nase putzen.

3. Die Spieler ärgern sich immer wenn sie verlieren.

4. Wenn wir uns nicht beeilen, werden wir unseren Flug verpassen.

5. Ich bin ziemlich sicher, dass du dir das Bein gebrochen hast.

Exercise 4

1. Am Abend putzt sich Michael die Zähne.

2. Er hat sich für das Geschenk bedankt./Hat er sich für das Geschenk bedankt?

3. Warum kannst du dich nicht benehmen?

4. Sie wird sich sicherlich bei den Behörden beschweren.

5. Bevor wir ins Restaurant gehen, ziehe ich mich um.

Workout 17 .... p. 34

Exercise 1

A. 1. Nein, das ist meiner.

   2. Nein, das sind meine.

   3. Nein, das ist meins.

B. 1. Nein, danke. Ich habe meine.

   2. Nein, danke. Ich habe meins.

   3. Nein, danke. Ich habe meine.

C. 1. Nein, ich fahre mit meiner.

   2. Nein, ich fahre mit meinem.

   3. Nein, ich fahre mit meinen.

Exercise 2

1. meine

2. ihren

3. unseren (or: unsren)

4. deins

5. seins

Exercise 3

1. meinetwegen

2. Deinetwegen/Euretwegen/Ihretwegen (informal forms capitalized as first word; formal capitalized regardless of position)

3. Ihretwegen (capitalized as first word)

4. unsertwegen

5. Ihretwegen (capitalized as first word)

Exercise 4

1. Das ist mein Rucksack. Wo ist deiner? Or: Wo hast du deinen?

Answer Key

2. Meinetwegen kann er am Mittwoch (damit) anfangen.

3. Ihre Papiere liegen auf dem Tisch. Hast du/Haben Sie unsere/unsre?

4. Enschuldigung! Mein Koffer ist auch schwarz. Ist das Ihrer?

Workout 18 .... p. 36

Exercise 1
1. der
2. Die
3. dem
4. Den
5. Das

Exercise 2
Possible answers:
1. Magst du Tobias?
Ja, der hat ja Talent.
2. Magst du Claudia?
Ja, die ist ja intelligent.
3. Magst du Berndt?
Ja, der ist ja großzügig.
4. Magst du Sabina?
Ja, die ist ja lustig.

Exercise 3
Wilhelm: Hast du den Markus gesehen?
Ute: Nein. Wo bleibt der denn? Auf den müssen wir immer warten!
Wilhelm: Tja, der hat aber einen langen Weg. Der wohnt doch in Littenweiler.
Ute: Das stimmt, aber trotzdem . . .

Workout 19 .... p. 38

Exercise 1
1. der
2. den
3. den
4. dem
5. dessen

Exercise 2
1. dessen
2. deren
3. deren
4. dessen
5. dessen

Exercise 3
1. Eine Banane ist eine Frucht, die man schält.
2. Ein Roman ist ein Buch, das man liest.
3. Eine Universität ist ein Institut, an dem man studiert.

Exercise 4
1. Das Restaurant, das „Zum Goldenen Löwen" heißt, bietet Platz für 150 Gäste.
Das Restaurant, das Platz für 150 Gäste bietet, heißt „Zum Goldenen Löwen".
2. Die Speisekarte, die jeden Monat verändert wird, hat zehn Seiten.
Die Speisekarte, die zehn Seiten hat, wird jeden Monat verändert.
3. Die Hauptspeisen, die zwischen 12,00 und 18,00 Euro kosten, sind hervorragend.
Die Hauptspeisen, die hervorragend sind, kosten zwischen 12,00 und 18,00 Euro.

Exercise 5
1. Meine Mitbewohner rauchen zu viel. Ich mache Urlaub mit ihnen.
Ich mache Urlaub mit meinen Mitbewohnern, die zu viel rauchen.
2. Das Haus ist sehr preiswert. Seit drei Jahren wohnen wir in dem Haus.
Seit drei Jahren wohnen wir in dem Haus, das sehr preiswert ist.

Workout 20 .... p. 40

Exercise 1
1. Hast du alles gegessen, was dein Freund gekocht hat?
2. Habt ihr nichts gekauft, was er sich zu Weihnachten wünscht?
3. Ein Fernseher ist etwas, was ich nicht brauche.

Exercise 2
1. Das ist das Schönste, was ich jemals bekommen habe.
2. Das ist das Beste, was wir seit langem gehört haben.
3. Das ist das Schlimmste, was man hier essen kann.

Exercise 3
1. Gestern hat sie mich beleidigt, wofür sie sich aber heute entschuldigt hat.
2. Im Winter fahren wir in die Berge, worauf wir uns sehr freuen.

Exercise 4
1. Bregenz, woher ich komme, liegt im Vorarlberg.
2. Basel, wohin meine Schwester heute fährt, liegt an der Grenze zu Deutschland.
3. Ihre Vorfahren stammen aus Biel, wo ihr Großvater noch wohnt.

Exercise 5
1. Das Gebäude, in dem ich arbeite, ist sehr groß.
Das Gebäude, wo ich arbeite, ist sehr groß.
2. Ich wohne auf einer Insel, auf der es keine Katzen gibt.
Ich wohne auf einer Insel, wo es keine Katzen gibt.

3. Die Tankstelle, bei der ich arbeite, hat jeden Tag auf.
Die Tankstelle, wo ich arbeite, hat jeden Tag auf.

Workout 21 .... p. 42

Exercise 1
1. Ich habe alles gelesen.
2. Wir haben viel zum Nachtisch gegessen.
3. Sofia hat nichts bekommen.
4. Georg will etwas schreiben.
5. David kauft nur wenig ein.

Exercise 2
Possible answers:
1. Man soll öfters spazieren gehen.
2. Man soll mehr Gemüse essen.
3. Man soll einen Abend in der Woche für sich nehmen.
4. Man soll jeden Tag etwas Neues lernen.
5. Man soll jedes Jahr etwas, was einen interessiert, einplanen.

Exercise 3
Hans: Herr Schmidt scheint viel über das Thema zu wissen. Haben wir einen besseren Kandidaten?
Helga: Eigentlich nicht, aber ich meine, man sollte auch etwas über die technische Seite unserer Arbeit wissen, und leider weiß er wenig darüber.
Hans: Tja, wenig ist besser als nichts, oder?
Helga: Man kann natürlich die technischen Sachen auch an der Arbeit lernen, nachdem man angestellt ist; solange man einem die Chance und das richtige Training gibt.

Workout 22 .... p. 44

Exercise 1
1. regnet
2. geht
3. gibt
4. schneit
5. gibt

Exercise 2
1. Hier gibt es einen Bleistift.
2. Hier gibt es eine Taschenlampe.
3. Hier gibt es ein Wörterbuch.
4. Hier gibt es ein Pflaster.
5. Hier gibt es eine Haarbürste.

Exercise 3
Possible answer:
Lieber Wilhelm!
Es tut mir Leid, dass ich seit langem nichts mehr geschrieben habe. Mir geht's gut. Es regnet heute nicht mehr, und ich kann endlich wieder spazieren gehen. Die Sonne scheint, und es gibt einen Park nicht weit von hier. Ich werde also dort einen Spaziergang machen. Nach dem kalten Winter ist es mir endlich wieder warm!
Wie geht es dir?
Deine Doris

Workout 23 .... p. 46

Exercise 1
Gestern stand ich **gegen** 8.30 Uhr auf. Als ich **durch** die Küchentür kam, sagte meine Mutter: „Schau was ich **für** dich gebacken habe!" Ich sah eine wunderschöne Sachertorte mit dreizehn Kerzen. Es war nämlich mein Geburtstag. **Um** den Tisch **herum** stand meine Familie mit vielen Geschenken **für** mich. Unter anderem bekam ich neue Schuhe, eine CD meiner Lieblingsband, ein Computerspiel und 50 Euro von meiner Oma, doch am besten gefällt mir meine neue Uhr. **Ohne** sie werde ich das Haus nie wieder verlassen.

Exercise 2
1. durch
2. Ohne
3. für
4. entlang
5. für
6. ohne
7. durch
8. entlang
9. bis

Exercise 3
1. Der Zug aus Wien kommt um 10.23 Uhr an.
2. Diese Blumen sind für meine Frau.
3. Ohne meinen MP3-Player gehe ich nirgendwo hin.
4. Gegen den Weltmeister hat er keine Chance.

Exercise 4
Possible answer:
Um 18.00 Uhr gibt es eine Geburtstagsparty **für** Monika. Die meisten Gäste kommen auch pünktlich **um** 18.00 Uhr an, aber einige kommen schon **gegen** halb sechs, um mit den Vorbereitungen zu helfen. Alle bringen Geschenke **fürs** Geburtstagskind, denn **ohne** Geschenke ist das keine Geburtstagsparty!

Workout 24 .... p. 48

Exercise 1
1. seinen Eltern
2. einer Stunde
3. dem Mittagessen
4. mir

Answer Key

Exercise 2
1. a
2. d
3. a
4. e
5. c

Exercise 3
1. seit
2. mit/bei
3. aus
4. bei
5. Nach
6. zur

Exercise 4
Possible answers:
1. Nein, ich bin mit meiner Schwester geflogen.
2. Wir kommen nach der Arbeit.
3. Ich arbeite im Supermarkt.
4. Er studiert erst seit einem Jahr in Bern.
5. Sie kommt aus einem Dorf.

Workout 25 .... p. 50

Exercise 1
1. D
2. D
3. A
4. D
5. A

Exercise 2
1. a. in das
2. b. neben dem
3. c. auf dem
4. d. Unter dem

Exercise 3
1. das
2. Ihnen
3. der
4. den
5. dem, der

Exercise 4
1. Das Wasser ist im Glas.
2. Die Kamera ist auf dem Tisch.
3. Die Schubkarre ist hinter der Scheune.
4. Die Tastatur ist vor dem Monitor.

Workout 26 .... p. 52

Exercise 1
1. seiner Handschrift
2. eines Wagens
3. des Urlaubs
4. ihrer Arbeit
5. des Hauses

Exercise 2
1. c.Trotz
2. Während
3. wegen
4. Statt
5. während

Exercise 3
Possible answers:
1. Wegen des Wetters sind wir nicht Ski laufen gegangen.
2. Trotz der vielen Arbeit haben wir viel Spaß gehabt.
3. Anstatt ins Kino zu gehen, sassen wir im Café.
4. Während des Filmes wollte ich keine Anrufe bekommen.
5. Während der Fahrt haben wir lange geplaudert.

Workout 27 .... p. 54

Exercise 1
1. denke
2. telefoniert (she)/telefonieren (they)
3. leidet
4. bittet (she)
5. sprechen

Exercise 2
1. über
2. an
3. mit
4. von
5. An

Exercise 3
1. Lachst du/lacht ihr/lachen Sie über sie?
2. Er fragt nach dir.
3. Ich denke an eine Geschichte.
4. Worüber schreiben sie?
5. Was hältst du/haltet ihr/halten Sie davon?

Workout 28 .... p. 56

Exercise 1
1. Machst/dich
2. freuen/uns
3. beklagen/sich
4. interessiert/sich
5. beschäftigt/sich

Exercise 2
1. um
2. über
3. auf
4. für
5. für

Exercise 3
1. Der kleine Thomas beschäftigt sich mit seinem Spielzeug.
2. Wir freuen uns auf die Ferien/den Urlaub.
3. Sie macht sich über mich lustig/lustig über mich.
4. Wofür interessierst du dich/interessiert ihr euch/ interessieren Sie sich?
5. Er beklagt sich darüber.

Workout 29 .... p. 58

Exercise 1
1. blöde
2. billige
3. gelbe
4. neue
5. komischen
6. karierte

Exercise 2
1. Ein Kunde kauft diesen hellen Bildschirm.
2. Eine Dame liest solche interessanten Bücher.
3. Mein Nachbar kennt den intelligenten Lehrer.
4. Ein Fotograph fotographiert beide lustigen Kinder.
5. Ein Gast umarmt die wunderschöne Braut.

Exercise 3
Possible answers:
1. Ich putze mir die Nase mit dem weichen Taschentuch.
2. Christian paddelt das Kanu bis zur blauen Brücke.
3. Robert hat erst nach der großen Pause Religion.
4. Das ist der Maulkorb vom schwarzen Hund
5. Es kommen viele Ameisen aus dem kleinen Loch heraus.

Exercise 4
1. teur**e**, reich**en**
2. schwarz**e**, einsam**en**
3. warm**en**, frish**en**
4. alt**e**, heftig**en**
5. weiß**e**, neu**en**

Workout 30 .... p. 60

Exercise 1
1. schlaue
2. dummer
3. frische
4. altmodisches
5. alte
6. weicher

Exercise 2
1. Der Mann hat eine weiße Katze.
   Der Mann mit einer weißen Katze heißt Peter.
2. Die Frau hat einen schwarzen Hund.
   Die Frau mit einem schwarzen Hund heißt Julia.
3. Das Kind hat ein braunes Pferd.
   Das Kind mit einem braunen Pferd heißt Ernst.
4. Das Mädchen hat keine grünen Frösche.
   Das Mädchen mit keinen grünen Fröschen heißt Andrea.

Exercise 3
1. Sie sind die Lehrer unserer besten Studenten.
2. Das ist das Bild unseres alten Freundes.
3. Sie ist die Schwester meiner wunderbaren Frau.
4. Das ist die Adresse seines ersten Hauses.
5. Das ist eine Auswahl ihrer besten Gemälde.

Exercise 4
1. nett**en**, rot**es**
2. lustig**e**
3. komisch**er**, groß**es**, schnell**es**
4. schön**e**, zauberhaft**es**
5. Mein**e**, mein**e** dreckig**en**

Exercise 5
Possible answers:
Ich wohne zusammen mit meinen Eltern. Ihr altes Haus war früher das Haus meiner Großmutter. Es ist kein modernes Haus. Die Küche ist sehr klein, aber groß genug für einen runden Tisch und vier Stühle. Das Wohnzimmer ist auch klein, aber gemütlich. Wir haben drei Schlafzimmer und ein Badezimmer mit Toilette . . .

Answer Key

Workout 31 .... p. 62

Exercise 1

	M	**F**	**Neuter**	**Pl.**
Nom.	exzellent**er** Wein	bitter**e** Schokolade	zäh**es** Fleisch	streng**e** Gesetze
Acc.	exzellent**en** Wein	bitter**e** Schokolade	zäh**es** Fleisch	streng**e** Gesetze
Dat.	exzellent**em** Wein	bitter**er** Schokolade	zäh**em** Fleisch	strengen Gesetzen
Gen.	exzellent**en** Weines	bitter**er** Schokolade	zäh**en** Fleisch**es**	streng**er** Gesetze

Exercise 2

1. gelber Senf
2. salzige Brezeln
3. grüne Äpfel
4. frische Milch
5. alkoholfreies Bier
6. leckerer Kuchen
7. gebratene Nudeln
8. bittere Schokolade
9. süße Erdbeeren
10. gesundes Müsli

Exercise 3

1. Romantisch**er**
2. lang**e**
3. durchsichtig**em**
4. einfach**en**
5. sein**er**
6. Gut**e,** hartverdient**es**
7. stressig**e,** ruhig**e**
8. Weiß**er,** grün**er,** grün**e,** rot**e**
9. Langweilig**e,** schön**en**
10. groß**en,** riesig**e,** köstlich**er**

Exercise 4

1. Er trinkt gern heißen Kaffee.
2. Ich höre gern klassische Musik.
3. Sie sitzen gern auf hohen Hockern.
4. Wir essen heute kalte Lasagne statt frischer Pizza.
5. Was kostet mehr? Eine Kiste guten Weines oder zwei Kisten schlechten Bieres?

Workout 32 .... p. 64

Exercise 1

1. blau
2. rosa ✓
3. teuer
4. schwarz
5. Münchner ✓
6. orange ✓
7. clever
8. Tiroler ✓

Exercise 2

1. x, Allgemein**e**
2. x
3. x
4. groß**en**, x
5. schön**e**, x

Exercise 3

1. Dieser lila Pulli ist wunderschön!
2. Hast du den Hamburger Hafen besucht?
3. Fahrt ihr mit dem orange oder mit dem schwarzen Schiff?
4. Haben Sie je Lübecker Marzipan gegessen?
5. Seine kleine beige Hose passt ihm nicht mehr.

Exercise 4
Possible answers:
Name: Beate
Alter: 15
Hobbies: Musik hören; Snowboarden; Windsurfen
Heimat: München
Ich über mich: Ich bin in München geboren und hier aufgewachsen. Ich habe mit 5 Jahren Ski fahren gelernt, und danach habe ich mit Snowboarden angefangen. Ich finde Snowboarden absolut **geil**! Im Winter bin ich oft in den **bayerischen** Alpen zu finden oder manchmal auch in den **Schweizer** Alpen . . . Das kommt immer darauf an, wo die Eltern Urlaub machen wollen. Mit 15 hat man selber **wenig** Wahl! Im Sommer bin ich oft am **Starnberger** See. Das ist gar nicht **weit** von uns, und ich kann dort windsurfen.

Workout 33 .... p. 66

Exercise 1

	Comparative	Superlative
1. nett	netter	am nettesten
2. klein	kleiner	am kleinsten
3. bequem	bequemer	am bequemsten
4. hübsch	hübscher	am hübschesten

Exercise 2

1. schneller
2. teurer
3. wärmeres
4. bekannteste
5. am höchsten

Exercise 3
1. Thomas ist am ältesten.
2. Jochen ist älter.
3. Jochen ist jünger.

Exercise 4
Possible answers:
Mein Bruder Robert ist **kleiner** als mein Bruder Mathias, aber Mathias ist **sportlicher**. Meine Schwester tanzt **besser** als meine Brüder, aber ich tanze **am besten**. In meiner Familie lächelt Maria **am meisten**. Sie findet mich lustig, und meine Brüder noch **lustiger**. Robert ist **der lustigste** von uns allen.

Workout 34 .... p. 68

Exercise 1
1. schneller, höher
2. jünger
3. gut
4. gesund
5. mehr, müder

Exercise 2
1. Das Benzin wird immer teu(e)rer.
2. Dieser Rock ist so lange wie der andere.
3. Je mehr ich übe, desto besser verstehe ich.
4. Uns(e)re Katze ist so groß wie unser Hund.
5. Dieser Film ist lustiger als der andere.

Exercise 3
Possible answers:
Die Reise nach München ist länger als die Reise nach Berlin. Die Reise nach Berlin kostet genau so viel wie die Reise nach München.

Workout 35 .... p. 70

Exercise 1
1. die Schlaue
2. der Große
3. die Blonde
4. das Gute
5. die Talentierte
6. der Schwache
7. das Lustigste
8. der Großzügige

Exercise 2
1. Kleiner
2. Neue
3. Interessante
4. Kranke
5. Deutschen

6. Alten
7. Beste
8. Bessere

Exercise 3
1. Der Arme hat Hunger.
2. Kennst du die Nette dadrüben?
3. Er findet immer das Gute (dabei/daran)
4. Sie hat es den Neuen erklärt.
5. Das Teuerste sind immer die Getränke.

Workout 36 .... p. 72

Exercise 1
1. das spielende Kind
2. das brechende Glas
3. das zu schnell fahrende Auto
4. der bellende Hund
5. die lachende Frau

Exercise 2
1. die geschlossene Tür
2. der gebackene Fisch
3. das gegrillte Gemüse
4. das gesprochene Wort
5. das gesparte Geld

Exercise 3
1. Ja, ich habe die tanzenden Kinder gesehen.
2. Ja, ich habe den (von ihr) getippten Brief gelesen.
3. Ja, ich habe die in München wohnenden Verwandten kennen gelernt.
4. Ja, ich kenne den Jazz singenden Musiker.
5. Ja, ich esse die von Ingrid gebackenen Kekse.

Exercise 4
1. Wir haben das von meinem Vater gegrilltes Fleisch gegessen.
2. Er hat das in der Bar singende Mädchen gesehen.
3. Das ist ein von meiner Großmutter selbstgemachter Pulli.
4. Sie kennt den Baseball spielenden Jungen.

Workout 37 .... p. 74

Exercise 1
1. jetzt
2. Früher; später
3. bald
4. täglich
5. selten
6. nie
7. lange
8. vorher
9. Manchmal

Answer Key

10. kurz

Exercise 2
Possible answers:
1. nachts
2. morgens
3. nachmittags
4. morgens
5. abends
6. morgens

Exercise 3
Pairings will vary. Possible sentence answers:
Vorgestern bin ich ins Kino gegangen.
Gestern habe ich Deutsch gelernt.
Heute werde ich Familie besuchen.
Morgen werde ich am Computer sitzen.
Übermorgen werde ich spazieren gehen.

Workout 38 .... p. 76

Exercise 1
1. schrittweise
2. alleine
3. Leider
4. Deshalb/Deswegen/Daher/Darum
5. Teilweise
6. zusammen
7. Deswegen
8. Daher
9. gern
10. langsam

Exercise 2
1. kaum
2. sehr
3. fast
4. kaum
5. sehr

Exercise 3
Possible answers:
1. Ja, ich gehe **gern** mit euch ins Konzert.
2. Ja, **manchmal** höre ich Rockmusik.
3. Du sollst das Projekt **schrittweise** durchführen.
4. Nein, du sollst **fast** nie laut schreien.
5. Nein, du brauchst nicht **alleine** zu arbeiten.

Workout 39 .... p. 78

Exercise 1
1. drinnen
2. weg
3. hier

4. geradeaus
5. unten
6. links
7. rückwärts
8. vorne

Exercise 2
1. Gehen Sie hinein!
2. Kommen Sie hinein!
3. Gehen Sie hinaus!

Exercise 3
Possible answer:
Leider habe ich mein Heft vergessen! Es liegt **oben** in unserem Zimmer! Kannst du es mir bringen? Ich bin **hier** im großen Hörsaal an der Uni. Nimm die U-2 bis zur Uni. Wenn du aussteigst, geh nach **oben** und dann **rechts**. Komm dann in das erste Gebäude **herein**. Geh dann immer **geradeaus**, bis du **links** zwei große Holztüren siehts. **Rechts** ist ein Schild: „Hörsaal 1". **Da** bin ich drin! Vielen Dank!

Workout 40 .... p. 80

Exercise 1
1. schreiben
2. komme
3. kaufen
4. macht
5. geht
6. kochen
7. arbeitest
8. sammeln

Exercise 2
1. die Kinder
2. ihr
3. Ich
4. dein Vater
5. du

Exercise 3
1. Er kauft ein Buch.
2. Sie joggt oft.
3. Die Kinder kochen die Suppe.
4. Sie antworten dir.
5. Ich wandere am Wochenende.

Exercise 4
Possible answers:
1. Ich suche einen Job.
2. Wir fahren nach Salzburg.
3. Er macht eine Lehre.
4. Sie joggen im Park.
5. Sie backt einen Kuchen.

Workout 41 p. 82

Exercise 1

	sprechen	braten	nehmen
ich	spreche	**brate**	**nehme**
du	**sprichst**	brätst	**nimmst**
er/sie/es	spricht	**brät**	nimmt
wir	sprechen	**braten**	nehmen

Exercise 2
1. Weißt
2. fällt
3. läuft
4. hältst
5. liest
6. Gibst
7. wirfst, Fängst
8. empfiehlt, Isst
9. stiehlst, hilfst
10. schläfst, liest

Exercise 3
Possible answers:
1. Was weißt du über die Geschichte Deutschlands?
2. Wenn ich ihm die Vase gebe, zerbricht er sie?
3. Wieso fährst du so schnell?
4. Sieht deine Schwester das Flugzeug dort drüben?
5. Frisst auch dein Hund Fleisch?

Workout 42 p. 84

Exercise 1
1. bin
2. hat
3. ist
4. sind
5. habt

Exercise 2
1. habe; hast
2. hat; haben
3. hat; habt
4. haben; haben
5. habe; haben

Exercise 3
1. ist; bist
2. ist; ist
3. sind; sind
4. bin
5. seid

Exercise 4
1. Sie hat ein Handy in ihrer Tasche/Handtasche.
2. Sind Sie Rechtsanwalt?
3. Die Kinder sind müde.
4. Elke und Rainer, seid ihr fertig?
5. Ich habe einen Computer zu Hause.

Workout 43 p. 86

Exercise 1
1. SEP
2. INSEP
3. SEP
4. SEP
5. INSEP

Exercise 2
1. siehst, aus
2. Rufen, an
3. räume, auf
4. fällt, auf
5. bringt, bei

Exercise 3
1. Wo gibt man das Gepäck auf?
2. Die Spieler hören dem Trainer immer zu.
3. Stimmt es, dass du kein Geld mitbringst?

Workout 44 p. 88

Exercise 1
1. umsteigen
2. bestellen ✓
3. entfernen ✓
4. überreden ✓
5. mitkommen
6. zerbrechen ✓
7. verzeihen ✓
8. umziehen

Exercise 2
1. verkauft; x
2. zerkratzt; x
3. erfährt; x
4. Kehren . . . um
5. beweist; x
6. ziehen . . . aus
7. bearbeitet; x
8. entziffert; x

Exercise 3
1. Ich bestelle die Bücher im Internet.
2. Entschuldigen Sie mich!
3. Er umarmt seinen Hund jeden Tag.

Answer Key

4. Verkaufst du das auf dem Flohmarkt?
5. Gefällt ihr das Haus?

Workout 45 .... p. 90

Exercise 1
1. heiraten sich
2. wünschen sich
3. putzt . . . dir
4. Wäscht sich
5. amüsieren . . . uns
6. umarmen . . . sich
7. Setzen . . . sich hin
8. wundere mich

Exercise 2
1. Ja, ich kämme mir die Haare am Morgen.
2. Nein, ich rasiere mich nicht jeden Tag.
3. Ich wasche mir fast jeden Tag die Haare.
4. Ich ziehe mir eine Krawatte zur Arbeit an.
5. Ich ziehe mir am Wochende meistens Jeans an.

Exercise 3
Beate: Sprichst du oft mit Katrin?
Berndt: Nein, aber wir schreiben uns oft per E-Mail. Oder manchmal tauschen wir SMS aus. Aber das kostet dann extra.
Beate: Wann habt ihr euch zum letzten Mal gesehen?
Berndt: Naja, das war schon vor zwei Wochen, aber wir treffen uns dieses Wochenende bei ihr.

Exercise 4
Possible answers:
Jeden Morgen **dusche ich mich** und **wasche mir die Haare.** Dann frühstücke ich mit meinem Zimmerkollegen zusammen. Oft muss **ich mich beeilen. Ich putze mir die Zähne,** aber wenn es zu spät ist, **rasiere ich mich** nicht. Dann **ziehe ich mich an, ziehe mir die Jacke** dazu **an,** und gehe aus dem Haus!

Workout 46 .... p. 92

Exercise 1
1. kann
2. darf
3. Darf
4. kannst
5. kann

Exercise 2
1. kann, kannst
2. kann, darf
3. dürfen
4. Darf
5. kann

Exercise 3
Possible answers:
1. Darf ich in die Stadt fahren?
2. Kannst du mir 10 Euro leihen?
3. Warum darfst du nicht fernsehen?

Exercise 4
1. Er kann kochen.
2. Darf ich bitte einen Stück Kuchen haben?
3. Sie kann das für dich machen.
4. Können Sie mir bitte sagen, wie spät es ist?
5. Mein Bruder kann sehr gut Französisch sprechen.

Workout 47 .... p. 94

Exercise 1
1. Er soll sich bei seiner Freundin bedanken.
2. Wir müssen arbeiten.
3. Nein, danke, ich möchte keinen Kaffee trinken.
4. Ich will von hier wegziehen.

Exercise 2
Possible answers:
1. (sollen)
Um gesünder zu werden, sollen meine Freunde und ich mehr Gemüse essen.
2. (müssen)
Um erfolgreich in der Schule zu sein, muss ich fleißiger werden.
3. (wollen)
Um die Wohnung schöner zu machen, will Erich Pflanzen kaufen.
4. (möchten)
Um Erfahrung im Ausland zu sammeln, möchte Linda in Italien arbeiten.

Exercise 3
1. Er mag diese Stadt nicht.
2. Ich muss ins Bett (gehen). Morgen will ich früh aufstehen.
3. Wir sollen jetzt nach Hause (gehen).

Workout 48 .... p. 96

Exercise 1
1. Martin will nicht im Lebensmittelgeschäft arbeiten.
2. Wilhelm soll mit ihr nicht singen.
3. Der Schauspieler muss morgen nicht anfangen.
Or: Der Schauspieler braucht morgen nicht anzufangen.
4. Der Autor will seinen nächsten Roman nicht schreiben.
5. Das Kind muss das Eis nicht essen.
Or: Das Kind braucht das Eis nicht zu essen.
6. Karolina möchte ihren Großvater nicht besuchen.
7. Das Radio kann ich nicht hören.

8. Helena soll die Medikamente nicht nehmen.

Exercise 2
1. Nein, ich will nicht Ski fahren.
2. Nein, ich will nicht fliegen.
3. Nein, ich kann nicht Französisch sprechen.
4. Nein, ich kann nicht Auto fahren.
5. Nein, ich will nicht erreichbar sein.

Exercise 3
1. Die Kinder dürfen nicht draußen spielen.
2. Sie kann noch nicht lesen.
3. Er will sein Gemüse nicht essen.
4. Wir sollen nicht zu lange warten.
5. Ich muss heute nicht in die Schule gehen.
    Or: Ich brauche heute nicht in die Schule zu gehen.

Exercise 4
Possible answer:
Mutter: Willst du mit mir in die Stadt?
Kind: Nein, ich **will** heute **nicht** in die Stadt.
Mutter: Wenn du zu Hause bleibst, **darfst** du aber **nicht** fernsehen!
Kind: Warum denn nicht? Ich **brauche nicht** für die Schule **zu** arbeiten.
Mutter: Hast du keine Hausaufgaben?
Kind: Nein, ich habe alles während der Pause gemacht.

Workout 49 .... p. 98

Exercise 1
1. wollten; schreiben
2. konnte; kommen
3. durfte; sein
4. soll; mitbringen
5. wolltest; bekommen
6. mussten; kochen
7. Durftet; schwimmen
8. sollte; einkaufen

Exercise 2
1. Ich musste gestern arbeiten.
2. Er sollte uns letzte Woche besuchen.
3. Wir wollten letzten Sommer eine Afrikareise machen.
4. Sie durften als Kinder nicht ohne Mantel nach draußen gehen.
5. Als Junge konnte er nicht Rad fahren.

Exercise 3
1. Er sollte ein Heft kaufen.
2. Kerstin konnte gestern Abend nicht zu uns kommen.
3. Die Kinder wollten heiße Schokolade trinken.
4. Wir durften ihnen nicht folgen.
5. Musstet ihr mit dem Zug fahren?

Workout 50 .... p. 100

Exercise 1
1. schmeckt
2. fehlt
3. passiert
4. gratulieren
5. gelungen

Exercise 2
1. ihm
2. mir
3. dir
4. Ihnen
5. euch
6. mir

Exercise 3
Possible answers:
1. Mir gefällt die Musik der Fanstastischen Vier.
2. Mir schmeckt ein Stück Linzer Torte am besten.
3. Ihm ist es nicht gelungen, weil er zu lange gebraucht hat.
4. Uns hast du eine Reise nach Leipzig versprochen.
5. Der rechte Arm tut mir weh.
6. Das kleine, schwarze Kleid passt ihr am besten.

Workout 51 .... p. 102

Exercise 1
1. Kennst
2. wissen
3. weiß
4. Weißt; kenne
5. kennst; weiß

Exercise 2
1. a. Ich weiß nicht. Ich habe Stollen noch nie gegessen.
2. b. Nein, ich weiß nicht, wann er Geburtstag hat.
3. c. Jeder weiß, dass sie rotes Haar hat.

Exercise 3
Possibe answers:
1. Weiß er, was Jutta studiert?
2. Kennst du den Weg nach Hause?
3. Kennst du meine Frau?
4. Wisst ihr, dass Harald Rechtsanwalt ist?
5. Wissen Sie, wo der Bahnhof ist?

Exercise 4
Maria: Weißt du, warum Jürgen nicht hier ist?
Berndt: Nein. Sollen wir ihn anrufen?
Maria: Kennst du seine Telefonnummer?
Berndt: Nein. Und ich weiß nicht, wie sein Vater heißt.
Maria: Ich kenne seine Schwester. Ich weiß, wo sie wohnen. Es ist nicht weit.

Answer Key

Berndt: Gehen wir zu ihm!

Workout 52.. p. 104

Exercise 1
1. gelassen
2. Lässt
3. lässt
4. lassen
5. lasse

Exercise 2
1. Lassen Sie
2. Lasst
3. Lass
4. Lass
5. Lass

Exercise 3
Possible answer:
In unserem neuen Haus gibt es noch so viel zu tun! Wir lassen zum Beispiel einen Zimmermann die Küche renovieren. Nachdem er fertig ist, lassen wir einen Schreiner kommen, um neue Schränke zu bauen. Im Wohnzimmer lassen wir einen Maler die Wände streichen und danach einen Designer die neuen Möbel installieren!

Workout 53.. p. 106

Exercise 1
1. lässt . . . schneiden
2. hörst . . . kommen
3. sehe . . . arbeiten
4. Bleiben . . . stehen
5. essen gehen

Exercise 2
1. putzen lassen
2. sitzen geblieben
3. schwimmen gegangen
4. stehlen sehen
5. spazieren gefahren

Exercise 3
1. Ich habe jemanden das Fenster hinten kaputt machen hören.
2. Ich habe Claudia die Polizei auf ihrem Handy anrufen hören.
3. Ich habe den Nachbarn nach hinten laufen sehen.
4. Ich habe den Nachbarn jemanden laut anschreien hören.
5. Ich habe den Verbrecher weg rennen sehen.

Exercise 4
1. Sie hat die Kinder spielen sehen.
2. Wir sind gestern Abend trinken gegangen.
3. Du sollst joggen gehen.
4. Sie sind im Flugzeug/an Bord sitzen geblieben.
5. Ich habe mir die Schuhe putzen lassen.

Workout 54.. p. 108

Exercise 1
1. versuchen . . . zu
2. Ohne . . . zu
3. hört . . . auf . . . zu
4. Hast . . . Lust . . . zu
5. um . . . zu

Exercise 2
Possible answers:
1. Ja, ich habe Zeit, dich abzuholen.
2. Nein, er hat nicht vergessen, etwas zu machen.
3. Statt ins Konzert zu gehen, will ich ins Theater.
4. Ich bin in die Stadt gefahren, um dort Arbeit zu suchen.
5. Ich hätte Lust, eine DVD auszuleihen, und zu Hause zu bleiben.

Exercise 3
1. Ich versuche abzunehmen.
2. Fängst du an, Deutsch zu lernen?
3. Wissen Sie, ober er Zeit hat, in die Buchhandlung zu gehen?
4. Sie kann zu ihm fahren, ohne auf den Stadtplan zu schauen.
5. Ich bin ins Lebensmittelgeschäft gegangen, um Milch zu kaufen.

Workout 55.. p. 110

Exercise 1
1. gekauft
2. gefragt
3. gespielt
4. getanzt
5. gehört
6. gemacht
7. gekehrt
8. geheiratet
9. geöffnet
10. geregnet
11. genannt
12. getippt
13. gewusst
14. gelegt
15. gedacht

Exercise 2

1. W; gekocht
2. W; gelernt
3. S; getroffen
4. W; gemerkt
5. S; gesungen
6. W; gefeiert
7. S; gewonnen
8. S; gelesen

Exercise 3

1. finden
2. sinken
3. schreiben
4. fahren
5. zurückfahren
6. empfangen
7. einladen
8. lesen
9. nehmen
10. steigen
11. helfen
12. missverstehen
13. abfahren
14. zerbrechen

Exercise 1

1. telefoniert
2. gewusst
3. studiert
4. gedacht
5. probiert

Exercise 2

1. getan
2. geholfen
3. geschält; geschnitten
4. gesehen; geschlagen
5. gestohlen/genommen; gestohlen/genommen

Exercise 3

1. Ich habe mit meinen Freunden ein Gartenhaus gebaut.
2. Martin hat die Werkzeuge gekauft.
3. Astrid und Ursula haben Löcher in die Wand gebohrt.
4. Moritz hat das Brett in zwei Stücke gesägt.
5. Wir haben viel an diesem Tag geschraubt.
6. Was haben sie zur Party gebracht?
7. Mathias hat jede Woche eine E-Mail an seine Mutter geschrieben.
8. Erika hat sehr mit den Kindern geholfen.

Exercise 1

1. Sein: wird; Haben: glaube, schneit
2. Sein: gehst, ist; Haben: habe
3. Sein: fahren, bleiben; Haben: machen

Exercise 2

1. ist
2. seid
3. sind; Haben
4. sind; haben
5. bist; hat

Exercise 3

1. bist; gelaufen
2. hat; gekauft
3. bin; gefahren
4. bin; geblieben
5. ist; gekommen

Exercise 4

1. Er ist nach Jamaica gesegelt.
2. Wir haben auf dem Bodensee gesegelt.
3. Wir haben in Hawaii gesurft.
4. Sie ist zur Insel gesurft.
5. Sie sind die ganze Nacht gefahren.
6. Er hat das Auto zum Meer gefahren.

Exercise 1

1. S; angezogen
2. I; gefallen
3. S; zurückgerufen
4. I; missverstanden
5. I; verursacht

Exercise 2

1. aufgehört
2. zugemacht
3. eingekauft
4. zurückgeholt
5. ausgerutscht
6. abgestürzt
7. losgekriegt
8. mitgemacht
9. weggefegt
10. ausgerichtet

Exercise 3

Ich bin um 6.00 Uhr aufgestanden. Zuerst habe ich mich geduscht. Dann habe ich mir die Beine rasiert.
Danach habe ich mich angezogen, mir die Zähne geputzt und mir nochmal die Hände gewaschen.

Answer Key

Dann habe ich mir das Haar gekämmt und mich geschminkt. Ich habe mich bemüht, und obwohl ich mich beeilt habe, habe ich mich geärgert, weil ich keine Zeit zum Frühstücken gehabt habe.

Exercise 4
Possible answers:
1. Ja, und heute hat er seine ganzen Klamotten weggeworfen.
2. Nein, und heute hat er mir auch nichts mitgeteilt.
3. Ja, aber heute haben sie entschieden, nach Kiel umzuziehen.
4. Ja, und heute hat ein Erdbeben unser Haus zerstört.
5. Doch, aber heute habt ihr mir empfohlen, beim Supermarkt einzukaufen.

Workout 59 .... p. 118

Exercise 1
1. Kerstin hat gern Tennis gespielt.
2. Mutti hat Kekse für uns gebacken.
3. Herr Wagner hat seinen Kollegen angerufen.
4. Der Sportler hat jeden Tag trainiert.
5. Der Zug ist am Abend angekommen.

Exercise 2
1. Die Prüfung wird von der Studentin geschrieben.
2. Das Auto wird von Hans gewaschen.
3. Die Kinder werden von Karla erzogen.
4. Deutsch wird von dieser Lehrerin unterrichtet.
5. Die Maschinen werden von Marcel verkauft.

Exercise 3
1. Gesuchte
2. verkauft
3. zerbrochenen
4. erledigt
5. Versprochene

Workout 60 .... p. 120

Exercise 1
1. regnete
2. fragte
3. machtest
4. verkauften
5. schauten

Exercise 2
1. stürzte
2. forderte
3. retteten
4. explodierte
5. wählten

Exercise 3
1. kam
2. ging
3. holte sich
4. zog
5. sich
6. aus
7. setzte sich
8. ass
9. schaltete
10. ein
11. freute sich

Workout 61 .... p. 122

Exercise 1
1. war
2. hatten
3. warst
4. hattet
5. Hatten

Exercise 2
1. wollte
2. sollten
3. musste
4. durften
5. Konntest
6. wolltet
7. musste
8. durften
9. konnte
10. wollten

Exercise 3
Possible answers:
1. Als ich jung war, hatte ich blonde Haare.
2. Als wir Urlaub machten, fuhren wir immer zusammen.
3. Als Karin Austauschstudentin war, wohnte sie bei einer Gastfamilie.
4. Als du in der Küche warst, passierte nichts im Film.
5. Als Heinz-Peter bei Siemens arbeitete, musste er mit der U-Bahn fahren.

Exercise 4
Possible answer:
Norbert: Was haben Sie am Wochenende gemacht?
Norma: Mein Mann und ich **waren** am Starnberger See.
Norbert: Und, wie **war** es?
Norma: Tja, wir **hatten** zum Glück schönes Wetter, denn wir **wollten** vor allem segeln.
Norbert: Habt ihr ein eigenes Boot?
Norma: Nein, wir **durften** das Boot von unseren Freunden benutzen.

Workout 62 .... p. 124

Exercise 1
1. hatte getragen
2. hatte gelesen
3. war Ski gefahren
4. hatte gewaschen
5. hatte gekostet
6. hatte vermietet
7. hatte geschlossen
8. war gestiegen
9. hatte geheißen
10. war geblieben

Exercise 2
1. Nachdem ich im Internet gesurft hatte, habe ich ein Hotel gefunden/fand ich ein Hotel.
2. Ich habe ein Zimmer gebucht/buchte ein Zimmer, nachdem ich ein Hotel gefunden hatte.
3. Bevor ich einen Flug gebucht habe/einen Flug buchte, hatte ich ein Zimmer gebucht.
4. Ich hatte einen Flug gebucht, bevor ich nach München geflogen bin/nach München flog.

Exercise 3
Possible answers:
Ich bin um 6.00 Uhr aufgestanden. Zuerst habe ich mich geduscht. Nachdem ich mich **geduscht hatte,** habe ich mich angezogen. Dann habe ich mir die Haare gekämmt. Erst nachdem ich **gefrühstückt hatte,** habe ich mir die Zähne geputzt.

Exercise 4
Martina: Wo warst du gestern?
Manfred: Ich musste in die Stadt, denn meine Chefin hatte gestern früh angerufen.
Martina: Weswegen?
Manfred: Sie konnte nicht ins Büro, weil sie ihren Schlüssel vergessen hatte.

Workout 63 .... p. 126

Exercise 1
1. werde
2. wird
3. Wirst
4. werdet
5. wird

Exercise 2
1. Ich werde das Geschirr spülen.
2. Karin wird staubsaugen.
3. Martin und Sabina werden die Wäsche waschen.
4. Thomas wird das WC putzen.

Exercise 3
1. Morgen werde ich mein Auto von der Reparatur abholen.
2. Nächste Woche wird er nach Düsseldorf fliegen.
3. Übernächste Woch werden sie in den Alpen klettern.

Exercise 4
1. Du wirst mir jetzt die Wahrheit sagen!
2. Sie werden mir sagen, mit wem Sie telefoniert haben!
3. Du wirst jetzt den ganzen Müll wegwerfen!

Exercise 5
Possible answers:
1. Zuerst werde ich aufstehen.
2. Dann werde ich mich duschen.
3. Danach werde ich mich anziehen.
4. Nachdem ich das mache, werde ich frühstücken.
5. Zum Schluss werde ich mir die Zähne putzen.

Workout 64 .... p. 128

Exercise 1
Possible answers:
1. Die zwei Verbrecher sind verhaftet worden.
2. Das Ehepaar ist vor einem Schloss fotografiert worden.
3. Die zwei Schauspieler sind geschminkt worden.
4. Das Baby ist in einer Kirche getauft worden.
5. Ein Fisch ist gefangen worden.

Exercise 2
1. Die Kühe werden gemelkt.
2. Der Stall wird ausgemistet.
3. Die Eier werden eingesammelt.
4. Das Pferd wird gefüttert.
5. Die Katze wird gestreichelt.

Exercise 3
Possible answers:
1. Zuerst war alles ausgepackt worden.
2. Dann war die Gebrauchsanweisung gelesen worden.
3. Dann war kontrolliert worden, ob etwas fehlt.
4. Danach waren die Batterien richtig eingelegt worden.
5. Danach war der elektrischer Rasierapparat eingeschaltet worden.

Workout 65 .... p. 130

Exercise 1
1. Der Autor schreibt das Buch.
2. Der Mechaniker repariert den Wagen.
3. Der Kapitän steuerte das Schiff.
4. Zum ersten Mal hat eine Frau die Sendung moderiert.
5. Der Babysitter hatte die Wäsche gewaschen.

Answer Key

Exercise 2

1. Das Feuer hat das Haus zerstört.
   Das Haus ist durch das Feuer zerstört worden.
2. Das Hochwasser hat die Brücke beschädigt.
   Die Brücke ist durch das Hochwasser beschädigt worden.
3. Ein Sandsturm hat die Ernte ruiniert.
   Die Ernte ist durch einen Sandsturm ruiniert worden.

Exercise 3

1. Es wurde bis Mitternacht gearbeitet.
2. Es wurde im Chatroom geflirtet.
3. Es wurde über die Entführung berichtet.
4. Es wurde drei Jahre lang Forschung betrieben.
5. Es wurden um 10.00 Uhr Getränke serviert.

Exercise 4
Possible answers:

1. In der Halle wird gespielt.
2. Auf der Party wird getanzt.
3. In der Bibliothek wird gelernt.
4. Im Restaurant wird gegessen.
5. Im Garten wird gegrillt.

Workout 66 .... p. 132

Exercise 1

1. kauf	kauft	kaufen Sie
2. mach	macht	machen Sie
3. finde	findet	finden Sie
4. schlaf	schlaft	schlafen Sie
5. sammle	sammelt	sammeln Sie
6. sei	seid	seien Sie

Exercise 2

1. Ruf die Polizei an!
2. Mach ein Foto von mir!
3. Gib ihm zehn Euro.
4. Schick mir eine SMS!
5. Iss mehr Gemüse!

Exercise 3

1. Helft ihr mal mit ihren Hausaufgaben.
2. Zieht euch andere Hosen an.
3. Lest mindestens ein Buch die Woche.

Exercise 4
Possible answers:

1. Haben Sie keine Angst! Ich beiße nicht.
2. Treiben Sie öfter Sport! Es wird Ihnen helfen, abzunehmen.
3. Werfen Sie bitte den Müll weg! Es stinkt hier langsam.
4. Sparen Sie Geld! Ohne Geld können Sie nichts kaufen.
5. Schreiben Sie mir eine E-Mail. Sagen Sie mir wie es Ihnen geht.

Workout 67 .... p. 134

Exercise 1

One-word Form	Two-word Form
1. wäre	würde sein
2. hätte	würde haben
3. tränke	würde trinken
4. führe	würde fahren
5. spielte	würde spielen
6. tanzte	würde tanzen

Exercise 2

1. würdest . . . laden
2. würden . . . mitkommen
3. würdest . . . machen
4. würde . . . treiben
5. würde . . . lesen

Exercise 3

1. käme; könnten
2. wäre
3. ginge; gäbe
4. Möchten
5. Hättest

Exercise 4

1. Ich wünsche, ich könnte ihm diese Jacke kaufen.
2. Möchten Sie heute nach Hause fliegen?
3. Wenn er das wüsste, würde er die Frage beantworten können.

Workout 68 .... p. 136

Exercise 1

1. c
2. a
3. d
4. b

Exercise 2

1. Ich hätte eine Suchmaschine gebraucht.
2. Wie hätten uns die großen Kakteen angeschaut.
3. Du hättest dich warm angezogen.
4. Sie hätten einen Film runtergeladen.
5. Ich wäre bei ihr geblieben.
6. Sie hätte den Schnee selber geschaufelt.
7. Ihr hättet einen Baum eingepflanzt.
8. Er hätte dir mit der Arbeit geholfen.
9. Wir wären nach Hause geflogen.
10. Wärest du umgezogen?

Exercise 3
Possible answers:
1. Wenn Richard die E-Mail verschickt hätte, hätten wir das früher gewusst.
2. Wenn Lena etwas anders studiert hätte, wäre sie schon längst mit ihrem Studium fertig.
3. Wenn Karl sein Handy bei sich gehabt hätte, hätten wir ihn erreichen können.
4. Wenn Monika früher zum Arzt gegangen wäre, hätte er ihr helfen können.

Exercise 4
Possible answer:
Wenn ich letztes Jahr das Geld und die Zeit dazu gehabt hätte, hätte eine Weltreise gemacht. Ich wäre zuerst nach Europa geflogen, um dort Freunde zu besuchen. Im Winter hätte ich auch das berühmte Eishotel in Schweden besucht, weil es so einmalig ist. In Deutschland wäre ich gerne mit Freunden unterwegs gewesen, die dort wohnen. Sie kennen sich mit den Sehenswürdigkeiten gut aus, und es hätte Spaß gemacht, etwas mehr Zeit mit ihnen verbringen zu können . . .

Workout 69 .... p. 138

Exercise 1
1. Möchte
2. dürften
3. müssten
4. Könntest
5. wollten

Exercise 2
Possible answers:
1. Ja, ich möchte noch warten.
2. Ja, ich möchte gern mit dem Manager sprechen.
3. Ja, ich bringe ihn gleich!
4. Ja, gern!
5. Ja, ich hätte gern noch eine Tasse Kaffee.

Exercise 3
1. Beate und Ludger hätten den Rasen mähen können.
2. Ich hätte den Kuchen essen dürfen!
3. Wir hätten das wissen sollen.
4. Du hättest selber zur Bank gehen müssen.
5. Wenn er den Wein nur hätte trinken wollen!

Exercise 4
1. Sie müsste vegetarisch essen.
2. Das Kind dürfte draußen spielen.
3. Ihr hättet das herunterladen können.
4. Wenn ich nur mehr Eis hätte essen können!
5. Die Studenten hätten ihre Hausaufgaben machen sollen.

Workout 70 .... p. 140

Exercise 1
1. komme
2. sei
3. habe
4. werde
5. wolle
6. könne
7. wisse
8. solle
9. möge
10. lasse

Exercise 2
1. Er kaufe ein Buch.
2. Sie jogge in dem Park.
3. Die Kinder nehmen ihre Bücher mit.
4. Sie räumen ihr Zimmer auf.
5. Er entscheide sich dafür.

Exercise 3
1. spreche
2. sei
3. steigen
4. werde
5. glauben

Workout 71 .... p. 142

Exercise 1
1. Monika sagte, sie seien sehr glücklich.
2. Christian sagte, der Kellner habe es empfohlen.
3. Die Dame sagte, die Putzfrau werde das aufräumen.
4. Der Student fragte, ob ich viel verdiente.

Exercise 2
1. Der Arzt sagte, ich solle abnehmen.
2. Der Arzt sagte, ich solle mehr Gemüse essen.
3. Der Arzt sagte, ich solle zwei Aspirin nehmen.
4. Der Arzt sagte, ich solle diese Übungen machen.

Exercise 3
Possible answers:
Maria sagte, sie **sei** in Berlin **geboren** und in Hamburg **aufgewachsen.** Sie sagte auch, dass sie jetzt 20 Jahre alt **sei,** und dass sie in Hamburg **studiere.** Sie erzählte mir dann weiter, dass sie noch bei den Eltern **wohne,** und dass sie Einzelkind **sei.**

Answer Key

Exercise 1
1. essen
2. liest
3. schläfst . . . ein
4. Erhält
5. Tragen

Exercise 2
1. Wir werden gesund.
2. Sie wäscht die Wäsche.
3. Du gibst ihm einen neuen Computer.
4. Ich lade Monika ein.
5. Er vergisst, wie sie heißt.

Exercise 3
Possible answers:
1. Der Mann sieht den Bus.
2. Er läuft zur Haltestelle.
3. Auf dem Weg fällt er hin.
4. Der Bus hält, und der Mann steigt ein.

Exercise 1
1. möchte
2. Gefällt
3. Mögt
4. habe
5. Gefallen
6. möchten
7. Habt
8. mag

Exercise 2
1. Gefällt
2. gern
3. Hast . . . gern
4. möchte
5. mag

Exercise 3
1. Sie spielt gern Klavier.
2. Sie möchten mit Kreditkarte zahlen.
3. Die Kinder spielen gern draußen.
4. Hast du sie sehr gern?/Magst du sie sehr?
5. Dein/Ihr neues Kleid gefällt mir sehr.

Exercise 1
Possible answers:
1. Nächstes Jahr zieht er nach Düsseldorf um.

2. Ihren Bruder nimmt sie nicht mit.
3. Mir haben sie nichts erzählt.
4. Wann Heinrich ankommt, weiß ich nicht.
5. Wenn wir genug Geld dazu haben, werden wir nach Deutschland fliegen.

Exercise 2
1. Tobias spielt heute Nachmittag Fußball.
2. Die Trainer arbeiten stundenlang mit den Spielern.
3. Gestern Abend haben wir gesungen.
4. Ich mag es, wenn er lächelt.
5. Maria kocht, wenn er arbeitet.

Exercise 3
Possible answers:
1. Ja, ich lese oft.
2. Mein Lieblingsroman ist *Nirgendwo in Afrika*.
3. Ich kaufe meine Bücher in der Buchhandlung ein.
4. Nein, ich gehe nicht oft in die Stadtbibliothek.
5. Ja, ich kann auf Deutsch lesen.

Exercise 1
1. Trinkt Stefanie immer Rotwein?
2. Isst Maximilian gern italienisch?
3. Wollen Birgit und Heike nicht ins Restaurant gehen?
4. Möchtest du lieber hier bleiben?
5. Fahren wir heute Abend in die Stadt?

Exercise 2
Possible answers:
1. Hans-Peter studiert Geologie, nicht wahr?
   Studiert Hans-Peter Geologie?
2. Monika schreibt heute eine Eintrittsklausur, oder?
   Schreibt Monika heute eine Eintrittsklausur?
3. Viele Studenten haben mehr als zehn Semester studiert, nicht wahr?
   Haben viele Studenten mehr als zehn Semester studiert?
4. Du hast einen Studienplatz bekommen, gell?
   Hast du einen Studienplatz bekommen?
5. Wir werden im Studentenwohnheim wohnen, oder?
   Werden wir im Studentenwohnheim wohnen?

Exercise 3
1. Arbeiten Sie im Garten!   Arbeiten wir im Garten!
   Work in the yard!   Let's work in the yard!
2. Gießen Sie die Blumen!   Gießen wir die Blumen!
   Water the flowers!   Let's water the flowers!
3. Pflanzen Sie Gemüse!   Pflanzen wir Gemüse!
   Plant vegetables!   Let's plant vegetables!
4. Mähen Sie den Rasen!   Mähen wir den Rasen!
   Mow the lawn!   Let's mow the lawn!

Workout 76 .... p. 152

Exercise 1
1. Ich weiß nicht, ob er morgen kommen wird.
2. Er interessiert sich für Deutsch, weil er nach Deutschland will.
3. Sie hat geschrieben, dass sie nicht nach Chicago will.
4. Weißt du, wo Ingolstadt liegt?
5. Der Schaffner hat gesagt, wann der Zug ankommen soll.
6. Das ist der Mann, mit dem wir geredet haben.
7. Sind das die Studenten, deren Eltern du kennst?

Exercise 2
1. haben wird
2. kennen lernen wollte
3. machen wollte
4. hätte mitbringen sollen
5. mitkommen wird
6. gekocht hat

Exercise 3
1. Wissen Sie, wo die Buchhandlung ist?
2. Sie fliegen nach Europa, weil sie dort Freunde haben.
3. Meine Schwester weiß, wer in meiner Klasse ist.
4. Weißt du, ob sie mit mir tanzen wird?
5. Das ist die Frau, deren Mann ich gestern kennen gelernt habe.

Workout 77 .... p. 154

Exercise 1
1. Wir gehen heute Abend zusammen ins Kino.
2. Sylvia und Karl essen um 18.00 Uhr mit Maria im Restaurant.
3. Ich wandere am Tag alleine im Wald.
4. Meine Eltern fahren dieses Wochenende schnell zu Oma.
5. Gregor arbeitet jeden Tag ständig am Computer.

Exercise 2
1. Morgen Abend arbeitet Jürgen mit seiner Lerngruppe im Gemeinschaftsraum.
2. Mit seiner Lerngruppe arbeitet Jürgen morgen Abend im Gemeinschaftsraum.
3. Im Gemeinschaftsraum arbeitet Jürgen morgen Abend mit seiner Lerngruppe.

Exercise 3
Possible answer:
Ich bin letztes Jahr mit einer Gruppe nach München geflogen. Wir haben nur eine Woche Zeit gehabt, aber wir hatten viel Spaß dabei. Am Montag bin ich mit meiner Freundin im Hotel geblieben, weil wir uns ausruhen wollten. Aber am Dienstag ging es los! Mit ihr bin ich am Morgen ins Deutsche Museum gegangen. Wir hätten dort den ganzen Tag verbringen können, aber am späten Nachmittag waren wir schon müde.

Wir setzten uns um 3.00 Uhr zusammen ins Café, wo wir uns beide einen Kaffee bestellt haben . . .

Workout 78 .... p. 156

Exercise 1
1. Margrit kocht ihnen eine Suppe.
2. Uwe singt es seiner Freundin.
3. Nina und Bettina backen sie ihren Eltern.
4. Wiebke und Dominik schreiben ihm einen Brief.
5. Wir bringen sie unseren Nachbarn.
6. Die Kinder schenken ihr frische Blumen.
7. Der Vater baut ihnen einen Schneemann.
8. Thomas erzählt ihn dem Publikum.

Exercise 2
1. Julia strickt ihn ihrem Freund.
   Julia strickt ihm einen Pullover.
   Julia strickt ihn ihm.
2. Ich zeige ihn dem Beamten.
   Ich zeige ihm einen Pullover.
   Ich zeige ihn ihm.
3. Karl erzählt ihn den Touristen.
   Karl erzählt ihnen einen Witz.
   Karl erzählt ihn ihnen.
4. Gibst du es der Kellnerin?
   Gibst du ihr das Trinkgeld?
   Gibst du es ihr?
5. Der Professor erklärt sie den Studenten.
   Der Professor erklärt ihnen die Aufgabe.
   Der Professor erklärt sie ihnen.

Exercise 3
Possible answer:
Ich schicke meinen Freunden Einladungen. Ich backe dem Geburtstagskind einen Kuchen. Alle Gäste bringen ihm ein Geschenk.

Workout 79 .... p. 158

Exercise 1
1. eintausendeinhundertfünf
2. dreihunderteinundzwanzig
3. vierundsiebzig
4. sechs Komma fünf
5. sechshundertzweiundachtzig
6. zweitausendsechshundertzehn

Exercise 2
1. acht
2. einundachtzig
3. vierzig
4. fünfundsechzig
5. zweiunddreißig

Answer Key

Exercise 3
1. im Jahre neunzehnhundertsiebenundachtzig
2. im Jahre neunzehnhundertsechsundneunzig
3. im Jahre zweitausendzehn

Exercise 4
1. null
2. sieben
3. neununddreißig
4. sechsundsiebzig
5. zweiundsiebzig

Exercise 5
1. fünf nach zwölf
2. elf Uhr morgens
3. acht Uhr dreißig
   halb neun
   zwanzig Uhr dreißig
4. vier Uhr fünfundvierzig
   Viertel vor fünf

Workout 80 .... p. 160

Exercise 1
1. ein Zehntel
2. zweieinviertel
3. fünf Achtel
4. drei Viertel
5. eineinhalb/anderthalb

Exercise 2
1. Ich habe am siebten neunten Geburtstag.
2. Der Sommer fängt am einundzwanzigsten sechsten an.
3. Der Tag der Arbeit ist am ersten fünften.
4. Man feiert den schweizerischen Nationalfeiertag am ersten achten.
5. Silvester ist am einunddreißigsten Dezember.

Exercise 3
1. Wir haben uns am fünften neunten kennen gelernt.
2. Hans ist in der fünften Klasse.
3. Vier Fünftel der Klasse verstehen ihn nicht.
4. Sie ist die erste in ihrer Klasse.
5. Sie fahren am dreißigsten fünften ab.

Workout 81 .... p. 162

Exercise 1
1. ein Kilo
2. zwei Meter dreißig
3. fünfzig Schweizer Franken
4. vier Kubikmeter
5. eineinhalb/anderthalb Kilo

Exercise 2
1. 3,50 SF
2. 30,- Euro
3. 50 Quadratmeter
4. 100 Kilometer
5. 3,1 Kilo

Exercise 3
1. Zwei Kilo Äpfel kosten drei Euro.
2. Er ist fast zwei Meter groß.
3. Wir wohnen vierzig Kilometer von Frankfurt entfernt.
4. Ich brauche einen Meter Stoff.
5. Wie viele Kubikmeter brauchen sie?

Workout 82 .... p. 164

Exercise 1
1. e
2. a
3. d
4. b
5. c

Exercise 2
Possible answers:
1. Ich weiß wie du heißt, und ich weiß wo du wohnst.
2. Ich gehe heute nicht ins Kino, sondern ich werde zu Hause bleiben.
3. Er schreibt eine E-Mail, denn ein Brief braucht zu lang.
4. Trinkst du einen Tee, oder trinkst du lieber einen Kaffee?
5. Gestern war ich krank, aber heute geht es mir viel besser.

Exercise 3
1. und
2. aber
3. denn
4. und
5. sondern
6. und
7. oder

Exercise 4
Possible answers:
1. Ich wollte spazieren gehen, aber ich musste oft zu Hause bleiben.
2. Wir wollten nicht zu Hause bleiben, sondern ins Kino gehen.
3. Ich wollte meinen Freund besuchen, und ich wollte meinem Onkel helfen.
4. Wir wollten in einem Café singen, aber es ist uns nicht gelungen.
5. Ich wollte einkaufen gehen, oder ich wollte abends tanzen gehen.

Workout 83 .... p. 166

Exercise 1
1. weil
2. ob
3. dass
4. ob

Exercise 2
1. ob
2. dass
3. wenn
4. weil
5. dass

Exercise 3
1. Ernst muß Geld sparen, weil er einen neuen Computer kaufen will.
2. Ich weiß nicht, ob es noch Eintrittskarten gibt.
3. Kirsten hat gesagt, dass sie ein Baby aus China adoptiert hat.
4. Wir gehen ins Café, weil wir einen Kaffee trinken wollen.
5. Er wird den Weg nicht mehr finden, wenn er nicht vorsichtig ist.

Exercise 4
1. Stimmt es, dass du in Zürich wohnst?
2. Peter isst eine große Portion Eis, weil er immer noch Hunger hat.
3. Wir haben keine Ahnung, ob wir morgen eine weitere Sitzung haben.
4. Ist es wahr, dass sie die Eishockey-Meisterschaft gewonnen haben?
5. Brigitte ist traurig, weil ihr Freund mit ihr Schluß gemacht hat.

Workout 84 .... p. 168

Exercise 1
1. Nein, das ist kein Stuhl.
2. Nein, das ist keine Tafel.
3. Nein, das ist nicht meine Mutter.
4. Nein, das ist kein Fenster.
5. Nein, es stimmt nicht, dass meine Lieblingsstadt Hamburg ist.
6. Nein, Luise fährt nicht nach Rostock.
7. Nein, ich habe keinen Wecker.
8. Nein, Julia schwimmt nicht jeden Tag.
9. Nein, ich kenne keine berühmte Schauspielerin.

Exercise 2
1. Die Schuhe wird er heute nicht kaufen.
   Er kauft heute keine Schuhe.
2. Die Geschichte werden wir heute nicht schreiben.
   Wir schreiben heute keine Geschichten.

3. Die Banane werden Sie heute nicht essen.
   Sie werden heute keine Bananen essen.
4. Den Stuhl wirst du heute nicht verkaufen.
   Du wirst heute keine Stühle verkaufen.
5. Das Geld werde ich heute nicht spenden.
   Ich werde heute kein Geld spenden.

Exercise 3
Possible answer:
Ist Angela Merkel Model? Nein, sie ist keine Model, sondern Politikerin, also hat sie keinen Fototermin.

Workout 85 .... p. 170

Exercise 1
1. nichts
2. Niemand
3. nie
4. nie/nirgendwo
5. nichts

Exercise 2
1. Nirgendwohin.
2. Nichts.
3. Nie.
4. Niemandem.
5. Niemals.

Exercise 3
1. Ich mache nichts am Wochenende.
2. Ich singe nie alleine.
3. Wir reden mit niemandem.
4. Sie hat niemanden angesprochen.

Workout 86 .... p. 172

Exercise 1
1. Er telefoniert.
2. Dreieinhalb Stunden.
3. Mit der U-Bahn.
4. Am kommenden Wochenende.
5. Thomas Mann.

Exercise 2
Possible answers:
1. Ich heiße Monika.
2. Ich wohne in Berlin.
3. Ich bin 22 Jahre alt.

Exercise 3
Possible answers:
1. Woher kommt Michael Schaumgartner?
2. Wie viele Geschwister hat Michael?
3. Wie heißt Michaels Bruder?

Answer Key

Exercise 1
1. woran
2. mit wem
3. wovon/von wem
4. woran/wem
5. wovon/worüber/von wem/über wen

Exercise 2
Possible answers:
1. Wonach riecht es?
2. Woran wird Susanna teilnehmen?
3. Auf wen warten Lorenz und Jürgen?
4. Worüber soll ich schreiben?
5. Wovor hat Jeanette Angst?
6. Womit schreibt Barbara?
7. An wen schreibst du einen Brief?
8. Woran erinnert ihr euch?

Exercise 3
Anja: Was hältst du von dem neuen Textverarbeitungsprogramm an der Arbeit?
Andreas: Tja, zuerst hatte ich mich davor gefürchtet, da ich mich nicht so sehr für die Technologie interessiere, und so was macht mir einfach Angst. Aber mit der Zeit geht's.
Anja: Christina hat sich darüber wirklich Sorgen gemacht. Aber ich weiß selber nicht, wovor sie uns warnen wollte. Ich finde das neue Programm einfach toll!
Andreas: Worauf wartest du denn dann? Zurück an die Arbeit!

Exercise 1
1. wo
2. bei wem
3. wie
4. wann
5. wer
6. warum
7. worauf/worüber
8. was
9. mit wem
10. wem

Exercise 2
Possible answers:
1. Nein, ich weiß nicht, wo er jetzt ist.
2. Ja, ich weiß, wer zuletzt mit ihm gesprochen hat. Monika hat mit ihm gesprochen.
3. Ja, ich weiß, wann er gestern das Haus verlassen hat. Es war um 9.00 abends.
4. Nein, ich weiß nicht, warum er weg will.
5. Ja, ich weiß, wie er normalerweise nach Berlin fährt. Er fährt normalerweise mit dem Zug.

Exercise 3
1. Wir wissen, wohin wir gehen/fahren.
2. Sie hat keine Ahnung, wo sie wohnen wird.
3. Er weiß genau, was er will.
4. Ich habe keine Ahnung, wofür er sich interessiert.
5. Weißt du, worauf sie warten?

Exercise 1
1. wann
2. Als
3. Wenn
4. Wann
5. wenn

Exercise 2
Possible answers:
1. . . . das Konzert beginnt?
2. . . . war es schon zu spät.
3. . . . der Thomas mitkommt.
4. . . . würde ich es dir sagen.
5. . . . sie fertig sein wird?

Exercise 3
Georg: Wann kommt der Klempner?
Gertrud: Ich weiß nicht, ob er heute kommt.
Georg: Wenn er erst morgen kommt, könnte er wenigstens anrufen.
Gertrud: Als ich mit ihm gesprochen habe, hatte er noch nicht Bescheid sagen können.

Exercise 1
1. falls/wenn
2. Wenn
3. Wenn
4. wenn
5. Wenn

Exercise 2
1. Scheint die Sonne, dann/so machen wir ein Picknick.
2. Wird das Haus verkauft, dann/so ziehen wir um.
3. Fängt das Semester an, dann/so haben wir weniger Freizeit.
4. Kommen sie nach Hause, dann/so bleiben sie bei uns.

Exercise 3
1. Falls wir Geld brauchen, werden wir die Wohnung vermieten.
2. Falls er mehr Zeit hat, wird er einiges in der Stadt erledigen.
3. Falls sie ihr Handy dabei hat, wird sie ihn anrufen.
4. Falls Nina das Geld hat, wird sie ihren Sohn in Belgien

besuchen.

5. Falls Markus hier ist, wird er uns besuchen.

Exercise 4
1. Wenn ich zur Uni ginge, würde ich mit der U-Bahn fahren.
2. Falls ich nicht mitfahre, kannst du mir bitte etwas mitbringen?
3. Wenn du einkaufen gehst, wirst du mir ein Brot mitbringen?
4. Wenn sie Zeit hätte, würde sie mehr lesen.
5. Falls er krank wird, werde ich für ihn eintreten.

Workout 91 . . . . p. 182

Exercise 1
1. Ja, ich bin für ihn.
2. Ja, ich bin dagegen.
3. Ja, ich sitze daneben.
4. Ja, das habe ich von ihm bekommen.
5. Ja, ich wohne dahinter.

Exercise 2

						D	A	R	I	N
						A				
						R				
						U				
		D	A	R	A	N				
						T				
						E				
		D	A	V	O	R				
		A								
D	A	R	A	U	F					
		Ü								
		B								
		E								
		R								

Across	**Down**
1. f.	**1.** d.
2. b.	**3.** c.
3. e.	
4. a.	

Exercise 3
1. Er hat uns davon erzählt.
2. Legen Sie/Leg das Buch darauf.
3. Gehst du/geht ihr/gehen Sie dazwischen?
4. Sie interessiert sich dafür.
5. Ich habe kein Geld dabei.

Workout 92 . . . . p. 184

Exercise 1
1. F
2. F
3. F
4. I
5. I

Exercise 2
1. Sie
2. du
3. dich
4. euch
5. Sie
6. ihr
7. du
8. Euer
9. du, deine
10. Sie

Exercise 3
1. Uwe, was möchtest du trinken?
2. Lutz und Karin, habt ihr schon lange gewartet?
3. Herr und Frau Holzer, haben Sie meinen Brief bekommen/erhalten?
4. Papa, ich Kann dich nicht hören.
5. Viktor und Maria, wir werden euch beide und euren Wagen/euer Auto brauchen.

Workout 93 . . . . p. 186

Exercise 1
1. Konstanza hat Durst.
2. Margrit hat Angst.
3. Robert hat Hunger.
4. Wilhelm hat Pech.
5. Diana hat Lust, etwas zu machen.

Exercise 2
1. Nein, ich habe kein Interesse daran.
2. Nein, ich habe kein Glück gehabt.
3. Nein, ich habe keine Angst dabei.
4. Nein, ich habe keinen Hunger.
5. Nein, ich habe keine Lust, ihren nächsten Roman zu lesen.

Answer Key

Exercise 3

1. Du hast ja/wirklich Glück gehabt.
2. Wir haben viel Spaß gehabt.
3. Warum hat er Angst?
4. Hat sie Durst?
5. Haben Sie Interesse daran?

Workout 94 .... p. 188

Exercise 1

1. machen
2. machst
3. getan
4. tut
5. tun

Exercise 2

1. Ausflug
2. Fotos
3. weh
4. Spaß
5. Hausaufgaben

Exercise 3

1. Er soll jeden Tag Gymnastik machen.
2. Sie macht die Hausarbeit nicht gern.
3. Es tat ihnen Leid, dass sie nicht bei dem Empfang dabei sein konnten.
4. Katja macht nie eine Pause.
5. Paul macht ein Schläfchen.

Workout 95 .... p. 190

Exercise 1

1. erledigt
2. erledigt
3. unerledigt
4. erledigt
5. unerledigt
6. unerledigt

Exercise 2

1. P
2. P
3. S
4. S
5. S

Exercise 3

Possible answer:

Wir ziehen nach Koblenz um! Beim Umzug gibt es immer viel zu tun. Einiges haben wir schon erledigt. Das übrige Essen wurde den Nachbarn schon geschenkt, die Zeitung ist abgestellt, das Telefon haben wir schon umleiten lassen, und die Rechnungen sind bezahlt. Jetzt müssen unsere Sachen eingepackt werden, und die Kisten dann aufgeladen werden. Am Ende lassen wir die Möbel transportieren!

Workout 96 .... p. 192

Exercise 1
1. In Paris spricht man Französisch.
2. Im alten Kino zeigt man klassische Filme.
3. Mit dem neuen Computer macht man die Arbeit viel schneller.
4. Im Winter schaufelt man Schnee.
5. Man liefert die Zeitung früh (am Morgen).

Exercise 2
Possible answers:
1. Es ist schwer, auf Deutsch zu schreiben.
2. Es ist unmöglich, diesen Computer zu reparieren.
3. Es ist einfach, Fahrrad zu fahren.
4. Es ist unkompliziert, mit ihm zu reden.

Exercise 3
1. Das Auto ist noch zu waschen.
2. Dieses Haus lässt sich leicht verkaufen.
3. Diese Möbel lassen sich leicht transportieren.
4. Die Kisten sind noch zu packen.
5. Das lässt sich elektronisch verschicken.

Exercise 4
1. Das ist noch nicht gemacht.
2. Die Karten sind noch zu verkaufen.
3. Dieses Foto lässt sich vergrößern.
4. Die elektronischen Rechnungen sind leicht zu bezahlen.
5. Am Samstag liefert man keine Blumen.

Workout 97 .... p. 194

Exercise 1
1. c
2. b
3. a
4. d

Exercise 2
1. b (wau wau)
2. d (miau)
3. e (piep piep)
4. f (kikeriki)
5. a (muh)
6. c (grunz grunz)

Exercise 3
1. Au! Mir tut der Finger weh!
2. Warum bellt der Hund?
3. Ach! Was haben wir denn hier?
4. Die Vögel zwitschern in den Bäumen.
5. Hörst du die Katze miauen?

Answer Key

Exercise 1
1. erst
2. denn
3. wohl
4. mal
5. aber

Exercise 2
1. Fahren wir doch bis zur nächsten Tankstelle.
2. Warum schaust du mich denn so an?
3. Er will erst morgen damit anfangen.
4. Tu das ja nicht!
5. Sie wird wohl die Nächste sein.

Exercise 3
1. Was ist denn hier passiert?
2. Das ist aber billig!
3. Es ist wohl zu spät.
4. Ich will mir den Film erst nächste Woche anschauen.
5. Fangen Sie doch morgen an!

Exercise 1
1. dass
2. wir mussten
3. du heißt [diphthong]
4. weiß [diphthong]
5. ich wusste
6. groß [long vowel]
7. er weiß [diphthong]
8. die Straßenbahn [long vowel]
9. der Großvater [long vowel]
10. sie isst

Exercise 2
1. die Telefonnummer
2. der Geschirrreiniger
3. Eis laufen
4. nacherzählen
5. das Balletttheater
6. Auto fahren
7. spazieren gehen
8. die Mittagspause
9. die Buchhandlung
10. loswerden

Exercise 3
Liebe Katja!
Weißt **du** was?! Am 6.8. ziehe ich nach Koblenz um!
Kannst **du** das glauben? Das heißt, wir werden jetzt gleich in der Nähe sein! Wir können zusammen **Rad fahren** gehen, und im Winter können wir zusammen Richtung Süden fahren und dort **Ski laufen** gehen!

Es ist kaum zu glauben, **dass** es schon 5 Jahre sind, seitdem wir uns zum ersten Mal **kennen gelernt** haben! Wir waren zusammen auf der **Schifffahrt** auf der Donau. Erinnerst **du dich** daran?

Tja, langsam **muss** ich gehen …
Bis bald!

Dein,
Stefan

Workout 100....................................... p. 200

Exercise 1

1. studieren
2. winken
3. blau
4. Gift
5. bekommen

Bonus: Student

Exercise 4

			B						
			R		B				
		F	A	B	R	I	K		
			V		O			W	
					T			I	
	B	E	K	O	M	M	E	N	
			L		A			K	
			A		S			E	
	B		S		C			N	
	L		S		H				
B	A	D	E	Z	I	M	M	E	R
	U				N				
					E				

Exercise 4

1. Wo
2. Geschenk
3. studiert
4. Badezimmer
5. Wer
6. Schüler
7. Gift
8. Toilette
9. lernt
10. Student